Praise for

Gender-Inclusive Treatment of Intimate Partne...

". . . a welcome and important contribution to the family violence and s_____ . . professional literature . . . Hamel's work is well-written, comprehensive, very practical, and easily surpasses the current books on the subject . . . This book will be useful and essential reading for all social workers, psychologists, family therapists, and victimologists interested in domestic violence."

—Albert R. Roberts, PhD
Professor of Social Work and Criminal Justice
Director of Faculty and Curriculum Development
Faculty of Arts and Sciences
Rutgers, The State University of New Jersey

"This book is a significant scholarly and practical contribution to the field of family violence. It is particularly relevant in its acknowledgment that men (as well as women) are frequent and serious victims of partner abuse."

—Martin Fiebert, PhD
Professor of Psychology
California State University, Long Beach

"John Hamel takes the discussion of family violence 'up a notch' by going beyond yet another convincing argument for the bilateralism of partner abuse. Indeed, Gender-Inclusive Treatment of Intimate Partner Abuse *provides well-thought-out and concrete treatment options that consider the reality of men and women who experience violence in their intimate relationships. Clearly, this book is evidence that society is finally ready to move forward in seeking more inclusive remedies to a very serious social problem."*

—Reena Sommer, PhD
Divorce Consultant
Winnipeg, MB, Canada

Springer Series on Family Violence

Albert R. Roberts, PhD, Series Editor

John Hamel, LCSW, has a B.A. in psychology and a Masters in Social Welfare from U.C.L.A. In 1992, Mr. Hamel began his training in family violence counseling with Don Mathews, MFT, and soon established John Hamel & Associates in Pleasant Hill, California. Later, offices were established in Berkeley, California and Greenbrae, California. Mr. Hamel, along with Darlene Pratt, MFT, and his other associates, provide a wide range of services for high-conflict families, including family violence assessments, victim services and advocacy, and specialized treatment programs for angry and abusive men, women, couples, parents and teens. Although many of his clients are voluntary participants, many are referred from Family Court or Child Protective Services, or mandated by the courts to participate in either a batterer treatment program, or a parenting program.

A recognized expert in the fields of anger management and family violence, Mr. Hamel has provided consultation and training for mental health professionals, shelter workers and victim advocates, court mediators and evaluators, teachers, attorneys and law enforcement. He has spoken at a number of events, including the California Dept. of Social Services 10th Annual Family Strengths Training Institute, and the FVSAI 9th Annual Conference on Family Violence. His manual on domestic violence characteristics and etiology, *Domestic Violence Today,* can be found on the website of the Family Violence Treatment and Education Association (www.FAVTEA.com). Mr. Hamel is married and lives with his wife, Judi, and their twins, Jacob and Aviva, in San Rafael, California. He can be contacted at his e-mail address: angercounsel ing@aol.com.

Gender-Inclusive Treatment of Intimate Partner Abuse

A Comprehensive Approach

John Hamel, LCSW

 Springer Series on Family Violence

To Judi, Jacob, and Aviva
Love and peace, always

Springer Publishing Company, Inc.
11 West 42nd Street
New York, NY 10036-8002

Acquisitions Editor: Lauren Dockett
Production Editor: Jeanne Libby
Cover design by Joanne Honigman

01 02 03 04 05/5 4 3 2 1

Library of Congress Cataloging-in-Publication Data

Hamel, John
  Gender-inclusive treatment of intimate partner abuse : a comprehensive approach / John Hamel.
     p. cm. — (Springer series on family violence)
    Includes bibliographical references and index.
    ISBN 0-8261-1873-9
    1. Family violence. 2. Conjugal violence. 3. Family psychotherapy. I. Title.
  II. Series.
RC569.5.F3H35 2005
616.85'822—dc22   2004028956

Printed in the United States of America by Capital City Press.

Contents

List of Tables

Foreword

Intimate violence is a problem whose seriousness has finally been recognized after years of denial and neglect. Social policy, including police service and court-mandated treatment, has been radically altered in the past twenty years to acknowledge and attempt to curb repeat intimate violence. Many positive advances have been made. Unfortunately, not all policy has been successful. Arrest does not have a long term effect on suppressing recidivist violence unless supported by effective treatment. Effective treatment, in turn, has not always been available, in part because rather superficial "psychoeducational models" have been mandated in many states. These models have failed to establish necessary therapeutic bonds between therapist and client and have blocked access of therapists to clients' partners. Alternative treatment forms have been ruled out by law when the law called for an "intervention" that has not shown any appreciable results in numerous outcome studies.

Since the early work of Daniel Sonkin, a variety of alternative treatments have been available and the current volume by John Hamel extends the choice for alternative therapies. Hamel rightfully eschews the overblown and undersupported gender paradigm for conceptualizing intimate violence and puts the emphasis where it belongs—on intimacy. This focus enables us to treat same and opposite sex intimate relationships the same and to see that violent women need therapeutic help as do violent men. In this sense, Hamel's book represents a breakthrough although the time is right for new approaches. Here's a new approach that deserves recognition.

Donald Dutton, PhD
Professor of Psychology
University of British Columbia
Vancouver, BC

Acknowledgments

By the Fall of 2001, having worked for nearly a decade in the field of family violence, I had become increasingly frustrated with the dearth of information on gender-inclusive approaches to treatment. The literature was, and continues to be, almost completely silent on this matter; and at the many domestic violence trainings and community roundtables I had been attending there was no mention of mutual abuse or male victims, and very little about the complexities of violent relationships and the different types of abuse, or of family systems. Particularly disturbing was the almost conspiratorial disregard for alternative points of view, a disregard which I now know to be based in fear and which has, unfortunately, limited our common efforts to reduce domestic violence in our communities.

Unexpectedly, I was invited by two judges in Contra Costa County, California—Commissioner Josana Berkow of the Family Court, and Judge Judith Craddick of the Misdemeanor Domestic Violence Court—to present some research I had done with divorced couples referred to my counseling program. This book has its genesis in that research. I wish to thank these two individuals for their courage in arranging for me to speak at that February, 2002 forum.

I want to thank my colleagues in the Family Violence Treatment and Education Association (FAVTEA)—Michael Carolla, Tom Chapman, Darlene Pratt, and Laura Petracek—for their continued support and encouragement. My long-standing business colleague, Don Mathews, who initially trained me in conducting batterer intervention programs, has also been a source of wisdom and strength. I continue to admire his professionalism and inquisitive spirit, and appreciate his disarming humor. David Fontes has been a wonderful mentor. I want to thank him for his pioneering research, for pointing out the important distinction between the terms "gender-inclusive" and "gender-neutral," for his gentle manner and, most of all, for inspiring me to persist in my research endeavors despite the resistance I have experienced in some quarters. "If you present them with the facts," he assured me, "you'll be surprised how they come around." How right he was.

Thank you, Judi, for your love and support, and for bearing with me the past three years, as I spent countless nights in our home office, transfixed to the computer screen. Phil Cook of SAFE has always been there to listen, on the many occasions I have telephoned him, seeking help on some matter or other, or just wanting to *kvetch*. It was Phil who suggested that I turn my research into the book it is today. I also want to give my sincerest, most effusive thanks to Sheila Smith, also of SAFE, who diligently toiled on the first two drafts of the manuscript, helping me prepare it for publication submission. Sheila insisted on clarity over vagueness, simplicity over redundancy, and directness over hesitation and qualification. I admire her candor, and her independence of thought. Thanks to the women who have attended my seminars and stayed to talk afterwards, for reminding me that feminism has always been about openness and inclusion, and for their unflinching embrace of truth over political correctness.

Many thanks to the staff at Springer, for the faith they have shown in this book, and their incomparable editorial advice and guidance. And, finally, thanks to the clients I have worked with the past fifteen years. Time and time again, they have shown me that we learn from both our successes and our failures, and that progress comes when we have the courage to overcome our fears.

Introduction

The Current Paradigm

Domestic violence, also known as intimate partner abuse, is generally understood as severe physical and emotional abuse perpetrated by a male against his female partner. For years, interventions in domestic violence have been based on this assumption. Consequently, the vast majority of individuals referred to anger management and batterer intervention programs have been men. Clinicians in the private and public mental health field, county agencies, and child protective services typically regard violence by women as rare, inconsequential, or symptomatic of underlying emotional issues, or as a reaction to violence perpetrated by males. A corollary assumption is that men are motivated by a need to dominate their women, and that the ultimate cause of partner abuse stems from a patriarchal structure that systematically oppresses women. Neither female initiated aggression nor mutually perpetrated aggression is a consideration within this theoretical construct. Asking a female victim to participate in counseling with her abuser would be regarded as dangerous and unjust, the moral equivalent of further victimization (Bograd, 1984). In many states, including California, individuals involved in court-mandated cases have been prohibited from participating in couples or family therapy, regardless of the couple's history or the possible value of these interventions. Most often, perpetrator and victim have been required to utilize treatment models based on sociopolitical theories of patriarchy.

But such models have not demonstrated higher rates of successful outcomes than those based on alternative theories (National Research Council/Institute of Medicine, 1998; Saunders & Hamill, 2003). Furthermore, the most reliable and empirically sound research indicates that although women sustain twice the number of injuries, men and women physically and emotionally abuse each other at equal rates, and that domestic violence is not a unitary phenomenon, but a complex one, involving multiple motives, various degrees of severity, and, as often as not, is mutual in nature. In fact, severe, unilateral violence by men represents less than 5% of spousal assaults (Straus et al., 1990). In previous years, individuals who entered the criminal justice system were likely to comprise the 5%, and more likely to fit a severe battering profile. However, with the advent of zero tolerance policies, law enforcement agencies and mental health professionals are encountering a much more diverse population of offender, including men with less severe abuse histories, a greater proportion of women, and gay and lesbian perpetrators. Most current treatment models have failed to tailor programs with these variables in mind.

This manual seeks to correct these shortcomings. It departs from the patriarchal paradigm, and offers a gender-inclusive systems approach to domestic violence.

BATTERING AND DOMESTIC VIOLENCE: STRUGGLING FOR DEFINITIONS

Current misconceptions about domestic violence exist largely because the shelter movement is often at the forefront of disseminating information and influencing public policy on domestic violence. An assumption of these service providers is that if serious consideration were given to other forms of violence, or to male victims, funding for battered women services would decrease.

Much of the confusion also concerns how domestic violence and battering are defined. Murray Straus and his colleagues, who conducted the National Family Violence Surveys, originally defined battering as the use of serious violence, that is, punching, kicking, or slapping, and very serious violence, such as beatings or weapon use. Indeed, men perpetrate the majority of the latter. The assaults by many of these men, labeled "Cobras" and "Pit Bulls" by well-known researchers Neil Jacobsen and John Gottman, or "intimate terrorists" by sociologist Michael Johnson, are particularly vicious and sometimes deadly. Naturally, serious assaults receive the most attention. Not surprisingly, they have come to represent all violent males. Furthermore, research indicates that some men, once they establish dominance with physical aggression, are able to intimidate their partners into submission with merely the threat of violence. But intimidation, as represented in the now-famous "Power and Control Wheel" (Pence & Paymar, 1993), is regarded as one tactic among the several power and control tactics these men employ, and the definition of "control" has been expanded beyond that of physical intimidation to include such tactics as isolation, emotional abuse, and using children (e.g., tell children negative things about partner, join children against partner, threaten to take children away).

This broader definition, together with a focus on more sensational cases of battering and the assumption that men enjoy greater control because of their dominant position of power in the household, has resulted in a highly distorted perception of domestic violence. That is to say, the vast majority of men whose use of power and control tactics are nonexistent or minimal, but who have perpetrated very minor violence (grabbing or pushing), tend to be characterized as batterers due to their presumed position of power in the household; whereas violent women are rarely categorized as batterers because they have erroneously been viewed as engaging in lesser levels of emotional abuse and controlling behaviors, and are considered to wield less power overall. But research indicates that women, although generally less able to intimidate their partners physically, are every bit as capable of exercising control through emotional intimidation, and through economic, legal, and other forms of manipulation. In essence, methods of defining a batterer and the creation of intervention policies have been based on a limited subgroup of the most extreme types.

Defined solely on frequency of assaults, battering is perpetrated at equal rates by men and women (Archer, 2000; Straus et al., 1990). But should all assaults, regardless of consequences, be lumped together as "battering"? Approximately 70% of domestic violence involves pushing, grabbing, and slapping, and does not lead to physical injury. Of those assaults that do, the greater proportion are perpetrated by men, because of their superior strength. From statistics provided by the National Violence Against Women Survey (Tjaden & Thoennes, 1998), Archer's meta-analysis of the literature (Archer, 2000), and the Department of Justice (2002), it can be roughly estimated that men cause approximately two-thirds of overall domestic violence injuries and three-fourths of very serious injuries, including those resulting in death. From these data, two conclusions can be drawn: (1) women are physically impacted by partner violence to a much greater extent then men, and (2) men suffer a substantial minority of injuries, in numbers too great to ignore.

High-Conflict to Battering

Below is a more sensible scheme for defining intimate partner violence. *High-conflict* involves verbal and symbolic aggression (e.g., breaking things). *High-conflict violence* includes assaults leading to negligible or no injury. This represents the majority of violence, and is perpetrated primarily by women. Individuals in high-conflict violent relationships use various "dirty fighting" tactics, such as mind-reading or cross-complaining, which reflect poor communication skills and a desire to win arguments; but typically engage in lesser levels of isolation, diminishment of the other's self-esteem, and other abusive/controlling tactics. *Common battering* involves the perpetration of more serious assaults (e.g., punching or biting) leading to visible injury, and is usually accompanied by moderate levels of emotional abuse/control tactics. The *severe battering* category is composed of men and women who engage in very serious violence including beating up and use of weapons and high levels of emotional abuse/control. Men account for approximately two-thirds of the first battering type, and a somewhat higher proportion of the latter. However, although the two typically co-exist (Johnson, 2000; Swann & Snow, 2002), extent of physical abuse and emotional abuse/control do not correlate perfectly. Some domestic violence, therefore, may be considered battering regardless of physical injury, when the nonverbal abuse has reached extreme levels. This type of abuse, perpetrated at approximately equal rates by men and women, can also be characterized as *emotional battering*.

FAMILY VIOLENCE

Domestic violence cannot be understood or treated outside the context of family. Children reared in volatile environments learn that violence is an acceptable way to resolve problems and that love and abuse go hand in hand. As adults, these children are more likely than those from nonviolent homes to become abusive, thus perpetuating the cycle from one generation to the next. Children who witness marital violence are more likely than children from nonviolent homes to exhibit depression, low self-esteem, and oppositional behavior. Although symptoms manifest differently depending on the type of violence, gender of the parent and developmental level of the child, children are affected whether the violence is perpetrated by the father upon the mother, or the other way around. Furthermore, research indicates that children who witness their parents emotionally abuse one another may develop levels of pathology comparable to those of children who see their parents physically fight (e.g., Fantuzzo et al., 1991; Grych & Fincham, 1990; Hershorn & Rosenbaum, 1985). In this respect, the distinctions between high conflict and battering types of spousal abuse are less crucial. But witnessing parental violence is only one problem. Research indicates a reciprocal relationship between marital abuse and child abuse. Parents who are physically aggressive with their children are prone to engage in marital violence, and parents who physically assault one another are more than twice as likely as nonviolent couples to assault their children.

The most problematic violence varies from family to family. In some, it is spousal abuse by the father, whereas in other families, the mother's violence against the children is more often the case. Although the consequences of direct physical or verbal abuse upon children may be greater than the consequences of having witnessed spousal violence, the behavior of each family member affects the whole unit. For this reason, whether the target of intervention is the marital dyad or the entire family, treatment must incorporate a systems perspective.

CULTURAL CONTEXT

The paradigms for understanding, assessing, and treating intimate partner violence as presented in this manual will, for some, seem counter to what is commonly known about the plight of women throughout history. How does one reconcile these paradigms with the bleak lot of females in many parts of the world today, where women are prohibited from showing their faces in public, and girls are genitally mutilated or murdered in ritual killings for being raped and dishonoring the family? Consider the following, from John Archer (2000) of the University of Central Lancashire, England:

> One may ask whether it is possible to explain the considerable number of women using physical aggression toward their partners from the background of coercive male power, which is crucial to both feminist and evolutionary explanations. It is certainly a finding that is predicted by neither approach and at first sight is more consistent with gender-free explanations emphasizing individual differences and relationship problems. . . . However . . . women's aggression can be explained in terms of two sets of beliefs about how men should treat their wives or partners. In western nations, there will be a greater impact of the norm of disapproval of men's physical aggression toward women and a lesser impact of patriarchal values. The pattern of physical aggression observed will be more influenced by individual and relationship variables and less by patriarchal power.
>
> This perspective would predict greater male than female physical aggression wherever there is the unhindered influence of patriarchal values. Ultimately, this is a consequence of the reproductive conflict of interests between the sexes, and it represents a form of default value that should be expected whenever men are able to control the reproductive interests of women. There will be a number of circumstances in which this pattern is overridden, with the result that female aggression increases. One is where there are modern secular liberal values together with economic and familial emancipation of women: Most of the studies finding frequent female aggression were located in such conditions. These values will have greatest impact in a relationship that can be ended by the woman at little cost and where the rate of male aggression is low. These may represent specific instances of a more general set of circumstances entailing a relative change in the balance of power between men and women. [p. 668]

Undoubtedly, in modern Western nations women have made unparalleled economic, social, and legal achievements, and yet men continue to exhibit considerably higher levels of physical aggression overall. One need only glance through the morning paper, or tune in to the first few minutes of a television news broadcast to learn of another school shooting, rape, or other violent crime that has been committed—usually by a male. However, although this is certainly the case outside the home, it is not the case within the home and in the context of intimate partner relationships. In a seminal paper, Murray Straus (1999) offers several reasons for the alarming rate of female-perpetrated assaults in the domicile:

- *Cultural norms:* Although it is considered "unfeminine" for females to hit others outside the home, assaults against intimate partners are widely accepted (e.g., slapping one's spouse for ogling another female).
- *Lesser size and strength:* Women give themselves permission to physically strike out because they consider their assaults to be inconsequential and because they are less fearful of retaliation by family members, who are committed to them.
- *Source of identity:* Due to prevailing cultural norms, women's identities are more strongly based on family than men's. Women thus have a corresponding need to defend their interests and reputation, with aggression if necessary.
- *Violence level of setting:* Women are less likely than men to work in highly aggressive occupations (e.g., law enforcement, construction); but spend more time at home, where they may acquire many years of practice hitting their children as a morally correct, socially sanctioned practice.
- *Criminal justice system involvement:* In intimate partner relationships, abused men are highly reluctant to call the police. Violent women therefore have less reason to stop their assaults.

Speaking at the 1995 Women's Freedom Network Conference, Reena Sommer made the following observations:

Twenty-five years ago, the problem of wife abuse went virtually unnoticed by the legal, medical, social and research communities. Up till that point, women caught in abusive relationships were left to suffer in silence with nowhere to turn to for help or understanding. Little support was provided by their own families because of strong adherence to the notion of "to death do you part." Much of the credit for the increased public knowledge about wife assaults is attributed to the women's movement which, through its tireless efforts, has brought the issue of wife battering to the forefront. Today, wife abuse has been identified as the single most important dimension of family violence. . . . However, the lobby for the protection of women has been at the expense of protecting other family members also at risk for abuse. In some quarters of both popular and media culture, as well as the legislative culture, violence against women by men has literally squeezed out recognition of other forms of family violence, including the violence perpetrated by women against other women (siblings, daughters, mothers and lesbian partners), against children, and indeed against male partners and elderly fathers . . .

At the center of the debate on family violence is the argument of who is more often the victim. Feminists assert that women are unquestionably the greater victims and men are the greater perpetrators—even at the cost of invented figures, illogical arguments and suppressed empirical data which dispel this position. It has been suggested that feminists fear that what is perceived as the more serious problem of wife abuse will be impeded by drawing attention to other forms of domestic violence . . . that by sharing the victim spotlight with men, funds will be diverted from women's shelters and advocacy and towards the needs of men and others suffering abuse. Is it too naïve of me to suggest that by viewing family violence—and specifically spouse abuse—as a much larger problem than it has been until now, more funds could be directed to domestic abuse programs which recognize the role of both partners?

These funds could then be used to bring about long term solutions by working with couples and their families instead of the current band aid strategies that shelters offer to women alone.

I cannot help being frustrated by attempts to resolve the abuse of women by turning a blind eye to those women who inflict serious physical and emotional abuse on their loved ones. By denying this fact, we do little to help women cope with life's stressors, to assist them in building more satisfactory intimate relationships and we fail to protect their victims . . . Even more damaging to the image of women is the label of victim. In doing so, we deny ourselves the empowerment that we have long strived for. As long as women subscribe to the notion of universal victimization, they will never experience the freedom that goes along with having control over their lives. (Sommer, 1995, p. 3)*

A New Look at Assessment and Treatment

Aside from problems involving public misconceptions about assault rates and confusion over terminology, interventions in domestic violence have also been stymied by poor assessment methods. On the one hand, women advocates and DV specialists have had good reason to be skeptical of traditional counseling interventions in domestic violence. Studies have shown that many licensed psychotherapists routinely fail to identify, or minimize, the significance of violence in their clients' relationships. Because therapists often lack an understanding of domestic violence dynamics, they cannot formulate an appropriate risk assessment. Without proper assessment, both the safety of victims and the viability of treatment are compromised. On the other hand, many batterer intervention specialists don't have clinical backgrounds. Lacking the knowledge of individual psychodynamics, developmental psychology, and family systems theory, clinicians cannot utilize a broad-based approach for the majority of high-conflict domestic violence cases. For treatment to be effective, it must draw both from the expertise of DV specialists and psychotherapy.

Treatment strategies ought to be empirically based and derived from the full range of research data. Specific treatment features ought to be based on a thorough assessment and the facts of each particular case, rather than on myth, tradition, or political agenda (see Table Intro.1). It is hoped that you find this manual a helpful tool in our common effort to reduce domestic violence in our communities.

---

*From *Controversy within family violence research* by Reena Sommer, 1995. Paper presented at "Women's Freedom Network Conference." Available at www.reenasommerassociates.mb.ca/a_wfn.html
Reprinted with permission of Reena Sommer.

TABLE Intro.1   Two Approaches to Domestic Violence Treatment

TRADITIONAL APPROACH	GENDER-INCLUSIVE APPROACH
Priority: Protect women and children from men's violence, and hold men accountable for their actions	**Priority:** Protect *all* victims of family violence and hold *all* perpetrators accountable
Focus: Male-perpetrated partner violence	**Focus:** Family violence
Based on: (1) Feminist sociological theory (2) Crime studies (3) Clinical data from battered women shelters and men's domestic violence programs	**Based on:** (1) Family systems, conflict, and social learning theories, and research on human aggression (2) National surveys and meta-analytical reviews (3) Clinical data from a wide range of sources
Current Policy and Treatment Consequences: Funding for women victims, but not for men Public information/outreach directed toward women victims Mandatory, "zero tolerance" arrests Arrest policies, based on men's greater physical strength and discouragement of mutual arrest, ignore problem of mutual abuse and violence by women State law mandates "one size fits all" group treatment, and prohibits individual therapy, or couples or family counseling Heterocentric bias discounts realities of gay and lesbian violence	**Alternative Policy and Treatment Consequences:** Funding priority would be for victims of the most serious violence, regardless of gender Public information/outreach would be directed toward all victims, including efforts to help men overcome stigma associated with reporting women's violence Possibility of diversion, such as "ticket system" requiring further assessment Gender-neutral arrest policies would be based on history of violence, including mutual abuse State law would allow interventions based on assessment and the needs of each particular family, with victim safety a primary concern Reality of gay/lesbian violence would be recognized
Impact on Families: Lower level perpetrators, usually men, forced to take responsibility for their behavior before it becomes more serious However, only designated "perpetrator" is mandated to treatment; others, whether victims or co-perpetrators, must voluntarily seek treatment Financial and legal costs Untreated spouse free to abuse partner and/or children, and is likely to carry dysfunction into the next relationship, further victimizing the children	**Impact on Families:** Lower level perpetrators of both sexes would be forced to take responsibility for their behavior before it becomes more serious Mandated treatment for both parties, unless contraindicated for safety reasons, would dramatically increase effectiveness of interventions Children would be less likely to be victimized in current family, or in the next family unit following a divorce

I

Assessment

1

Domestic Violence Today

DATA SOURCES

Research data on domestic violence comes from three general sources: agency/archival data, crimes surveys, and general survey data. Agency/archival data and crime surveys are limited in that the population samples do not readily generalize to the larger population, but the advantage is that they give more precise information about the particular sample being studied. General survey data are preferable, primarily because more general conclusions can be drawn; however, they may provide only superficial information regarding specific populations. The Conflict Tactics Scale (CTS) is by far the most widely used instrument for measuring the frequency of family violence (Archer, 1999). Its strength lies in the way questions are framed, maximizing the odds of truthful responses; however, the original CTS did not ask about the context in which the abuse occurred.

PREVALENCE RATES

Both men and women tend to underreport assaults they perpetrate against their partners. Some surveys indicate that men tend to underreport somewhat more than women whereas others show no such gender difference. Men also underreport assaults perpetrated against them (Archer, 1999).

According to general surveys, such as the National Family Violence Surveys (NFVS), approximately 12% of couples experience at least one incidence of physical partner violence each year, about equally divided between men and women (Straus & Gelles, 1990). Crime surveys, such as the National Crime Victimization Survey, indicate much lower overall rates, around 1%, with assaults by men 5 to 6 times higher than those by women. The differences between surveys, according to Straus (1999) and Fontes (1998), are due to the particular interview formats utilized. Inherent in crime survey questionnaires are *demand characteristics*, such as the kinds of questions asked, which elicit information on only the most severe assaults, more often perpetrated by men. General survey questions, usually framed in terms of conflict resolution, elicit more truthful responses and correspondingly higher assault rates.

Approximately one-third of physical assaults can be classified as serious, and these include punching, kicking, biting, choking, beating, and the use of objects or firearms.

Women and men perpetrate this level of violence at roughly equal rates. Men choke more often, and are far more likely to beat up their partner; women punch and kick more, and also use objects at a higher rate. Firearms are used at about the same frequency by both sexes (Archer, 2002; Straus & Gelles, 1990). There is a somewhat higher overall incidence of physical abuse in lesbian and gay relationships than in heterosexual ones (West, 1998a).

CONTEXT

Physical assaults are highly correlated with the use of verbal and emotional abuse and control tactics (Johnson, 2000; Murphy & O'Leary, 1989; Simonelli & Ingram, 1998; Stacey, Hazlewood, & Shupe, 1994). More than half, and perhaps as high as 83% of partner violence is mutual, and men and women initiate assaults overall at equal rates (Langhinrichsen-Rohling, Neidig, & Thorn, 1995; Moffitt & Caspi, 1999; Morse, 1995). Rates of female-initiated violence are high, even among court-mandated cases in which the man has been arrested for spousal abuse. For example, the female partners of men attending batterer treatment in Gondolf's (1996) large, multi-site study admitted to having initiated the physical assaults in 40% of the cases in which the men re-offended during a 1 year follow-up. In cases of unilateral violence, women are the perpetrators three times more often than men. However, the number of assaults perpetrated by the average man who is violent is somewhat higher than for the average woman (Straus et al., 1990).

Shelter interviews indicate that self-defense is often a motive when battered women are themselves violent toward their partners (Saunders, 1986). The literature lacks sufficient data to determine how much self-defense is a factor for battered men. However, it is not the predominant motive in most cases of partner violence. Trying to "get through" to the partner, or to inflict retribution, is far more common (Carrado, George, Loxam, Jones, & Templar, 1996; Fiebert & Gonzalez, 1997; Sommer, 1994). Self-defense is very rare in cases of male-perpetrated homicides (Felson & Messner, 1998). Women who murder their spouses often claim self-defense, but genuine self-defense is infrequent, less than 10% of the time (Felson & Messner, 1998; Mann, 1988). However, women who kill their male partners are more likely to have previously experienced physical assaults against them.

Approximately 25% to 30% of all intimate partner assaults lead to injury. Women incur injuries two to three times as frequently as men. The vast majority of injuries are minor or moderate, but women who have been injured are 3% to 33% more likely than men to have sustained a serious injury (Archer, 2000; Tjaden & Thoennes, 1998). About 78% of homicides are perpetrated by a male upon his female partner (Department of Justice, 2002). Due to men's greater physical strength a level playing field does not exist between men and women in physical combat. However, a woman gains some advantage by using objects and by striking when her partner is in a vulnerable state (Archer, 2000; Mann, 1988).

In the National Family Violence Survey (Straus & Gelles, 1990), abused women reported somewhat higher levels of anxiety, fear, missed work days and psychosomatic symptoms compared to men, and they reported significantly higher levels of depression. An analysis of the National Violence Against Women Survey, involving 16,000 respondents, found no gender differences for the effects of emotional and physical aggression on depression, health problems or drug abuse (Pimlott-Kubiak & Cortina, 2003). Abused men more often report problem drinking (Hines & Malley-Morrison, 2001; Pimlott-Kubiak & Cortina, 2003). A male-specific consequence of partner violence is the ridicule men suffer when they admit to an assault by a female partner (Cook, 1997; Fontes, 1998; Pearson, 1997).

Because of new domestic violence laws, and proactive enforcement policies, most of the individuals mandated to batterer treatment have perpetrated less severe types of violence. According to a study conducted by this author, 53% of male participants in batterer treatment fall within the high conflict-violence category.

RISK FACTORS

Risk factors for domestic violence include having experienced or witnessed violence in one's family of origin or community; aggressive temperament; personality characterized by lack of empathy, impulsivity, poor social skills, high dependency needs, and negative attitudes about the opposite sex; high stress levels; alcohol and drug use; and being in a high-conflict, unhappy relationship (Hamberger & Hastings, 1986; Hotaling & Sugarman, 1986; Sommer, 1994; Straus et al., 1990). See Table 1.1.

According to Holtzworth-Munroe and Stuart (1994), the majority of batterers fall into the "family-only" category, and the rest are equally divided between "dysphoric/ borderline" and "generally violent/antisocial." The primary distinction between the family-only types and the others is that individuals in the first group are generally less violent and controlling and tend to act out within the context of an argument rather than for internal reasons. The most severe types of abuse are correlated with personality disturbance in populations of both male (Dutton, 1998) and female perpetrators (Johnston & Campbell, 1993). A recent study comparing men and women arrested for spousal abuse (Simmons, Lehmann, & Cobb, 2004) indicates that women are significantly more likely than male offenders to exhibit personality disturbance in general, especially histrionic and narcissistic traits.

RELATIONSHIP DYNAMICS

Men with borderline personality disorder perpetrate some of the most dangerous and unpredictable battering. It is this type of abuse, according to Dutton (1998), that Lenore Walker's well-known three-stage theory describes (tension building, battering event, contrition).

Most partner violence is mutual, less severe, and most often the result of escalating conflict. The interaction variables in violent relationships include high conflict, anger, negative communication, poor impulse control, mutual dependency, approach–avoidance and attack–defend cycles, and poor assertiveness skills (e.g., Babcock, Waltz, Jacobson, & Gottman, 1993; Burman, John, & Margolin, 1992; Cordova, Jacobson, Gottman, Rushe, & Cox, 1993; Neidig & Friedman, 1984). This author's typology (see Table 2.2) describes violent relationships according to where they fall on the continuum of two axes: (1) severe abuse (physical assaults leading to serious physical injury, and high-frequency emotional abuse and control tactics) at one end, and minor abuse at the other, and (2) unilateral violence at one end of the second axis, and mutual assaults at the other.

TABLE 1.1 Summary of Etiology and Risk Factors in Partner Violence

Distal Correlates (Genetic and Past Influences)	Proximal Correlates (Immediate, Current Factors)

1. *Genetic/Organic*
  aggressive temperament
  temporal lobe epilepsy
  head injury
  attention-deficit disorder
2. *Socialization in Family of Origin*
  witnessing parental violence
  experiencing child abuse
3. *Socialization Outside Family*
  "culture of violence"
  violent peer relations
4. *Violence in Past Relationships*
	1. *External Stress*
	  unemployment
	  other life events
	2. *Personality/Behavior*
	  borderline, antisocial, narcissistic and
	   histrionic personality disorders
	  depression
	  attachment disturbance
	  impulsivity (including anger)
	  poor social skills
	  negative attitudes about other sex
	  positive attitudes about violence
	  alcohol/drug abuse
	  violence against children
	  violence outside the home
	3. *Relationship Conditions/Dynamics*
	  high conflict
	  low overall satisfaction
	  mutual dependency
	  resistance to change
	  drive to maintain homeostasis
	  verbal abuse
	  controlling behaviors
	  generally negative reciprocity
	  approach–avoidance patterns
	  retributional behaviors
	4. *Other*
	  under age 25
	  not married

The literature is mixed on how violence escalates and desists over the course of a relationship (Morse, 1995; O'Leary, Barling, Arias, & Rosenbaum, 1989). Research indicates that most violent couples are rarely assaultive, and that violence occurs during extreme periods of stress, such as separation and divorce. However, the use of even minor, expressive violence can lead to more frequent and instrumental violence (Straus, 1993), due to the behavioral principle of reinforcement (see page 22—"Anger and Coercion: Taking Responsibility"). Physically assaultive couples typically begin with verbal and emotional abuse, although some highly violent men may assault their spouses right away, during times of intimacy such as their honeymoon or first pregnancy. Such men may perpetrate significantly fewer physical assaults after a few years, but most continue verbal and emotional abuse of their partners (Jacobsen, Gottman, Gortner, & Berns, 1996).

Victimized men and women remain in abusive relationships for many of the same reasons, such as emotional dependency or economic insecurity. However, women are more likely to stay out of fear of physical retribution; men, out of fear of being ridiculed or losing their children in a custody dispute (Cook, 1997; Hines & Malley-Morrisson, 2001; Walker, 1979). Repression, denial, projection, blaming others, and the use of entitlement are some of the ways abusive individuals avoid responsibility for their actions.

SOCIALIZATION

Ours is one of the most violent industrialized nations in the world. The home is the most violent institution a citizen is likely to encounter (Straus, Gelles, & Steinmetz, 1980). The general acceptance of corporal punishment, the proliferation of family violence, and the number of marital assaults point to this fact. According to social learning theory (O'Leary, 1988), having witnessed marital violence or experienced direct parental abuse establishes an internalized model of violence used to deal with adult conflict. Adults who engage in partner abuse are more likely than nonviolent adults to have been recipients of parental assaults, or to have witnessed their parents assault one another in their families of origin (Carter, Stacey, & Shupe, 1988; Sommer, 1994; Straus et al., 1990). Violence by the mother has a somewhat stronger effect on adult partner violence by both sexes. However, violence by either mother or father is associated with other adult psychosocial problems such as depression, stress, and alcohol and drug abuse (Straus et al., 1990).

Family-of-origin violence accounts for only some of the variation in adult partner violence. In one study, 80% of assaultive adults reported witnessing no violence as children. Childhood violence more strongly predicts adult partner violence when coupled with the following variables: stress, borderline or anti-social personality, alcohol/drug abuse, and a couple's interaction style (Sommer, 1994). For assaultive men with Borderline Personality Disorder, theories related to attachment disturbance and childhood trauma provide more thorough explanations for partner violence than does social learning theory. Within this population, both physical abuse and rejection by the father have a stronger influence than the mother's behavior or having witnessed the parents fight (Dutton, 1998).

GENDER ROLES

Patriarchal explanations for partner violence assert that men's assaults are natural extensions of patriarchy in which men maintain dominance over women as their inherent right, and by doing so deny women access to political, economic, legal, and educational resources (Dobash & Dobash, 1979). This patriarchal model of causality has several significant flaws. First, in recent years the social status of women has rapidly approached parity with men, and very few households are characterized as male-dominant with respect to decision-making (Coleman & Straus, 1990). Secondly, patriarchal attitudes do not significantly distinguish violent men from nonviolent ones (Sugarman & Frankel, 1996). And third, this theoretical perspective does not adequately account for the existence of partner violence by lesbians, or the fact that the majority of men do not abuse their partners.

Gender differences do persist in many respects (Tannen, 1990). Men tend to value autonomy more than women, and women place a higher value on intimacy. Whereas men may regard women as *sex* objects, women tend to regard men as *success* objects (Farrell, 1988). Research on aggression indicates that women are less overtly aggressive outside the home when compared to men. Although this is the case for direct confrontation, it is not the case for women's use of indirect, covert forms of aggression, such as ostracism or spreading malicious rumors (Björqvist, 1994; Eagly & Steffen, 1986; Frodi et al., 1977). At home, a man's wish to be king of the castle is balanced by a woman's wish to be queen of the castle (Straus, 1999). As discussed earlier, women are motivated by cultural norms to defend their interests in the home and to take charge in areas they regard as their responsibility, such as housekeeping and child care. By engaging in practices such as "maternal gatekeeping" (Allen & Hawkins, 1999), in which she expects her husband to carry out household tasks but then criticizes him or insists on re-doing the job herself, a wife invariably invites conflict.

POWER AND CONTROL

Emotional abuse and coercive control include threats, isolation and jealousy, economic abuse, diminishment of the partner's self-esteem, general control, obsessive relational intrusion, passive-aggressive behavior and withdrawal, using children, legal system abuse, and sexual coercion. Women perpetrate most forms of abuse and control at similar rates to men (Straus, et al., 1980; Kasian & Painter, 1992; Graham-Kevan & Archer, 2002; Coker, Davis, Arias, Desai, Sanderson, Brandt, & Smith, 2002). Women are more likely to engage in verbal abuse (Coker, et al., 2002), deny access to children and other family members and withdraw affection (Stacey, et al., 1994). Men more often use physical threats and intimidation, and perpetrate severe forms of sexual coercion (Felson & Messner, 2000; Tjaden & Thoennes, 1998). Most partner violence occurs within the context of a mutual, escalated conflict, and is *expressive* in nature, involving poor impulse control. In some cases, the violence may be *instrumental*, that is, intentionally used for the purpose of exercising power and control over the other. Instrumental motives reflect some immediate or future goal, whereas expressive motives are spontaneous acts committed in anger, often after a provocation, for the purpose of self-expression.

In a study of dating couples (Follingstad, Wright, Lloyd, & Sebastian, 1991), 250% more women than men reported that controlling their partner was a motive for their violence. In a sample of college students (Makepeace, 1986), three times more men than women reported intimidation as a motive for their assaults, whereas three times more women than men said their assaults were intended to cause harm. In a British study by Carrado and colleagues (1996), an equal number of men and women, about 25%, stated that they had assaulted their partner "to make him/her do what I wanted." But twice as many of both sexes said they were either trying to "get through" to the other or were retaliating for something said or threatened.

EFFECTS OF DOMESTIC VIOLENCE ON CHILDREN

Over 10 million children are exposed to marital violence annually (Straus, 1992). Children exposed to marital violence run a higher risk of exhibiting anxiety, depression, self-blame, anger, oppositional behavior, and a host of physical, social, and school-related problems (Edleson, 1999; Kolbo, Blakely, & Engleman, 1996; Wolak & Finklehor, 1998). The effects of marital violence are greatest on young children, who have fewer coping resources and tend to take responsibility for the abuse.

The work of Johnston (Johnston & Roseby, 1997), Salzinger and colleagues (Salzinger, 2002), and English and associates (English, 2003) indicates that children are negatively affected by marital violence whether the perpetrator is the father, the mother, or both. The research is inconclusive on the differential impact of living in a high-conflict family versus witnessing marital violence (Fantuzzo et al., 1991; Grych & Fincham, 1990; Hershorn & Rosenbaum, 1985; Wolak & Finkelhor, 1998). The research is also inconclusive on the differential impact of witnessing marital violence versus experiencing direct verbal and physical abuse. However, in a well-designed study by Moore and Pepler (1998), children were found to be more adversely affected by the mother's verbal abuse toward them than by having witnessed their father assault the mother.

2

Issues and Problems in DV Assessment

CATEGORIZING DOMESTIC VIOLENCE

Effective intervention in intimate partner abuse requires a thorough assessment, as well as an awareness of the full spectrum of research on the subject, including such neglected areas as mutual abuse and the characteristics of male victims. Overall, there are a number of variables to consider. Clinicians presented with a case of intimate partner abuse may therefore be overwhelmed, unless they have some sensible means by which to organize the data. In the sections below, a variety of typologies and other information are presented to help guide the clinician through the treatment process.

Holtzworth-Munroe and Stuart's Three Subtypes of Batterer

Although the typology below (Holtzworth-Munroe & Stuart, 1994) was derived from research on men, work with female perpetrators suggests a similar constellation of traits. The following table (Table 2.1) has important clinical applications. Successful treatment outcomes are highest among family-only types and lowest among generally violent/antisocial types, who require special attention.

Family-only types are often good candidates for conjoint couples counseling. Dysphoric/borderline individuals may benefit from conjoint sessions if the victim's safety can be assured, and from group interventions, although some formats may be too threatening. More severe cases require intensive individual psychotherapy. Keep in mind that these categories overlap a great deal. For instance, a number of "family only" men *are* hostile to women; and some borderline or antisocial types may maintain control over their partners with only emotional abuse, once they have established domination with severe violence early in the relationship.

Typologies of Violent Relationships

Partner violence involves two individuals. Typologies such as Holtzworth-Munroe and Stuart's are therefore of limited use. The typologies below expand upon those models and provide an understanding of the dynamics of violent relationships.

**TABLE 2.1   Domestic Violence Perpetrators
Descriptive Dimensions and Variables According to Subtype***

Dimension	Family-only	Dysphoric/Borderline	Generally violent/ Antisocial
Severity of marital violence	low	moderate-high	moderate-high
Psychological/ sexual abuse	low	moderate-high	moderate-high
Extrafamilial violence	low	low-moderate	high
Criminal behavior	low	low-moderate	high
Personality disorder	none or passive-dependent	borderline or schizoidal	antisocial/psychopath
Alcohol/drug abuse	low-moderate	moderate	high
Depression	low-moderate	high	low
Anger	moderate	high	moderate
Variable			
Genetic influences	low	moderate	high
Parental violence witnessed as a child	low-moderate	moderate	moderate-high
Child abuse/rejection	low-moderate	moderate-high	high
Deviant peer group	low	low-moderate	high
Attachment	secure/ preoccupied	preoccupied**	dismissing
Dependency	moderate	high	low
Empathy	moderate	low-moderate	low
Impulsivity	low-moderate	moderate	high
Marital social skills	low-moderate	low	low
Nonmarital social skills	moderate-high	moderate	low
Hostile attitudes toward women	no	moderate-high	high
Attitudes supporting violence	low	moderate	high

*Psychopaths, otherwise known as sociopaths, have similar characteristics, but are different from antisocial types. Refer to Robert Hare's book, *Without Conscience* (1993), for more information.
**Recent research suggests that borderline batterers often exhibit a fearful-disorganized attachment style.

Jacobsen and Gottman

Based on interviews with couples recruited through radio advertisement, Jacobsen and Gottman (1998) categorized severely abusive relationships into three groups. The first two are characterized by male-dominated violence, by now fairly well known among domestic violence specialists:

- *Pit Bulls*—These men, akin to Holtzworth-Munroe's dysphoric-borderline type, may appear as well-functioning citizens in the outside world, but within the home can be extremely violent and abusive, particularly when their emotional needs are not met.

- *Cobras*—Unlike pit pulls, these men are not so emotionally dependent on their wives. They have much in common with Holtzworth-Munroe's generally violent/antisocial type, with sociopathic traits and an inability to provide love and intimacy. Cobras are more abusive than pit bulls, and their violence is more deadly. However, once a cobra wife decides to leave the relationship, she is in less danger than the pit bull wife, who is likely to be stalked and pursued. An important distinction between pit bulls and cobras is that whereas the Pit Bulls tend to become physiologically aroused when battering, Cobras tend to calm down, as measured by their heart rate (Jacobsen et al., 1994).
- *Bonnie and Clyde Couples*—A small number in Jacobsen and Gottman's sample included couples who mutually engaged in high levels of verbal, emotional, and physical abuse.

    A striking feature of Jacobsen and Gottman's typology is the absence of female-dominated battering, a consequence of sampling procedures that focused on male perpetrators.

Michael Johnson

Michael Johnson's (2000) model attempted to reconcile survey data showing comparable rates of violence between the genders (e.g., NFVS), and agency/archival data, which often show a high degree of gender asymmetry. The model was derived from both community and court-mandated/shelter samples. Johnson's four categories, based on physical violence, coercive control, and degree of mutuality, are as follows:

- *Mutual violent control*—Both parties are violent and controlling, akin to the Bonnie and Clyde couples described by Jacobsen and Gottman.

Steve, who is very possessive, constantly interrogates his wife, Lenore, about the men she works with. Lenore withdraws affection and verbally abuses Steve. When their conflicts escalate, there is always the possibility of physical violence, which has on more than a few occasions led to injuries of both individuals.

- *Intimate terrorism*—Only one person is violent and controlling and there is a high number of more severe assaults. Johnson focuses his attention on *patriarchal terrorism*, perpetrated by men. Intimate partner terrorists can exhibit either Pit Bull or Cobra traits.

Luke, who has been in and out of jail most of his life for various crimes, including felony assaults, treats his girlfriend, Leah, like a doormat, ordering her around and calling her "bitch." Luke hasn't worked in years, and Leah has supported him with a waitress job. Early in their relationship, Luke broke Leah's jaw when she talked back to him, and since then she has been terrified to say anything about his employment status.

These men can be highly manipulative. A client in the Duluth, Minnesota, Domestic Abuse Intervention Project (Pence & Paymar, 1993) admits that "Sometimes I would really push her to hit me or to brush up against me and then I would really feel justified in hitting her. I'd just think she hit me first" (p. 5).

- *Violent resistance*—One person is both violent and controlling; the other is violent (assumed to be self-defensive, in response to the other).

> Doug, a carpenter in his late 20's, constantly monitors his wife Tracy's whereabouts and expenses, although she has never cheated on him nor spent more than they could afford. In an attempt to "get her attention," Doug has frequently grabbed her by the arm, while verbally disparaging her. At times, when she has had enough of his bullying, Donna will hit back.

- *Common couple violence*—Both parties are violent, but neither exhibits highly controlling behavior. The physical assaults arise within the context of escalating anger. There are fewer assaults and they are less severe.

The following is an example of common couple violence, from one of our own cases:

> Don Kimble, a carpenter in his mid-thirties, sought treatment after his wife, Donna, a 28-year-old retail clerk, threatened to leave him. A week before, he had shoved Donna, causing her to fall on a coffee table and bruise her right forearm. He insisted to the intake counselor that he had not meant to push her, but had done so because he was trying to leave an escalating argument and she wouldn't move away from the front door. In his view, he did not deserve to be seen as the "bad guy." He stated that he and Donna normally get along, but have had some mutual verbal arguments throughout their 6-year relationship, and that Donna had even slapped him on two occasions. Don sometimes finds his wife's criticism and nagging "depressing."

> In a separate interview, Donna indicated that Don had grabbed her on one other occasion during a heated argument (not leading to injuries), and that he has slammed doors and once threw a remote control across the living room. Donna admitted having slapped her husband, each time for coming home late and lying to her about his whereabouts. She says Don doesn't listen, and often chooses to play pool with his buddies, rather than spend time with her.

> A psychosocial history revealed no significant physical abuse in either partner's family of origin, nor in any prior intimate relationships, and neither has any criminal history. However, Don's mother frequently used corporal punishment to discipline him, and Donna remembers her parents openly arguing.

Johnson determined that intimate terrorism represents only 11% of all couple violence, and that it is perpetrated by the man in 97% of the cases. Violent resistance and mutual violent control were estimated to be rare phenomena, with violent resistance overwhelmingly female. Although the model acknowledges some important differences in domestic violence, its conceptual and methodological flaws limit its usefulness: The model assumes a gender asymmetry in the use of coercive control that is unsupported by research (conceptual). Only women were surveyed, and the questions on control were derived from the Duluth Model, which focus on male tactics (methodological). A recent study (Graham-Kevan & Archer, 2004) tested Johnson's categories with a population of both male and female university students and staff and found no significant gender differences in the number of intimate terrorists, or in the number of violent resisters. "These findings," the authors concluded, "suggest that research that has used single-sex samples to provide information on their own and opposite-sex partner's aggressive behaviors may have drawn conclusions about sex differences when in reality the effects were driven by self versus partner report bias" (p. 26).

Johnston and Campbell

Johnston and Campbell (1993) have proposed an alternative typology based on a sample of 140 couples engaged in child custody disputes. Unlike Johnson, the Johnston and Campbell model was derived from extensive in-depth interviews and a battery of psychological testing of both male and female combatants, as well as their children. The five categories are presented as follows, with a description of perpetrator and victim characteristics, and their representation within the sample:

- *Ongoing or episodic male battering*—This characteristic represents 13.6% of the sample. It most closely resembles the classic battering husband/battered wife sceanrio, as reflected in the media. Violence is unilateral, frequent, and severe, and stems from internal pathological causes and chauvinistic attitudes. "Vulnerable to humiliation and often very dependent upon the women they abused, these men generally increased the intensity of the violence at the threat of separation" (Johnston & Campbell, 1993, p. 194). Stalking is common. Victims are fearful, chronically depressed, and mostly submissive, but one subset of women were assertive and had good self-esteem.
- *Female-initiated violence*—This element represents 13.5% of the sample. There is frequent violence, mostly unilateral, but not as severe as male-perpetrated battering in terms of physical injuries inflicted. This violence stems from internal, pathological causes. "The wives in these cases were assertive, willful women who neither looked nor described themselves as fearful" (p. 195). Male victims were depressed, passive-aggressive, or inhibited in their ability to resolve conflict. Although Johnston did not elaborate, she described some of the men as "too inhibited to act or communicate clearly with their wives" (p. 195). Of course, another possibility is that some may simply have used self-restraint, with strong moral objections to hitting a woman.
- *Male-controlled interactive violence*—This accounts for 19.3% of the cases. Violence was mutual, arising primarily from disagreement between the spouses, and escalated from mutual insults and verbal provocation into physical altercations. "Neither the woman nor the man appeared fearful of the other spouse. Both were assertive, feisty, and quick to respond to a perceived confrontation with a counterattack. Interestingly, in a subgroup of this profile of violence there seemed to be a degree of sexual excitement generated by their mutual brawls" (p. 196). When violence escalated to higher levels, generally, the man physically dominated.
- *Separation and postdivorce violence*—This was the largest group, representing 46.7% of the sample. In these cases, there had been little or no violence prior to the separation. "In general, physical violence was perpetrated by the partner who felt abandoned, and this could be either the man or the woman" (p. 197). Violence was limited to a few incidents, some episodes quite severe, during the separation and divorce. Perpetrators later expressed contrition and embarrassment about their behavior.
- *Psychotic and paranoid reactions*—Only 5.7% of couples fell into this category. The separation triggered a psychotic break, wherein "the disturbed partners perceived their ex-spouses as aggressive, persecutory figures and their actions in the separation and request for custody as deeply humiliating attacks. . . . Ex-

pecting trickery and deceit, their policy was to attack before being attacked" (p. 198).

Johnston and Campbell's typology accounts for much of the heterogeneity and complexity of partner violence. However, the postdivorce and separation violence category does not apply to intact, nondivorcing relationships. In order for the typology to generalize to all couples, it would need to be broadened to represent the phenomenon of infrequent, crisis-related violence.

Additional Subtypes

Research by Holtzworth-Munroe, Jacobsen and Gottman, Johnson, and Johnston and Campbell, provide a broad picture of domestic violence subtypes. Unfortunately, these were limited samples, and represented tendencies in the data, based on statistical analysis rather than on absolute realities. The dynamics and subtle nuances of partner violence are more complex than what neatly falls within the demarcated categories outlined above. Research and clinical experience suggest the existence of additional domestic violence configurations:

Female Controlled Interactive Violence

Johnston's observations about mutually violent couples suggest that when the conflict reaches a certain point, the man is able to protect himself and end the conflict through physical force. Although this is often the case, there are situations in which the man is weakened by illness or old age or the woman is the physically dominant partner because of superior strength or martial arts training.

> Mrs. Smith, a healthy, vibrant 48-year old, slaps her frail, wheelchair-bound 72-year-old husband when she is angry with him. Her husband shoves her and yells. When Mr. Smith won't stop yelling, his wife pushes his wheelchair over.

> Jackie, a proficient kickboxer, ends a pushing/grabbing altercation by fracturing her boyfriend's jaw.

> Veronica, a jealous 25-year-old crack user, regularly has verbal and physical altercations with her boyfriend, Joe. Sometimes, she waits until he comes home from the bar and passes out, or falls asleep, and then pummels him with household objects. Veronica always has the last word.

Male-Dominated Nonviolent Control

Many emotionally abusive men do not typically perpetrate physical assaults, but the degree of emotional abuse these men inflict can be severe.

> Dan, a narcissistic mechanical engineer with strong religious views, insists on absolute control of his household. He constantly questions his wife about how she looks and her whereabouts, and gives her money only when she grants him sexual favors. Generally he nitpicks, criticizes, nags, and orders her around. Consequently, his wife suffers from severe depression.

> When Albert, a 20-year-old construction worker, is stressed from work, or when he's had too many beers, he unleashes vitriolic tirades at his girlfriend, Vivian, calling her "cunt," "fat pig" and "stupid bitch."

Matriarchal Terrorism

Johnson refers to intimate terrorism as patriarchal terrorism because of research suggesting that high levels of physical violence and control occur almost exclusively with male perpetrators. By limiting his sample to reports by women, and in particular battered women, his research is gravely flawed. In reality, the percentage of female terrorists to male, although smaller, is considerably greater than 3%, possibly as high as 25%–35%, if we consider injury rates.

> Throughout his eight-month relationship with Laura, Bill's life has been hell. Laura is highly critical of Bill, and will force him to stay up until three a.m., browbeating him with complaints. As a result of not sleeping and Laura's harassing calls to his workplace, Bill was fired from his job. Now she refers to him as a "loser" and "a worthless piece of shit." When he shows lack of interest in sexual relations, she ridicules him, questioning the size of his penis, and calls him a "faggot." During her rages, she bites, kicks, punches, slaps, and throws objects at Bill. Altercations have led to serious injuries, and she once scratched his face so ferociously that he had to have stitches. When Bill attempted to call the police, Laura threatened to fabricate spousal abuse charges, claim self-defense, and have Bill arrested, boasting that "they'll believe me because I'm a woman."

Female-Dominated Nonviolent Control

Like men, women can dominate relationships without using physical violence, by resorting to verbal and emotional abuse and coercive control tactics. Men more frequently instill fear of violence, even in the absence of violence. But fear of violence is not the only kind of terror. The emotional consequences of abuse go beyond one particular emotion. Both men and women can be dominated and devastated by abuse intended to cause emotional hurt, confusion, anxiety, embarrassment, shame, depression, and degradation.

> In her ten-year marriage to Desmond, Lauren only struck him once, a noninjurious slap to the face. However, she maintains absolute control over the household and her husband through a variety of coercive and manipulative tactics such as nagging, withholding affection, persistent criticism, and feigning helplessness and depression to instill guilt. She assigns him chores, but insists on supervising, and corrects him when tasks are not performed to her liking, often referring to Desmond as a lame brain. Lauren has discouraged Desmond from participating in the children's upbringing and has established alliances with the children against him. Having grown up in a wealthy family, she has demanded that they spend beyond their means, necessitating that he work a second job. His absences from the family further alienate him from the children. Desmond feels insignificant and humiliated, and has confided to his friends, "I have no life."

Mutual Nonviolent Control

Relationships in which both partners employ emotionally abusive and coercive control tactics with very little or no physical violence.

The Smiths have had a volatile relationship from the very beginning. Brittany tends to yell, nag, and criticize, and Steve frequently reciprocates with hurtful name-calling. When this happens, Brittany will then not speak to him for days at a time. Lately, she has been telling their mutual friends what a "jerk" her husband is. Steve has closed their joint checking account, as punishment for Brittany going to Las Vegas with her sister.

A Continuum of Violence

The model below (Table 2.2) focuses on two significant variables—severity of violence and extent of mutuality—and places violence on a continuum rather than in categories. Clearly, there are many ways to categorize domestic violence. We should, however, be careful when using certain terminology, or when trying to fit a client into a particular category. Individual behavior and personality characteristics are varied and relationships are complex. A client may have antisocial tendencies, may in fact be a psychopath, without having come from a violent home. Another with a volatile temper and intimacy issues may not have a borderline personality. Every situation is different. The ideal scheme, although unwieldy, would incorporate all the major

TABLE 2.2 Domestic Violence Continuum

SEVERE BATTERING

High frequency, injury, abusive and controlling behaviors. Instrumental violence, used to dominate others, arises from gender-based beliefs and/or psychopathology.

U	*Quadrant #1: Unilateral Severe Battering*	*Quadrant #2: Mutual Severe Battering*	M
N	COBRAS/PIT BULLS (Jacobsen & Gottman)	BONNIE & CLYDE COUPLES (Jacobsen & Gottman)	U
I	INTIMATE TERRORISM (Michael Johnson)	MUTUAL VIOLENT CONTROL (Michael Johnson)	T
L	ANTISOCIAL TYPE and DYSPHORIC/BORDERLINE (Holtzworth-Munroe)	MALE-CONTROLLED INTERACTIVE and SEPARATION/TRAUMA VIOLENCE	U
A	ONGOING/EPISODIC MALE BATTERING	(Janet Johnston)	A
T	and FEMALE-INITIATED BATTERING (Janet Johnston)		
E			L
R	*Quadrant #3: Unilateral Common Battering/High-Conflict Violence*	*Quadrant #4: Mutual Common Battering/High-Conflict Violence*	
A	FAMILY ONLY (Holtzworth-Munroe) *Some cases of:*	COMMON COUPLE VIOLENCE (Michael Johnson) *Some cases of:*	
L	FEMALE-INITIATED BATTERING	MALE-CONTROLLED INTERACTIVE SEPARATION/TRAUMA VIOLENCE	

HIGH CONFLICT

Low frequency, injury, emotionally abusive and controlling behaviors. Violence is often "expressive" and arises from conflict and poor impulse control.

traits as outlined by Holtzworth-Munroe and Stuart and others and would include all interactional possibilities, literally thousands of combinations.

The above model may be sufficient for heuristic and conceptualization purposes, but has its limits. As mentioned in the introduction to this manual, the extent of physical assaults and emotional abuse/control do not always correlate. Some domestic violence may be considered emotional battering regardless of physical injury, when the nonverbal abuse has reached extreme levels. And, as we will explore in a later section, the differences between expressive and instrumental violence are not always clear. Responsible treatment requires an open mind and a thorough and objective assessment. Typologies may help organize and make sense of the data gathered, but interventions should always be determined from the facts of the case.

DOMINANT AGGRESSOR ASSESSMENT

Mutual vs. Unilateral

One of the dimensions of domestic violence concerns whether only one party or both parties perpetrate the assaults. As illustrated earlier, this dimension may be visualized on a continuum, from unilateral to mutual. The literature indicates that the majority of domestic violence is mutual, and the number of couples who engage in mutual abuse ranges from approximately 50% to 60% of the total (Moffit & Caspi, 1999; Morse, 1995; Straus et al., 1990; Vivian & Langhinrichsen, 1994) to 83% (Langhinrichsen-Rohling et al., 1995).

The term *mutual* is ambiguous, with a number of possible meanings. Obviously, a relationship characterized by one individual who initiates aggression and whose partner fights back in self-defense would not be characterized as mutual. In the studies cited, mutuality did not include such obvious exceptions. It was based primarily on whether both parties had initiated physical assaults in the time period studied by the researchers. For instance, in the National Family Violence Survey of 1985, the wives reported that they had initiated violence 53.1% of the time, and their husbands 42.3% of the time. Determining whether a relationship involves mutual abuse is fraught with limitations, and depends on definitions of such terms as *abuse* and *self-defense*. Some questions to ponder in assessing mutuality:

- Who initiates the physical assaults?
- How repetitive or excessive are the physical assaults?
- When the other person responds to a physical assault, is it in self-defense or is it retaliatory?
- When one person initiates physical assaults, is it typically in response to intense emotional and verbal abuse and/or controlling behaviors, and not simply to common provocations, such as nagging?
- How frequent and severe is the nonphysical abuse?

Dominant Aggressor Issues

As the above questions suggest, there may be a number of types of mutually abusive relationships. A relationship can be mutually abusive but not necessarily mutually violent. Also, the violence or abuse may have generally been mutual over the course of the relationship, but not in the recent past. One must also inquire as to the broader context of the violence and abuse, and include factors such as power and control, and the impact of the abuse on each partner.

Law enforcement authorities have recognized the need for such an inquiry because of legal requirements, such as those of California Penal Code Section 13701 (b) and the problems inherent in determining whom to arrest following a domestic violence call. According to guidelines followed by law enforcement (Contra Costa Sheriff, 2002):

> Dominant aggressor is the person determined to be the most significant, rather than the first. Officers SHALL consider the intent of the law to protect victims of domestic violence from continuing abuse, the threats creating fear of physical injury, the history of domestic violence between the persons involved, and whether either person acted in self-defense.

When determining who is the dominant aggressor, police consider:

- Age, weight, and height of the parties
- Criminal history
- History of domestic violence assaults, including convictions and probation
- Strength and special skills, such as martial arts training
- Use of weapons (e.g., knives, guns, objects)
- Whether the injuries are offensive and or defensive
- Seriousness of injuries
- Use of alcohol and drugs
- Who called 911
- Who is in fear
- Presence of behaviors of power and control in the relationship
- Details of statement
- Demeanor of the parties
- Existence of corroborating evidence

To provide for the safety of all parties, police feel compelled to take decisive action when responding to domestic violence calls. This is as it should be. It is always preferable to err on the side of caution rather than risk the possibility of subsequent abuse reaching lethal levels because a dangerous perpetrator was allowed to go free. If police faithfully and thoroughly adhere to the procedures outlined above, they may be able to determine which person may be most at risk in that particular situation. However, due to constraints in training and time, it would be unreasonable to expect that any police officer, during a routine domestic violence call, could determine with any degree of certainty who is the dominant aggressor overall. This is a crucial distinction because treatment requires an understanding of the larger picture, not simply of one incident. As mentioned earlier, men rarely call law enforcement because they fear appearing weak and unmanly, and possibly being subjected to ridicule (sometimes by the police).

Mental health professionals are not bound by such time constraints, and should have a more complete grasp of DV dynamics and mental health issues in order to conduct a more thorough assessment. In addition, it is crucial *how* the factors listed above are considered. The guidelines do not indicate how much importance should be attached to each factor, or how the factors are combined to determine who is the dominant aggressor. For instance:

Age, Weight and Height, Strength and Special Skills

The fact that one person, usually the woman, is smaller and weaker, is a crucial consideration in determining who is potentially at greater risk. This variable is far more important if there has been a history of physical assaults, especially when the assaults have been serious. The potential for violence is less relevant if there is no history of assault in an ongoing, long-term relationship, and there is no intent to harm. An individual may have strong convictions against the use of violence.

Presence of Power and Control Behaviors

Power and control, unless specifically defined, have no meaning. How do we measure power? Does the person earning the larger paycheck automatically have more power? What about non-economic forms of power, such as withholding cooperation, affection, and sex? Power is usually defined in terms of who makes the decisions, who has the most education, who earns the greater income, and who is physically stronger. Control can be exerted by physical intimidation, behaviors designed to isolate the partner, emotional abuse, using the children, and a variety of other methods. Particular types of power and control tactics need to be considered, as well as frequency and ultimate impact.

Communication style can be used to establish power. It is with communication that one negotiates needs. Resource-exchange theory (Bagarozzi & Wordarski, 1977; Gelles, 1983) postulates that the health and stability of relationships depend on the balance, or perceived balance, of interpersonal resources—"rewards" in behavioral terminology. If one party does not adequately reciprocate the distribution of rewards to the other party, the principle of "distributive justice" is thereby violated. The result can be anger, conflict escalation, and violence. Individuals verbally and physically abuse one another in order to redress an actual or imagined imbalance. But there are social controls, such as prevailing laws and ethical norms about the use of violence, that limit the extent of the abuse and how it is carried out. The abuser must factor into his/her decisions the costs of being abusive, such as the possibility of arrest, losing a partner's love and respect, or violating his/her own sense of right and wrong.

Fear Factor

Sometimes, it is quite apparent from observing a couple for only a few minutes which one fears the other. But the person who exhibits less fear is not necessarily the dominant aggressor. Due to socialization or personality structure, some individuals are unwilling to express fear. A man whose girlfriend has attacked him while he's asleep may be quite afraid of her and feel powerless, but embarrassed to admit this to a male police officer. It may be more face-saving for him to claim she is "crazy" or "PMS-ing." The fact that someone expresses fear of another does not mean there is any objective reason to be fearful, or that the other person means any physical harm. Individuals who have previously been victimized tend to experience high levels of anxiety in nonthreatening situations because of past conditioning. The degree of fear one experiences is assumed to be directly proportionate to the level of violence or threat of violence. This is not the case. Some women are terrified when men raise their voices, whereas others have little fear at all. It is equally true that most men are uncomfortable with any type of interpersonal aggression and are deeply affected by a partner's assaults. Violence, even at lower levels, is inherently frightening simply by transgressing sacred personal boundaries, in the same way that a person whose house was robbed of a few dollars in cash, feels intensely violated and unsafe. Furthermore, victims frequently have more reason to fear emotionally abusive and controlling behaviors than physical assaults. A woman whose partner calls her a "stupid cunt" or a man who is referred to as a "pathetic fag" may not fear gross bodily injuries, but may be continuously tormented by emotional assaults. Physically and emotionally battered men, just like female victims, walk on eggshells, in constant fear of what their partner will do next.

Who Is the Dominant Aggressor?

Establishing who is the dominant aggressor can only be determined on a case-by-case basis (see Table 2.3). Clearly, there is no template with which to determine who is the dominant aggressor in a relationship. Several factors need to be considered, and may be combined in a variety of ways. Some examples are outlined below. Patricia Pearson (1997) writes:

> On the whole, men do indeed have a more powerful left hook. The problem is that the dynamic of domestic violence is not analogous to two differently weighted boxers in a ring. There are relational strategies and psychological issues at work in an intimate relationship that negate the fact of physical strength. At the heart of the matter lies human will. Which partner—by dint of temperament, personality, life history—has the will to harm the other? [p. 117]

ANGER AND COERCION: TAKING RESPONSIBILITY

During a domestic violence conference this author heard a batterer intervention specialist state the following, in response to a question about anger management: "Domestic violence is all about power and control. Problems with anger management—well, that's something else altogether." The statement suggests that there are two radically different types of violence: one used to dominate and establish control over the partner, and the other involving poor impulse control or frustrated attempts to communicate. The first is often known as *instrumental*, the second as *expressive*. In this manual, a distinction is also made between *battering* and *high-conflict violence*. Typically, severe forms of battering have an instrumental component, whereas high-conflict incidents more often than not arise from expressive impulses. But this is not always the case. We have seen that coercion can be maintained without the use of physical violence, in the male or female nonviolent control types. Lesser forms of violence may be perpetrated out of instrumental motives, whereas expressive anger may lead to serious injury.

TABLE 2.3   Who Is the Dominant Aggressor?

1.	The man is not very big but has a history of grabbing, slapping, and on one occasion choking his smaller, weaker wife. She sometimes yells or swears at him, and once broke a plate out of frustration, but he initiates most of the verbal abuse.	Man—due to extent of both physical and verbal abuse
2.	A couple both yell at each other, and sometimes get into pushing and shoving matches, none leading to injury. The man complains about her nagging and silent treatment; the woman complains about his jealous interrogations.	Neither
3.	The woman is petite, but has a fiery temper. She is highly critical of her husband whom she sometimes assaults with her fists. Once, after coming home drunk, the woman hit him with a high-heel shoe while he was asleep, causing a deep gash on the side of his head. The man defends himself as best he can, but won't strike back out of fear of hurting her or being arrested. He claims to be unafraid of her, but sometimes sleeps with one eye open.	Woman—because of her physical abuse
4.	The man tends to pick fights with his girlfriend, teases her about her weight, and generally puts her down. An attorney, he argues every point and seeks to win every argument. He has never hit her, nor has he threatened to do so. His wife is depressed and feels helpless to do anything about her situation.	Man—maintains dominance with verbal and psychological abuse
5.	A couple argue and trade insults, especially when they've been drinking. They have a divided power relationship and rarely argue about chores. However, both are jealous and possessive. Over their ten-year marriage, the woman has slapped her husband three times, and once threw a pack of cigarettes at him when she suspected he was flirting with other women.	Neither—woman's physical assaults are relatively infrequent
6.	The woman holds down a $200,000-a-year job as a marketing vice-president, whereas her husband works in an auto parts store. Because of poor social skills, he has few friends and doesn't relate well to his children. By dint of her verbal skills and personality, she makes most of the decisions in the relationship, and cultivates the children's loyalty. She perceives him to be lazy, and will sometimes browbeat him or call him names.	Woman—maintains control with her economic and personality resources

Rod gets irritated by Jenny's forgetfulness. After having neglected to pay the mortgage, Jenny hands Rod an overdue notice from the bank. Rod blows up, yelling, calling her "stupid," and throws a stapler to the side. The stapler shatters a mirror, and its broken pieces cause a deep gash in Jenny's leg. "I'm sorry," he later says, after calming down. "I just lost my cool."

Was the motive driving Rod's behavior instrumental or expressive? How would Rod have acted had he been presented with a speeding ticket by a police officer carrying a gun, rather than a bill from his wife?

Stephanie feels ignored by her husband, Craig, who seems glued to the television every weekend throughout the football season. One day, after he tells her to "shut up," she punches him repeatedly on the face. "I can't stand this anymore!" she screams. Afterwards, she apologizes, explaining, "I'm sorry about what happened. But it was the only way to get through to you."

Was Stephanie's behavior instrumental and coercive, or expressive? One could argue that because of the verbal abuse, and the mounting frustration she had been experiencing, Stephanie's violence should be characterized as expressive. On the other hand, she admits to having had a motive—to "get through" to her husband. This and the above examples illustrate how difficult it sometimes is for a clinician to determine with certainty what sorts of behaviors he or she is dealing with. In fact, few behaviors are driven by a single, pure motive, and motives can exist at varying degrees of conscious awareness. Furthermore, behavior theory tells us that behavior that is reinforced—that is, behavior that has a positive outcome, whether intended or not—tends to re-occur. In this way, abuse has an instrumental, controlling component when it "works," and the individual does not take adequate steps to stop doing it. This can be illustrated in the following excerpt from a counseling session with a violent male, courtesy of Rosenbaum and O'Leary (1986).

THERAPIST: Tell me how the violence occurs?
PATIENT: Well, usually we'd be having an argument and she wouldn't listen to anything I'd say, and she'd keep at me, and I'd just lose control. Before I knew it, I'd be hitting her.
THERAPIST: So, what you're telling me is that you lose control and become violent. You feel you can't stop yourself from hitting her.
PATIENT: Yeah, that's right, Doc.
THERAPIST: Let's talk about the argument for a minute. If I understand what you're saying, when you and your wife get into an argument, you have a hard time getting her to listen to you.
PATIENT: Exactly, sometimes I can't get a word in edgewise.
THERAPIST: She just keeps after you, yelling and criticizing, and you can't get her to stop.
PATIENT: No way.
THERAPIST: Except by hitting her.
PATIENT: It's the only way to shut her up.
THERAPIST: So, actually, hitting her is your way of taking control of the argument.
PATIENT: (*after an embarrassed silence*): Well, when you put it that way, I guess it is.
THERAPIST: It may be a little hard to take responsibility for the violence at first, but when you think about it, it's a lot less scary than being out of control.

Indeed, the line between expressive and instrumental motives may not be so clear. A large, imposing man may only be talking to this wife, but if he is standing very close to her and glowering, his anger can be intimidating and have the desired result of getting her to back off, whether he is consciously aware of his motives or not. If a woman is frustrated with her husband's lack of attention and begins screaming at him, one may argue that her behavior is driven by poor impulse control, and therefore expressive. But her behavior additionally serves the instrumental goal of being heard.

Abuse, whether instrumental or expressive, is almost always associated with anger. Anger generally precedes and fuels abuse—except perhaps among Jacobsen and Gottman's Cobras, who tend to calm down internally even as their violence increases. It is fear, of course, that drives the most intense anger and rage reactions—fear of losing control over one's partner, and fear of losing the partner's love. These attachment issues ultimately must be addressed. But because anger is more often the stated problem, and because anger is used as a justification for abuse, it is this emotion that requires initial attention. To the extent that anger is an unpredictable and at times a very difficult emotion to manage, then violence must be understood within that context. However, if anger is assumed to cause abuse, then all violence is expressive, and by implication somewhat excusable. On the other hand, society holds individuals accountable for their actions, and we know that it is possible for the most impulsive individuals to control their anger under certain circumstances (e.g., when a job is at stake, or with a policeman wielding a gun). The man who slaps his wife after a difficult day at the office does so because he can get away with it, not because he can't help it.

With respect to clearly coercive abuse, the underlying motives are not always clear. The batterer intervention specialist quoted at the beginning of this chapter had been referring exclusively to male-perpetrated domestic violence, which, in his view, is rooted in the patriarchal need to maintain male privilege and dominance. However, the literature (e.g., Neidig, 1986; Sugarman & Frankel, 1996) indicates that violent men, on the whole, do not harbor more patriarchal attitudes than nonviolent men. As Dutton (1994) has argued, the most violent abusers control their partners mostly out of pathological factors, rather than from patriarchal ideology per se. Moreover, if patriarchal abuse is defined as behavior used to enforce traditional sex roles, then such behavior would serve either male or female interests. The desire of some men to maintain head-of-the-household status is balanced by women's identity in the family, creating a greater need for women to defend their interests and reputation (Straus, 1999). Whereas some men may use isolation tactics to keep their women in the home cooking and caring for children, some women may recruit the children as allies, act helpless, and make financial demands on the husband to reinforce his role as provider. Leaving aside men's use of physical intimidation and rape, women wield comparable decision-making power in the household (Coleman & Straus, 1990), and their use of coercive control tactics is as extensive as those of men. Power and control is less grounded in patriarchy or gender factors than in human desire.

The perpetrator typically has a well-intended reason for aggression, such as a need to communicate something important. As the table below illustrates (Table 2.4),

TABLE 2.4 "Well-Intended" Motives for Anger

Motive	Example
Make a connection	Latishia hurls a coffee pot at Rodney in a desperate attempt to get his attention.
Express moral outrage	Steve slaps his drug-addicted girlfriend after she leaves their toddler unsupervised for hours.
Communicate something important	Lupe comes home at three a.m., drunk again, and Manuel grabs her by the neck when she tries to laugh it off.
Set limits/assert oneself	Tired of Craig's verbal abuse, Joanne cracks a vase over his head.
Resolve a problem	Tom keeps his wife up past midnight, yelling and carrying on about their money issues, insisting that "we're going to solve this *now!*"

some motives seem understandable, even noble. Still, attempts to "get through" to one's partner involve some element of power and control. Moreover, victims rarely care if the aggressor's motive for intimidation and aggression is well intentioned or not. Unfortunately, the release of anger for expressive purposes is widely accepted in our society, and often actively encouraged by mental health professionals. Tavris (1989) challenges the view that ventilating our anger automatically leads to psychological and physical well-being. Rather than being cathartic, temper tantrums, aggression, and even some forms of talking it out are nothing more than practicing anger. Research indicates that ventilation in adults and aggressive play in children increase aggressive tendencies and solidify angry attitudes (Tavris, 1989).

In most cases, couples fight because their desires and needs are incompatible and they don't have the will, or the skills, to negotiate mutually acceptable solutions. When not consciously used to maintain dominance and control, the abuse is a conditioned response, the result of behaviors that have historically been successful. The essential difference between coercive and expressive aggression is thus one of conscious versus unconscious intentions. The usefulness of the distinction lies in its clinical application, in distinguishing between personality-disordered batterers who require intensive, lengthy psychotherapy, and those with less pathology, who are amenable to briefer psychoeducational interventions. In either case, it is the clinician's task to help clients take responsibility for their actions—regardless of motive.

A PRISONER IN HER OWN HOME

The combination of a therapist's failure to ask the right questions and a client's lack of disclosure can be a deadly combination in severe abuse cases. One might assume that assessment of severe abuse would be easier than less dangerous forms because victims would evidence signs of physical injuries and psychological trauma. However, severe physical abuse is typically intermittent, and control is maintained on a day-to-day basis with psychological abuse and the suggestion of further violence. Unless a victim appears in a clinician's office soon after an assault, a pattern of severe battering may not be readily apparent. Victims tend either to deny or minimize abuse and can be so traumatized by the abuse that they feel helpless, ashamed, and fearful of further abuse.

According to Sheridan (2001), severely abused women remain in battering relationships and avoid disclosing the abuse to others for a variety of reasons. He offers three psychological explanations: brainwashing and mind control, the Stockholm syndrome, and traumatic bonding.

Brainwashing and Mind Control

Beginning early in the relationship, the batterer subjects his victim to behaviors often used in cults, including social isolation, guilt induction, threats of harm interspersed with offers of love, and attempts to convince the victim that the victim is crazy. Through the use of verbal and physical dominance, along with isolative behaviors that separate the victim from friends and family, the batterer "fosters the development of a partner who is more docile and behaviorally malleable" (Sheridan, 2001, p.

206). After hearing repeatedly that she is to blame for the abuse, the victim begins to blame herself.

The Stockholm Syndrome

If sufficiently traumatized, battered individuals will literally fear for their lives, even as they intermittently experience kindness from the abuser. In order to survive, psychologically and physically, victims align with the perpetrator by being overly friendly and accommodating and sometimes seeing things from the perpetrator's perspective. When this happens, a victim is unlikely to complain or confront the abusive behavior.

Traumatic Bonding

Sheridan's forensic experiences and those of other researchers (Dutton & Painter, 1993) and clinicians (Cusik, 2000) suggest a very powerful mechanism of bonding. In traumatic bonding, the perpetrator exerts increasing control over the victim, and the abuse renders the victim powerless and dependent on the perpetrator. At the same time, the perpetrator becomes dependent on the victim to maintain his self-image. As he becomes aware of his dependency on his victim, the perpetrator attempts to gain even more power over her. This mutual dependence is strengthened by an alternating cycle of abuse and conciliatory behavior. Professions of love and contrition serve as intermittent rewards, the kind of reinforcement that produces the most hardened and persistent emotional bonds. To reconcile her need for the abuser with the harm it is causing her, the victim may psychologically split the perpetrator into good man and bad man parts, with the former fueling fantasies of change and an eventual end to the abuse.

Sheridan offers a list of obstacles, the "12 F's," that prevent victims from leaving extreme battering relationships. Although they were developed from observations of abused women, there is good reason to assume that these obstacles, as well as the phenomena discussed above, exist regardless of the gender of perpetrator or victim. In the absence of physical intimidation, traumatic bonding can be maintained by intense psychological abuse and manipulation.

- Fear: She is afraid of the abuser.
- Finances: She is economically dependent on the abuser.
- Father: She doesn't want the children to lose their father.
- Faith: Her religious beliefs tell her that marriage is for better or for worse.
- Forgiveness: She has seen the good, caring side of him. "When he tells her he is sorry for hurting her," Sheridan writes, "often with tears in his eyes, she wants to believe that he will change. . . . She wants to believe he will change back to the man with whom she fell in love" (p. 209).
- Fantasy/Fix: The abused woman fantasizes that somehow, someday, if she loves him a little more and does what he asks, she will be able to fix him.
- Family: The abused woman does not have extended family support, either because they don't know about the abuse and she feels disconnected, or because they know about it but disapprove of her staying with the perpetrator.

- Friends: She lacks a network of social support to help her leave.
- Familiarity: She has grown up in an abusive home and accepts the abuse in her own marriage as normal.
- Full: Sometimes a battered woman is ready to leave, but there are no shelter beds available.
- Find: From previous experience, she knows that her batterer will pursue her and eventually find her if she leaves.
- Fatigue: She has become too exhausted, physically and emotionally, to escape.

WHY MEN DON'T TELL

Ken, a 28-year old man, appeared in court on an assault charge brought against him by his former live-in girlfriend. He pleaded not guilty and flatly denied ever having been violent with her. He reported that he ended the relationship because she had a drinking problem, became violent whenever she drank, and refused any professional help.

> Since leaving he has moved twice because his former girlfriend came to his apartment and, when he refused to let her in, would yell threats, break windows, and scream until neighbors called the police. About a month ago she came to Ken's new apartment and talked Ken's roommate into letting her into the apartment while Ken was sleeping. She came into Ken's bedroom and stabbed at his groin with a pair of scissors, puncturing his scrotum. He remained in the hospital after being admitted into emergency. Since that time he has had all four of his car tires slashed. Yet Ken refused to file any kind of charges against her, or take out peace bonds or any protective orders, because she is a woman. [Shupe, Stacey, & Hazlewood, 1987, p. 55]

Depending on the nature of the survey, and the severity of the violence being reported, research shows that between 8% and 26% of women who are physically assaulted by an intimate partner report the abuse, and the percentage of male victims who report partner abuse is even lower, between 1% and 13% (Fontes, 1998; Tjaden & Thoennes, 1998). According to the National Family Violence Survey (Stets & Straus, 1989), women are five times more likely to discuss the abuse with a friend or a relative. This partially explains why the overwhelming number of arrests in spousal abuse cases involve male perpetrators. The research is clear on the comparable rates of violence between men and women overall. Yet if female victims report abuse at a higher rate than male victims, males will be overrepresented as batterers and underrepresented as victims.

Abused men stay for many of the same reasons as abused women do, including guilt, dependency needs, a sense of responsibility to the family, a desire to protect the children from mom's violence, and fear of losing the children in a custody dispute (Cook, 1997; Hines & Malley-Morrison, 2001). In addition, men fear the ridicule that follows an admission of having been attacked by a woman.

Why Men Avoid Discussing or Reporting Assaults

The following are reasons men are reluctant to discuss or report assaults by female partners (David Fontes, 1998):

The "Wimp" Factor

A male victim of spousal abuse feels humiliated by his partner's assaults and shamed by society for his failure to control her. Men are considered to be unmanly and weak when they allow an assault by a female or complain. "Taking it like a man," means that men should not complain, exhibit vulnerability, or express pain. "With the prospect of being viewed as 'wimps,' writes Fontes, "and/or having the assaults by their wives unbelieved or minimized by the general public and law enforcement, it's no wonder few men report their abuse or discuss it openly" (p. 32).

Male Socialization

Men are expected to be self-sufficient: This means that they should never need to be helped by others. Men are expected to be strong: This means they cannot express physical pain or the vulnerable feelings of fear, hurt, or sadness. Men are expected to be protectors of women and children: This means they cannot present themselves as victims or appear to need protection. To be a male victim of domestic violence means to be weak. And, because a man who would complain about his wife's assaults is viewed as unable to provide for the safety of either himself or his children, being a male victim also indicates an abdication of his responsibility to protect.

Suppression of Pain

From a young age, males face a common dilemma. When a boy is hit by another boy on the playground, he has three options: hit back—which labels him as aggressive; cry or run away—which labels him a wimp; deny he is hurt or in pain—which labels him as strong. Male socialization promotes and prefers this option. Suppression of pain is considered a sign of strength. When men *do* admit to an assault, especially by a woman, they tend to minimize its impact.*

Results from Two Illustrative Studies

Studies by Linda Marshall, drawn from samples of college students and community residents in Texas, indicate that men minimize both the physical and the emotional harm of assaults against them. The scores for estimated emotional impact of each of the 46 items of violence/threat of violence, on Marshall's Violence Against Men Scales (Marshall, 1992a) were lower than the corresponding items on the Violence Against Women Scales (Marshall, 1992b). One might assume that because men are less likely to be physically injured, they ought to be less distressed about the assault. However, it remains unexplained why the impact weights of emotional harm of being burned, or shot with a firearm, should be lower for men than for women. The emotional toll of having a pot of scalding water poured over one's head, or suffering a gunshot wound to the abdomen, ought to be equally devastating to a burly, 300-pound man as it would be for a petite woman.

---

*From *Violent Touch: Breaking Through the Stereotype* by David Fontes, 1998, available online at www.safe4all.org Adapted with permission of David Fontes.

WHY PARTNER VIOLENCE IS UNDERDETECTED BY THERAPISTS

Victim advocates have long been skeptical of traditional psychotherapeutic treatment of domestic violence, and for good reason. Research indicates that licensed therapists often fail to identify, or minimize the significance of, domestic violence in their clients' relationships (Hansen, Harway, & Cervantes, 1991). The following, adapted from Aldarondo and Straus (1994), are intended as general guidelines for mental health practitioners:

A. Client-based Reasons
    1. *Perception of physical violence as trivial or tolerable:* The couple regards minor acts of violence, such as grabbing or slapping, as not important enough to bring up in therapy.
    2. *Physical violence viewed as a way to resolve conflict:* Physical violence is considered quasinormal behavior, particularly with couples who have witnessed parental violence as children.
    3. *Too narrow a focus:* Some clients fail to recognize that the violence is related to their other problems. Others dismiss the aggression as merely symptomatic of deeper, more fundamental issues.
    4. *Public image:* Admitting to violence would be inconsistent with the positive self-image these clients present in their social lives.
    4. *Shame:* The abuse is concealed in an attempt to avoid public condemnation and humiliation. Men, who are socialized to present a brave façade, are especially reluctant to be viewed as victims, and tend to underreport assaults against them.
    6. *Fear of further victimization:* Chronically and severely abused clients fear the perpetrator may learn of the disclosure and attack them again.
    7. *Love and dependency concerns:* Many victims are reluctant to disclose information that may result in the arrest and incarceration of someone they love or depend on, or may otherwise contribute to the breakup of the relationship.

B. Therapist-based Reasons
    1. *Failure to ask:* The primary reasons therapists don't obtain adequate information about partner violence is that they

        *   Focus on what they perceive as more important issues
        *   Are reluctant to appear overly intrusive, or as though imposing their own agenda on the clients
        *   Want to avoid taking sides
        *   Minimize partner violence, for personal or theoretical reasons
        *   Assume that men can't be victims
        *   Underestimate the human capacity for evil. It's hard to imagine that well-dressed, seemingly upstanding citizens could perpetrate or be the victims of reprehensible and criminal behavior.

    2. *Terminology:* Certain words tend to affect clients negatively. The words *battering, abuse, perpetrator,* and *victim* may be inaccurate or offensive to

some clients. Especially in cases of minor assaults, such as pushing or slapping, the use of the words *violence* or *assault* can result in lack of disclosure.

3. *Failure to ask both partners:* Abusive individuals, both men and women, typically underreport their own violence. They do so to avoid being seen in a negative light, and to avoid taking responsibility for their behavior. In addition, most assaults arise out of incidents of high anger and confusion. Often, the most sincere and honest individuals simply don't recall, at least consciously, certain details of their assaults.

4. *Disclosure in the presence of the partner:* In many cases, questioning both parties simultaneously can engender greater honesty and trust, and lessen the perception of therapist–client alliances. However, individuals who have reason to fear their partner may fail to report, or underreport if their partner is present.

DIAGNOSING ANGER AND AGGRESSION

Perpetrators

No *DSM-IV* diagnosis perfectly corresponds to the various DV categorizations. Some types, such as Holtzworth-Munroe's Generally Violent/Antisocial, seem to fit a diagnosis of Antisocial Personality Disorder, but others overlap with several *DSM-IV* diagnostic categories. Possible diagnoses for individuals with anger/aggression problems follow.

Intermittent Explosive Disorder (312.34)

Characterized by "discrete episodes of failure to resist aggressive impulses that result in serious assaultive acts or destruction of property," according to the *DSM-IV* (American Psychiatric Association, 1994). "The degree of aggressiveness expressed during an episode is grossly out of proportion to any provocation or precipitating psychosocial stressor. The individual may describe the aggressive episodes as 'spells' or 'attacks' in which the explosive behavior is preceded by a sense of tension or arousal and is followed immediately by a sense of relief" (p. 610).

Impulse Control Disorder, NOS (Not Otherwise Specified) (312.30)

This term is used to describe an aggression problem that doesn't fit a diagnosis of Intermittent Explosive Disorder—for instance, if the assaults are less than "serious," or if they seem more appropriate to the provocation or precipitating stressor. Neither 312.34 nor 312.30 is a useful diagnosis for chronically angry individuals who are not outwardly aggressive, nor are they appropriate for individuals whose violence is instrumental.

Major Depressive Disorder (296.2, 296.3)

Aggressive individuals often suffer from depression (e.g., the "dysphoric-borderline" types described by Holtzworth-Munroe). When the depression is less severe, a diagnosis of Dysthymic Disorder (300.4) may be made.

Bipolar Disorder—Bipolar I (296.XX) and Bipolar II (296.89)

The literature and clinical experience suggest that a high number of assaultive women suffer from Bipolar Disorder.

Attention-Deficit Disorder (314.XX)

Individuals suffering from this disorder, both children and adults, exhibit higher than average tendencies toward aggression. It is an alternative diagnosis to Impulse Control Disorder, NOS.

Borderline Personality Disorder (301.83)

A common diagnosis for intensely angry and violent clients, whose behavior is not merely a reaction to stress, this diagnosis accounts for 25% of male batterers in treatment, according to Holtzworth-Munroe and Stuart (1994), and according to Dutton (1998), represent the majority of severe batterers. Also see page 52.

Antisocial Personality Disorder (301.7)

Characterized by "a pervasive pattern of disregard for and violation of the rights of others occurring since age 15," Antisocial Personality Disorder is an appropriate diagnosis for many abusive individuals with criminal tendencies, such as the "Cobras" described by Jacobsen and Gottman (1998), and other highly controlling, severely assaultive individuals. This diagnosis should not be confused with the interchangeable terms *psychopathy* and *sociopathy*, as explained on page 54.

Other Personality Disorders

Narcissistic Personality Disorder (301.81) and Histrionic Personality Disorder (301.50) have also been found in abusive individuals. Together with the Antisocial and Borderline categories, they comprise the related "cluster B" grouping in the DSM-IV. Narcissists are characterized by a grandiose sense of importance and entitlement, lack empathy and will exploit others. Histrionics need to be the center of attention, exhibit inappropriately provocative behavior and shallow but exaggerated displays of emotion, and are easily influenced. It is not uncommon for a particular client to meet the criteria for more than one of these diagnoses.

Adjustment Disorder, with Disturbance of Conduct (309.3)

This diagnosis can be applied when anger outbursts and/or violence follows an identifiable event, series of events, or conditions.

Adjustment Disorder w/Mixed Disturbance of Emotion/Conduct (309.4)

This diagnosis is similar to 309.03, except that symptoms of anxiety and/or depression accompany the aggressive behavior.

V61.1, Physical Abuse of an Adult

This is an all-purpose diagnosis for perpetrators of physical abuse.

V61.1, Partner Relational Problem

This diagnosis is reserved for high-conflict individuals and couples who aren't physically assaultive.

Substance Abuse Diagnoses

Aggression is highly correlated with alcohol abuse and the abuse of drugs such as methamphetamine. Often, the aggressive outbursts occur only in association with substance abuse, either during intoxication or during the withdrawal phase.

Medical Conditions

A number of medical conditions are associated with aggression. These include head injury, stroke, and epileptic seizures.

Victims

Besides physical injuries, spousal abuse victims experience fear, anxiety, depression, and psychosomatic symptoms (Follingstad et al., 1991; Morse, 1995; Straus et al., 1990).

Post-Traumatic Stress Disorder (309.81)

According to the *DSM-IV*, a diagnosis of PTSD can be made when:

- An individual has experiences outside the range of normal human experience, such as a threat to one's life
- The traumatic event, or events, are continually reexperienced, as in nightmares
- The individual avoids anything associated with the traumatic event or events, and/or experiences a numbing of general responsiveness
- The individual experiences persistent symptoms of increased anxiety
- The symptoms persist for more than a month

Research by Cascardi and colleagues (1995) indicates that 33% of physically abused women fit the PTSD criteria. Housecamp and Foy (1991) found that women whose injuries required medical attention, who had weapons used against them, and felt their lives were in danger, were more than twice as likely to meet PTSD criteria than women who experienced less severe abuse.

The domestic violence literature has concerned itself almost exclusively with female victims; therefore the data on men who may be suffering from PTSD as a result of spousal abuse are scant. Because women comprise roughly three-fourths of severe assault victims and are more likely to express fear, PTSD symptoms in domestic violence cases are not usually associated with male victims. However, anecdotal and clinical data (Pearson, 1997) and survey data (Hines & Malley-Morrison, 2001) suggest that men quite often experience PTSD symptoms resulting from a partner's assaults.

Acute Stress Disorder (308.3)

This disorder occurs when a victim exhibits less frequent and less intense PTSD.

Other Diagnostic Possibilities

Victims of domestic violence may fit other diagnostic categories, depending on their symptoms. Many of the same diagnoses are appropriate for perpetrators, such as Major Depression, Dysthymic Disorder, various Adjustment Disorders, and Partner Relational Problem. It should be noted that alcohol and substance abuse might be a *response* to abuse, as well as a precipitant. Cases of mutual abuse often include various combinations, such as a man with Intermittent Explosive Disorder and a woman with Bipolar Disorder, or a man with Major Depression and a spouse with Borderline Personality Disorder.

Battered Woman Syndrome

Although not included in the *DSM-IV*, Battered Woman Syndrome is often used to describe women who have been subjected to severe, chronic forms of abuse. Walker (1983) postulated that female victims suffer from a type of learned helplessness as a result of the unpredictable nature of the aggression, in combination with gross power imbalances in the relationship in which women are powerless to fight back during an attack. The syndrome is recognized in all 50 states as a legal defense for women who kill their abusive husbands.

But the term does not apply in the vast majority of spousal abuse cases, which are less severe and less chronic. In addition, flaws exist in the cycle part of the theory, which was based on limited samples and interview protocols high in demand characteristics. Research with female victims who have come to the attention of the police (Apsler et al., 2002) indicate that as many as 61% think future abuse is "not at all likely" or only "slightly likely." The same study questions the validity of learned helplessness, in that only 48% reported to have been "not at all afraid" or only "slightly afraid" of their perpetrator. Finally, women often leave, or fight back (Faigman, 1986). Referring to the female victims of episodic/ongoing battering, the type of violence their study identified as most closely resembling Walker's conception, Johnston and Campbell (1993) observed that "a subgroup of them did not tolerate the abuse. They left the marital relationship early, soon after the abuse was first manifest. These were assertive women with high self-esteem and good reality testing" (p. 194).

3

Conducting DV Assessments

ASSESSING FOR PARTNER VIOLENCE:
GENERAL GUIDELINES FOR MENTAL HEALTH PROFESSIONALS

The following sections provide detailed, step-by-step procedures with which to properly assess cases of intimate partner abuse. Here is a summary of some general guidelines.

A. Know the warning signs of possible partner violence:
   1. Frequent conflicts and high relationship dissatisfaction. (Some physically and verbally aggressive couples [see Lloyd, 1996] will not report distress. They accept the aggression as normal, sometimes as evidence of love.)
   2. Verbal and emotional abuse, especially disparaging statements and name-calling (e.g., that characterize the partner as fat, ugly, or a loser).
   3. Symbolic violence (e.g., breaking partner's valued possessions).
   4. Alcohol or drug abuse.
   5. Evidence that one partner is afraid of the other.
   6. Evidence of aggressive personality and controlling behaviors. In addition to physical intimidation, look for verbal abuse, jealousy, and isolating behaviors (from friends, family, or children), economic abuse, emotional withdrawal, and diminishment of self-esteem.
   7. Psychopathology (Borderline, Antisocial Personality, Bipolar Disorder).
   8. Corporal punishment of the children.
   9. Violence in family of origin.
   10. Violence in previous relationships.
B. Ask specific questions:
   1. Both men and women tend to underestimate the violence they perpetrate on their partners, and men also tend to minimize the seriousness of assaults perpetrated upon them. Avoid global questions, such as, "Has there been violence?" Many people don't consider pushing or slapping as violence. Avoid words like *abuse* and *battering*, which are nebulous and foster denial.
   2. Frame questions in terms of conflict resolution, for example, "When you have had disagreements with your partner, how have you tried to resolve them?" This is less threatening and elicits more candid responses.

3. Inquire about verbal abuse first, then symbolic violence (e.g., breaking things), then about physical violence, from minor to serious. Clients are sometimes more willing to disclose severe episodes of violence when they have already admitted to lesser ones.

4. Once you have obtained data about acts of aggression, then ask about context—who tends to initiate the aggression, self-defense, and injuries.

C. Be familiar with the various assessment instruments (e.g., Conflict Tactics Scale, Staxi II Anger Inventory, and the Controlling and Abusive Tactics Questionnaire [CAT]).

D. Determine the type and severity of partner violence:

1. Severity: punching or choking versus grabbing or pushing, injuries, and whether the violence is mutual or one person perpetrates the assaults.

2. Lack of remorse and other psychopathic traits.

3. Whether the violence appears to be primarily *expressive* (impulsive, "heat of battle" response) or *instrumental* (intended to dominate, intimidate, and control).

4. Whether one person is generally more dominant. The dominant aggressor is not necessarily the one who hits more often, but the one who maintains control through verbal and emotional abuse and various control tactics.

E. Put safety first:

1. Expect that both perpetrator and victim will minimize the abuse. The most serious battering is often not immediately evident. Always err on the side of caution when determining risk potential.

2. The smaller partner is not always the most at risk; the perpetrator must have both the means and the will to hurt the other. Men use fists, but women use objects and weapons at equal or higher rates than men.

3. Determine if violence might escalate to dangerous levels according to prior history and credibility of threats, not only on expressions of fear. Men, in particular, are socially conditioned to present a brave façade, and are reluctant to verbalize fear.

F. Conduct a family violence assessment:

1. Always interview both partners, separately at first, but then together if that is possible, and if the safety of all parties can be reasonably assured.

2. Interview the children, separately or with the parents, about family violence. Older children and adolescents usually give more accurate information.

3. Ask children first about sibling violence, which is less threatening. Then ask about spousal and parental violence.

4. Always frame questions in terms of conflict and avoid loaded words such as *abuse*. Because children are more suggestible than adults, start with open questions, then ask about specific acts, or compare to sibling or parental abuse: "When your parents aren't getting along, what do they do?"

A format for conducting collateral interviews with children can be found on pages 188–189.

SUGGESTED ASSESSMENT PROTOCOL

Depending on the number of people to be interviewed, the client's degree of cooperation, and the number of documents to be reviewed (police, court, medical, and psychological reports), a domestic violence assessment can be conducted in two or three 50-minute sessions. The following protocol is suggested for conducting a domestic violence assessment. This protocol is appropriate for voluntary clients, as well as those mandated by the court to complete a 52-week batterer program, with a few exceptions noted.

It is always preferable to interview both the identified patient/designated perpetrator and his/her spouse, who may be either a victim or a co-perpetrator. For reasons of safety and to obtain the most accurate, truthful information, the parties ought to be seen separately at the initial session. If the parties are self-referred as a couple, the clinician should conduct a preliminary screening on the phone to determine the appropriateness of seeing them conjointly for the first session. The fact that a couple voluntarily seeks help does not necessarily mean that one party is not in fear of the other.

CLIENT SESSION #1

Part 1 (see pages 157–159) consists of a general psychosocial assessment. It should include basic demographic information, referral source (who referred the client, and why?), who lives in the home and what children or ex-spouses are living out of the home, and presenting problems.

The counselor begins with an open-ended question, such as, "What brings you here today?" For most people, this implies the last incident, or series of incidents, of domestic violence, but many clients are often evasive and don't answer in a straightforward fashion. Clients may claim they don't know why they have been referred, when they do know but are reluctant to admit it. The information obtained is important in determining the client's level of motivation and the extent of projection, minimization, or denial defenses.

Considering the unethical, destructive, and illegal behaviors perpetrators have engaged in, domestic violence clients are usually defensive. As a typical ploy they may focus on the events leading up to the last abuse incident. To some extent, providing a context for the behavior is healthy and normal, but some clients obscure the reality of their actions to avoid accountability. The counselor needs to obtain only general background information at this time; specific details of the events immediately leading up to the incident can be obtained later, when the attention is directed to the client's abuse history.

The counselor must identify other significant events that may have recently occurred in the client's life, including illnesses, deaths, change in employment status, moves, and other stressors. The counselor ascertains the client's mood and mental status, and begins to speculate about a possible diagnosis. Comparing data obtained from the interview protocol with information presented elsewhere in the assessment section of this manual, the counselor also begins to categorize the perpetrator's violence.

It is especially important to assess the overall functioning of the client's family and any problems individual members may be having. How do people get along? Are there alliances? Scapegoats? At this point, the counselor would inquire about parent–child relationships, particularly the style of punishment used. The counselor should not be confrontational or judgmental. When the client discloses that the children often act up the counselor might ask, "Sounds like you've got your hands full. How do you usually deal with that?" In a later session, a more thorough parent–child assessment may be conducted.

The counselor inquires about previous mental health treatment, anger management and/or batterer intervention, and any counseling obtained in childhood or adolescence. Questions to ask might include: "Why did you go into counseling at that time?" "What was the focus of the sessions?" "How do you think they went?" The information gathered can determine whether violence is a recent or chronic problem, and how amenable the client will be to treatment. If the session is conjoint, the counselor inquires about the partner's counseling history. Once this phase of the interview is concluded, the counselor administers the domestic violence questionnaires.

For anger management/domestic violence assessment, Part 1, the recommended instruments for gauging the severity of intimate partner abuse are the Conflict Tactics Scale, or CTS (page 161), the CTS-2, and the CAT (Controlling and Abusive Tactics Questionnaire). The CTS is administered orally by the counselor. It is a brief instrument, however, and should be used in conjunction with the CAT (pages 172–177) when working with difficult and complex cases, such as those involving child custody disputes, or when a thorough evaluation has otherwise been deemed necessary. An alternative is the CTS-2, a self-administered instrument that takes fifteen to twenty minutes to complete, and includes items on injury and sexual assault. A sample of the self-administered CTS-2, known to the client under the title, "Relationship Behaviors," can be found on page 163.[1]

If the self-administered CTS-2 is used, it is advisable that the client complete it at the counselor's office. Clients are more likely to give truthful answers if they don't have too much time to think about it. While the client is completing the questionnaire, the counselor, provided he/she has secured the necessary releases, may contact other parties relevant in the case, and/or review any documents the client may have brought in to the session (such as probation or police reports). The CTS and CTS-2 are especially useful when clients are asked not only about their own abusive behaviors, but also any abuse perpetrated by their partner. This even-handed approach helps to reduce resistance and elicits more truthful responses.

When either version of the CTS has been concluded, the remainder of the session (time permitting) can be spent interviewing the client in greater detail about abuse in his/her current relationship. Because of time constraints, the CTS-2 usually needs

---

[1]Sample items from the CTS-2 have been duplicated in this manual for illustrative purposes only. The CTS-2 is an instrument which can be obtained at Western Psychological Services, 12031 Wilshire Blvd., Los Angeles, CA 90025, (800) 648-8857. Journal articles on the CTS-2 can be obtained from author, Murray Straus. He can be reached at the Family Research Laboratory, University of New Hampshire, Durham, NH 03824, by calling (603) 862-2594, by faxing a request to (603) 862-1122, or through e-mail correspondence at: http://pubpages. unh.edu/~mas2. (No permission is necessary for use of original CTS.)

to be scored later; however, by quickly reviewing the form, the counselor can immediately gauge the general severity level of abuse. The questionnaire, "Relationship Behaviors, Part 2," asks about possible motives for the violence (page 165). The questions have been used in DV research, most notably in Carrado and colleagues' British study (1996). Keep in mind that the questionnaire only identifies the stated motives, and from the perpetrator's point of view; actual motives may be different.

The next steps are as follows: Inquire about context, and obtain information about specific incidents of domestic violence (page 166). It is here that the counselor wants the client to go into detail about some of the more significant incidents. But the focus should be on *behavior*, and the counselor should ask questions such as, "What happened after that?" or "Then what did you do?" At this time, it's advisable to discourage clients' attempts to overly explain their reasons for their behavior. After the counselor has documented the basic facts of the client's domestic violence history, the counselor can fully address the client's motives within the context of needs, treatment, and goals.

Finally, the counselor presents the questions in parts B through E on page 166, inquiring about initiation of aggression, self-defense, extent of blaming and contrition, and use of alcohol and drugs. It is here that the counselor should take the opportunity to conduct a more thorough substance abuse interview. If the client reports that the couple has rarely or has never been under the influence of alcohol or drugs when violent, the counselor may still want to inquire about the use of substances at other times, because their use may be relevant to the client's overall functioning. If there are indications of substance abuse, a more thorough intake can be conducted, using the two questionnaires on pages 190–191.

Controlling and Abusive Tactics Questionnaire (Pages 172–177)

If the CTS-1 was utilized, rather than the more extensive CTS-2, it is essential that the counselor administer the CAT (created by the author). This gender-inclusive questionnaire asks about behaviors that correlate with severe physical violence (e.g., harming pets, rape), as well as more commonplace behaviors, such as nagging and ordering one's partner around. The questionnaire contains 50 items and 10 subscales: threats and intimidation (1–4), isolation and jealousy (5–11), economic abuse (12–16), diminishment of self-esteem (17–29), general control (30–33), obsessive relational intrusion (34–36), passive-aggressiveness/withdrawal (37–41), using children (42–45), legal system abuse (46–47), and sexual abuse (48–50).

Because this instrument is relatively new, there is as yet no information on prevalence rates or norms for scoring. The author created it from several instruments (see references in appendix), and from twelve years clinical experience working with violent men and women and their victims.

Following the first session, the counselor obtains legal, medical, and psychological reports and contacts relevant outside agencies and individuals, including the referring party, current and past psychotherapists, probation officers, case managers, mediators, and so forth. For cases involving disputed child custody, a separate information sheet (pages 158–160) may be used. The counselor will compare all of this data with the client's answers in the first interview session, and look for any discrepancies.

If the client's partner is available, the counselor is advised to schedule an interview with that individual prior to session #2.

PARTNER AND CHILD INTERVIEW(S)

There are many reasons the counselor will want to interview the client's partner and/or the children. First, it is usually but by no means always the case that the partner can provide more accurate information about the client's abuse. Clients often minimize their own violence, and sometimes lie outright. In addition, the partner can provide additional information regarding child abuse and neglect, and a differing perspective on overall family functioning. It should be kept in mind, however, that victim reports cannot be trusted in every case. Many victims, out of fear or for other reasons, will minimize the violence perpetrated against them. Others, usually for purposes of retribution, may exaggerate the client's abuse. Clients involved in disputed child custody cases often exaggerate, or outright fabricate, incidents of domestic violence and child abuse allegedly perpetrated by their part-ners. In addition, the partner could be a co-perpetrator of abuse, against the client, the children, or both. It cannot be assumed that because the referral source desig-nated one person as the perpetrator and the other the victim, this is necessarily the case. Interviews with partners ought to be conducted in the same manner and with the same forms as those used with referred clients. A problem that often arises is that of the partner's victim status. If the partner has not joined the client in the assessment process as a co-perpetrator from the start, the partner may be taken aback by the counselor's queries regarding his/her own use of violence. The coun-selor remains matter-of-fact, friendly, and non-confrontational, and reassures the client that the gathering of information is a normal part of the interview process.

When the parents are unable to provide adequate information, the counselor is advised to bring the children in for a separate interview. A format can be found on pages 188–189.

One must be careful when working with court-referred cases in which the perpetra-tor has been convicted of or pleads guilty to spousal abuse. Not all states have adopted standards regulating batterer intervention programs, and the ones that have vary in many respects. California law, for instance, requires that clinicians providing batterer intervention services contact the victim, to notify him or her of the client's participa-tion in the program, and request that the victim inform the program of any further re-offenses. In the vast majority of states, couples counseling is expressly prohibited as an alternative to group treatment, and some states, such as New York, discourage victim contact of any kind by the program, due to presumed safety concerns (Austin & Dankwort, 1998). Clinicians are well advised to become thoroughly familiar with the guidelines established in their own particular state.

If evidence is found of abuse by the partner, the counselor should proceed with additional partner assessment sessions, following the same procedures as in client sessions 2 and 3. Whether the abuse is unilateral or mutual, the counselor should always be on the alert for signs of severe violence and the possibility of a lethal assault. In addition to the CTS and CAT questionnaires, the counselor may want to administer to the victim(s) the *Campbell Danger Assessment*, which can be found on page 186. The CDA measures the perpetrator's lethality potential and the extent of victim risk. It has been developed for battered women, but can be used, with minor modification, in work with male victims (e.g., remove question about pregnancy and change pronouns).

CLIENT SESSION #2

This is Part 2 of the general psychosocial assessment. The counselor now resumes the general psychosocial history (page 158).

Client's Developmental History

It is not necessary to obtain a detailed history. However, information about family relationships is crucial. The counselor asks: "Tell me, briefly, about your childhood. Where did you grow up, and with whom did you grow up? What was it like, in general?" If the client provides information about childhood abuse, the information can be recorded here, or in the "Childhood" section of the domestic violence assessment (page 166). Then the counselor asks what the client's relationships with parents and siblings are today. If they are problematic, why is that? To learn about the client's adult history, the counselor should inquire about significant events in the client's adult life (e.g., marriage, major moves, illnesses, or deaths) and about employment problems. The counselor should be mindful of any significant gaps in the narrative that may be contributing factors of anger and domestic violence issues, like time spent in prison or long layoffs from work.

Anger Management/Domestic Violence Assessment, Part 2

CTS-2 Score

If the self-administered CTS-2 was used, the counselor would have scored the instrument between sessions and can go over the results with the client. This is an important part of the overall assessment protocol because, at this point, the counselor can begin to address any minimization and denial. Without having to directly confront the client, the counselor allows the facts to speak for themselves. A powerful technique to put the abuse into perspective and overcome resistance is to compare the client's scores to standardized norms.[2]

Assuming that the partner has been seen between sessions 1 and 2, information from the interview can be compared to the client's responses to determine veracity. The client's version of events can also be checked against any reports that may have been received and/or contacts made with relevant individuals and agencies. When

---

[2]In general, findings from the National Family Violence Surveys indicate that the average spouse, male or female, will engage in about 4 incidents of verbal aggression toward his/her partner each year, and that any physical aggression is perpetrated by only 15% of spouses. More complete norms are available from the Family Violence Laboratory in New Hampshire by calling (603) 862-2594, or through e-mail correspondence at: http://pubpages.unh.edu/~mas2.

alternative data are not available, but there is the suspicion that the client is lying about something, the counselor may want to ask the client previously asked questions again, during the second interview. Discrepancies between the client's own statements can then be addressed.

Childhood and Previous Relationships

The counselor inquires about childhood abuse, using the questions on page 166. Moving chronologically, the next series of questions concern the client's abuse history as an adult, prior to the current relationship (page 167). Considering that previous violence is the best predictor of future violence, including lethal assaults, history is a crucial part of the assessment process. Ask open-ended questions, such as, "Tell me about your previous relationships, starting with the one before your current relationship. What was it like?" If the client does not volunteer information about abuse, ask about how the couple dealt with conflicts, and specifically whether there was any verbal or physical abuse. To determine the relevance of alcohol or drug use, ask, "What percentage of your conflicts, especially those that led to violence, involved alcohol or drug use?"

Criminal History, Medical Conditions, and Current Parenting

Antisocial individuals, many of whom have histories of criminal behavior, perpetrate some of the most severe and chronic spousal assaults. These individuals are typically manipulative and charming, and the counselor can be misled to underestimate the seriousness of the violence. Information about criminal behavior is a necessary part of a complete assessment. Even if the client minimizes or attempts to explain away the history, the fact that he/she has been arrested, more than once, is telling. Obtain information regarding the client's medical history, or any other conditions that may have a bearing on the use of aggression and violence. Head trauma and PTSD have long been associated with aggression. Now the counselor seeks information about current parenting practices, using the questions on page 167. The counselor will want to ascertain how the client copes with the children's misbehavior, and in particular whether the client or the spouse have used abusive disciplinary tactics. In addition, the counselor will want to find out if there is abuse going on between the children, or directed by the children against one or both parents. Information on the use of the CTSPC Family Behaviors questionnaire, which examines possible child abuse in much greater detail can be found on page 187.

Assessment of Self and Partner's Relationship Functioning

The counselor concludes the second interview with the questionnaire (page 170) and a discussion of the treatment plan. An alternative is to have the client return for a third session. Based on the pioneering work of Peter Neidig and Dale Friedman (1984), this modified version of their original instrument explores seven areas of relationship functioning that are correlated with domestic violence:

- Personal responsibility
- Anger management

- Coping with stress
- Communication
- Conflict resolution
- Control
- Isolation vs. social support

Like most instruments, this one should be administered to both client and partner. When the partner is not available, ask the client to indicate how the partner would answer each item. This allows for more honest responses.

CLIENT SESSION #3

Useful Questionnaires

A third session is required when there is serious pathology, or when the counselor simply needs more information (e.g., when a client has not been forthcoming, and in difficult "he-said, she-said" cases). During this final session, the counselor finishes the interview protocol as outlined in session #2, and may administer to the client any of the following instruments. If indicated, these can also be administered to the partner.

Potter-Efron Anger-Styles Questionnaire (Page 169)[3]

This clear, simple tool categorizes anger into ten dimensions, or categories. The 10 categories fall into three major groups: masked anger (questions 1–9), explosive anger (questions 10–21), and chronic anger (questions 22–30). They are:

- Anger avoidance (questions 1–3)
- Sneaky (passive-aggressive) anger (questions 4–6)
- Paranoid anger (questions 7–9)
- Sudden (explosive) anger (questions 10–12)
- Shame-based anger (questions 13–15)
- Deliberate (instrumental) anger (questions 16–18)
- Addictive anger (questions 19–21)
- Habitual anger (questions 22–24)
- Moral anger (questions 25–27)
- Hate (questions 28–30)

Staxi-2 Anger Inventory (State-Trait Anger Inventory[4])

The Staxi-2 is another self-administered anger questionnaire. It contains 57 items divided into three major groups: "How I feel right now," "How I generally feel," and

---

[3]For a complete discussion, the counselor is urged to read R. Potter-Efron and P. Potter-Efron (1995), *Letting Go of Anger.*

[4]The Staxi-2 is available through PAR, Inc., P.O. Box 998, Odessa, FL, 33556, (800) 331-TEST

"How I generally act when angry or furious." There are several subscales, grouped along the following dimensions: state anger (how the client feels at the moment of taking the test), trait anger (how angry the client is prone to become in general, and across different situations), anger expression in (internalized anger), anger expression out (aggression), anger control in (self-soothing) and anger control out (behavior management). Unlike the Potter-Efron instrument, norm tables are available so that clients can get a sense of where they fall compared with others within their gender and age group.

Marital Happiness and Communication Test (Pages 178–179)[5]

Research shows that marital dissatisfaction is highly correlated with domestic abuse. This questionnaire identifies the various areas of relationship dissatisfaction. It's particularly useful when a counselor is assessing both parties, and when conjoint therapy is an option. An alternative instrument that has been in use for years is the Locke-Wallace Marital Satisfaction Questionnaire.

Experiences in Close Relationships—Revised (Pages 180–183)[6]

This 36-item, Likert scale self-report deconstructs adult intimate partner attachment on two continuums: degree of abandonment anxiety and degree of avoidance. Individuals categorized as "secure" are low in anxiety and avoidance. "Preoccupied" types are high in anxiety and low in avoidance. "Dismissing" types are low in anxiety and high in avoidance, and "fearful" types category are high in both anxiety and avoidance. The three insecure styles roughly correlate with Holtzworth-Munroe's typology: family only = preoccupied, dysphoric/borderline = fearful, and generally violent/antisocial = dismissing.

Obsessive Relational Intrusion/Stalking Checklist (Pages 184–185)

This instrument measures dangerous forms of stalking, such as physical confrontations, and various types of intrusive, unwanted behaviors. It was developed from the work of Davis and Frieze (2000). This version is for victims, but one can easily adapt it for perpetrators.

CTSPC—Family Behaviors (Page 187)[7]

With any indication of child maltreatment, the counselor would be advised to use this excellent, well-researched instrument, developed by one of the pioneers in the field of family violence, Murray Straus. It contains four primary scales:

---

[5]Information about this test can be found in *The Marriage Clinic* (1999) by John Gottman.
[6]Information on the original version of this test, along with the questionnaire and scoring instructions, can be found in Brennan, Clark, and Shaver (1998), "Self-Report Measurement of Adult Attachment: An Integrative Overview," in J. Simpson and W. Rholes (eds.), *Attachment Theory and Close Relationships*. Information on the revised version can be found at www.geocities. com/research93/. Clients can take the test online in less than ten minutes, and a profile is generated immediately upon completion. One option is for the client to complete a hard copy, as reproduced on pages 180–183, and have the counselor enter the data and obtain the profile on his/her computer.
[7]Sample items from the CTS-PC have been duplicated in this manual for illustrative purposes only. The CTS-PC is a copyrighted instrument, which can be obtained at Western Psychological Services, 12031 Wilshire Blvd., Los Angeles, CA 90025, (800) 648-8857. Journal articles on the CTS-PC can be obtained from the author, Murray Straus, by calling (603) 862-2594, by faxing a request to (603) 862-1122, or through e-mail correspondence at: http://pubpages.unh.edu/~mas2.

- Nonviolent discipline
- Physical assault
- Psychological aggression
- Neglect

Supplemental Questionnaires

Parent–Child Relationship Inventory[8]

This is a well-known instrument for obtaining information about general parenting practices and the overall parent–child relationship. It has been extensively researched, and comes with norm tables. There are 78 items, and 8 subscales:

- Support
- Limit setting
- Satisfaction with parenting
- Autonomy
- Involvement
- Role orientation
- Communication
- Social desirability

Child Abuse Potential Inventory[9]

This is a 160-item, self-report questionnaire, containing a 77-item physical child abuse scale and three validity scales, including a lie scale.

Minnesota Multiphasic Personality Inventory (MMPI)

It is not necessary to administer such a lengthy, time-consuming test in most domestic violence assessments. As indicted in previous sections, the perpetrators of the most serious battering are generally personality disordered. Elevated levels on the Pd scale, in particular, have been strongly correlated with domestic violence. Scores on the Lie Scale may be helpful in child custody evaluations, and other complex cases. The MMPI can be useful anytime the counselor has questions about the client's personality, motives, or veracity, or when more information is needed before determining treatment.

Adult Attachment Interview[10]

By obtaining information on individuals' state of mind about their attachment history, the AAI can predict both their parenting approach and their children's attachment style. It cannot be administered without considerable training (Hesse, 1999), and is

---

[8]Available through WPS.
[9]Available by purchasing the manual by J. S. Milner, *The Child Abuse Potential Inventory Manual*, 2nd ed. (1986), Psyctec, Webster, NC.
[10]Available by contacting Erik Hesse at the University of California at Berkeley, Psychology Dept.

not available to most clinicians, but can yield a wealth of information not accessible through the usual interview protocol.

Psychopathy Checklist[11]

This is the most widely used instrument for diagnosing psychopathy (alternatively known as sociopathy). Not all clients who fit the *DSM-IV* diagnosis of Anti-Social Personality Disorder are psychopaths, but many are. Reliable identification is essential, because this population is beyond the scope of practice for most therapists and domestic violence treatment providers. Psychopathic symptoms are listed on page 54 of this manual, but the checklist should be used only by qualified professionals with specific training.

Wrap-Up/Discussion of Treatment Plan

By the time the counselor has arrived at this final phase of the assessment process, he/she should have formulated a diagnosis (see pages 31–34) and have categorized the client's violence according to the information presented in the "categorizing domestic violence" section, particularly the charts on pages 12 and 18. Considerations for treatment planning should include the following:

1. *Is the victim in immediate physical danger?* Complete the lethality checklist (p. 168), and review results of the Danger Assessment. Mental health professionals have an ethical and legal obligation to notify the victim and police in such cases. Even if the danger is not imminent, moderate to high scores on the lethality check list have treatment implications. The counselor will discourage conjoint treatment, and may urge the victim to obtain a restraining order against the perpetrator.
2. *Is the client motivated?* An unmotivated client will resist interventions, will be a detrimental influence in group settings, and is likely to drop out before the conclusion of treatment. In these cases, the counselor may need to extend the assessment process a little longer, to develop a working therapeutic alliance (see next section), or refuse to treat the client altogether.
3. *What interventions are best suited to the client's needs?* Effective treatment can be conducted using various therapeutic modalities, depending on the case, as long as the counselor works within a family systems perspective. Part Two of this manual provides an in-depth exploration of treatment possibilities.

Although it is not necessary to share with each client every detail of the assessment, the counselor should provide a general summary of the findings. Afterwards, the counselor discusses treatment goals and interventions, and has the client sign any necessary paperwork or agreements. For clients going into group the counselor goes over the program rules regarding attendance, participation, etc.

---

[11]For more information read Robert Hare's *Without Conscience: The Disturbing World of the Psychopaths Among Us* (1993). His Psychopathy Checklist, the standard assessment tool, can be obtained from Multi-Health Systems, 908 Niagara Falls Blvd., North Tonawanda, NY, 14120-2060.

Developing a Therapeutic Alliance

Assessment has important functions besides information-gathering (e.g., helps over-come resistance, motivates the client to change, and establishes treatment goals). Abusive clients arrive with different levels of motivation. Many have had no prior counseling and are apprehensive. They may worry about being judged or told that they are inadequate or bad. The counselor's role is to elicit more truthful responses and facilitate accountability without alienating or shaming them. Gaining the client's trust is essential.

Interviews should be conducted in a respectful, non-threatening, businesslike manner. The counselor must show he/she is incapable of being manipulated and yet capable of caring and understanding. For instance, rather than suggesting that the client is a liar, the counselor matter-of-factly addresses discrepancies between what the client has said and information provided by other family members, outside sources, and court records. "Your version of the events," the counselor might say, "is different from so-and-so's." Most clients minimize their violence out of guilt and embarrassment or fear of disapproval, in contrast to the calculated lying of psycho-paths and some antisocial individuals, who lie purely out of self-interest. The first type of lying represents common denial, which can be dealt with and overcome during the course of treatment; the latter type indicates an unwilling, and most likely unsuitable, candidate for treatment.

The counselor should convey disapproval of all abusive behavior; otherwise, the client will think the counselor condones violent aggression and will lose respect for the counselor. Clients usually know that violence is wrong. However, the counselor must also express an understanding of clients' situations, the stresses they may have experienced, and their helplessness. When clients complain about abuse by their partner, the counselor should not automatically interpret this as an attempt to blame or as a means to deflect attention from their own behavior. Although this can be a motive, clients also need to feel they are being treated fairly and see that their partners will be held to the same standard of conduct. The counselor acknowledges that violence, other than self-defense, is always wrong, and that "two wrongs don't make a right."

Perpetrators often believe they have a good reason for resorting to violence. Typically, however, their focus is on the partner's negative behavior, which leads to blaming and denial. The counselor's task is to help each client identify his/her *positive intentions* behind the abuse. Beneath the surface motives of control, retribution, and so on is often a separate desire to have a better relationship, to gain intimacy, or to feel respected. Clients may want to change, but for external reasons—to avoid incarceration, separation, or divorce. Eventually, the client must find an *internal* basis for change. On the other hand, clients have a legitimate reason for wanting to advance their own interests. At odds with their partners, many feel legitimately hurt, abused, or taken advantage of, and are not motivated to please them. At least in the short run, it's therefore important that they find in treatment something of value for themselves. The counselor helps clients understand how their behavior has undermined their own best interests. Even clients who are unwilling to admit they are wrong can nonetheless understand cause and effect—the negative consequences of their actions. The counselor uses information gathered during the interview process to point out how abusive behaviors appear to bring about temporary success (getting a spouse to stop nagging), but ultimately fail by causing more dissension and chaos (withdrawal, more fighting).

Once the counselor facilitates the client's discovery of how self-defeating the current behavior has been, the counselor introduces some alternative means of communicating, healthy expressions of power, and effective methods of coping. Thus, the counselor becomes an ally, rather than an extension of the judicial system or an antagonist.

4

Special Considerations in DV Assessment

ETHNIC MINORITY CLIENTS

The assessment and treatment of an ethnic minority individual may vary little from procedures used with Caucasians, or the process may require a great deal of specialization. The type of ethnic minority group and the level of acculturation are factors for consideration. Many ethnic minority clients avoid help-seeking altogether, or withhold information needed for a competent assessment if the service provider is Caucasian. Some clients cannot be assisted unless they work with someone from their own ethnic group. If the clinic does not have the appropriate staff, the client will need to be referred elsewhere. Many ethnic minority clients are willing to work with Caucasians if the service provider has an understanding of cross-cultural issues. The following factors (Malley-Morrison & Hines, 2004; West, 1998b) can be obstacles that impede assessment and treatment. Providers should take these into account when working with either perpetrators or victims. For more information on ethnicity and family violence, refer to the outstanding new volume by Kathleen Malley-Morrison and Denise Hines, *Family Violence in a Cultural Perspective*.

Cultural and Institutional Considerations

Some ethnic minority clients have a general distrust of Caucasians, simply because of the racism and mistreatment their group has suffered in the past, or may continue to suffer. There are other factors, specific to particular cultures. Many African Americans have strong religious beliefs that emphasize faith and prayers over professional counseling. Asian Americans often fear that they will bring shame upon their family and "lose face," if they discuss problems with an outsider. Latino women are also reluctant to report abuse, and the subject of husband abuse is essentially a taboo subject. A number of Asian Americans and Native Americans believe that problems may not have a solution and ought to be endured. Attention also needs to be paid to problems such as lack of culturally appropriate materials, inadequate grasp of the client's culture by the counselor, and lack of available staff who can translate or speak the client's language.

Stereotypes and Misperceptions

In the larger culture, including the media, numerous stereotypes are perpetuated about ethnic minorities.

1.   Minority clients are viewed as innately violent. African-American men, particularly young men, are considered aggressive *and* likely to engage in criminal activity. National surveys do indeed indicate a greater extent of intimate partner abuse among African Americans, with homicide rates for both male and female victims considerably higher than those of whites. Furthermore, African Americans, along with Asians, are more accepting of corporal punishment than whites are. However, most of these differences disappear when socioeconomic factors and historical racism are considered. For instance, a disproportionate number of African Americans live in poverty, and the high murder rates can be partially explained by the proliferation of firearms in their communities. Also, traditional West African cultures, from which African Americans are descended, have among the lowest rates of wife abuse and male dominance in the world.

2.   Certain minorities, such as Latinos, are considered more accepting of violence due to patriarchal values, and/or are stereotyped as hot blooded and impulsive. In fact, Latinos place a high value on family. This serves both as a risk factor for maltreatment (by inhibiting disclosure), and as a protective factor (by providing a buffer against external stressors, such as poverty and isolation). *Machismo* may be interpreted in a positive or a negative manner. The hyper-masculine type of machismo is certainly associated with wife abuse, and prevents help-seeking by the batterer, who would interpret it as a sign of weakness. However, most Latinos value the more honorable form of machismo, in which women are to be protected and honored, as well as *respeto*, the ethic of obedience, duty, and deference to one's elders, which serves as a check against elder abuse. In sum, Latinos are no more impulsive or harbor more pro-violence beliefs, nor are Latino men any more misogynistic than whites.

3.   A victim's ability to cope may be overestimated. For example, African-American women are perceived to be either strong (typically as dominant matriarchs), or bad in some way, and therefore less in need of assistance. They are rarely seen as weak, passive, or as victims.

4.   Ethnic minority subgroups are assumed to have the same characteristics. Thus, Cuban Americans and Mexican Americans, despite the substantial differences in their cultures, are regarded as Latino or Hispanic, and Korean, Japanese, Chinese, and South Asian Americans are lumped together as Asians. Asians do share some common characteristics, but they also have significant differences. Chinese, for example, are much less accepting of domestic violence than Vietnamese or Laotians are. Some minority groups, such as Jews, are so diverse as to make any generalizations almost meaningless. Certain sects of Orthodox Jews can be quite insular, and almost fanatical in their religious beliefs, whereas others have so thoroughly blended into the secular, Gentile population as to be nearly invisible.

5.   It is often not recognized that individuals within a particular minority group are at different levels of acculturation. A third-generation Chinese American going to a university is likely to have values and live a lifestyle far different from a recent immigrant who does not speak English. More acculturated clients will relate more easily to the treatment provider and may, in fact, feel patronized if they are treated differently from their white counterparts.

SUBSTANCE ABUSE AND DOMESTIC VIOLENCE

High correlations have been found between domestic violence by men and alcohol abuse (e.g., Gelles & Loseke, 1996). Domestic violence by both sexes has also been correlated with overall substance abuse.

To evaluate a case for the presence of substance abuse or addiction, one is advised to inquire indirectly. Alcohol and drug abusers typically deny or minimize their use. The counselor should ask within the context of the domestic violence questionnaire (e.g., "When you have been verbally or physically aggressive, what percentage of the time were you under the influence of alcohol or other drugs?" In our experience, clients are disarmed by this question and readily concede to rates of 50% or more). The chart on page 53 may be helpful in detecting alcohol and drug use. With any evidence of possible drug abuse, the forms on pages 190–191, are useful.

According to Potter-Efron and Potter-Efron (1991), substance-induced aggression is dependent upon several variables. The setting is an important mediating variable—if there are threats in the environment, or if the person feels "closed in." Aggression is more likely while the drug is beginning to take effect, and less likely when the effects are decreasing. The person's mood and mental condition prior to taking the substance are key factors. Aggression may be induced through a variety of mechanisms and drug effects, including diminishment of ego controls and release of submerged anger, impairment of judgment, impulsiveness and irritability, paranoia, feelings of omnipotence, fugue states, and amnesia. The following table (Table 4.1), from Potter-Efron and Potter-Efron (1991), illustrates the relationship between

TABLE 4.1 Various Ways That Substance Abuse Leads to Aggression

(The numbers are for comparative purposes, with 0 = no association and 4 = very strong association)	Production of irritable, short-fused state	Induction of acute paranoid thoughts/ behavior	Exacerbation of underlying paranoid state	Disinhibition of intrinsic anger
Alcohol or sedative intoxication	2–3	1	0–2	3
Alcohol/sedative withdrawal	3–4	1–2	1–2	0
Stimulant intoxication	3–4	3–4	3–4	0
Stimulant withdrawal	0	0	0	0
Opiate intoxication	0	0	0	0
Opiate withdrawal	3	0	0–1	0
Hallucinogen intoxication	0–1	0–1	1–3	1
Cannabis intoxication	0–1	1–3	2–4	1
Phencyclidine intoxication (PCP)	2–4	4	4	0

substance abuse and the emotional/psychological states associated with anger and aggression.

Clinicians assessing for possible substance abuse should become familiar with their behavioral signs. Most clients know better than to come for their first interview intoxicated, but their between-use appearance and behavior may betray an ongoing problem. Table 4.2 also provides information about the psychological and physical dependency potential of various drugs.

BORDERLINE PERSONALITY DISORDER

Throughout the assessment process, the counselor must be on the alert for signs of personality disorder, including Narcissistic, Anti-social, and Borderline traits. Borderline personality disorder, in particular, has been implicated in the classic male-on-female battering cycle, as well as in more severe forms of female-perpetrated abuse. Borderlines have significant deficits in two key areas of functioning: self system and interpersonal/intimate relationships and social relationships. These deficits are exhibited in the following problem behaviors (Marziali, 2002):

- Repeated conflicts and intense disappointments in important relationships.
- Pervasive problems in distinguishing self-motivations and affects from those of significant others. The BPD client's observations, feelings, and motivations are projected indiscriminately onto others. For instance, batterers, without any external corroboration, decide that their partners are angry and want to control them.
- Difficulty managing emotions, especially anger, which erupts in disproportionate response to perceived threats of criticism, rejection, and abandonment.
- Impulsive behaviors that are potentially harmful to self (including suicidal attempts) or harmful to others (including violent attacks) and that are in response to disappointments in key relationships. The aggression, frightening and unpredictable, has been identified by researchers as cyclical in nature, responsible for the traumatic bonding phenomenon observed in severely abused victims.
- Multiple unsatisfactory experiences in all areas of functioning that reinforce low self-esteem and malevolent representations of others.

Wallace and Nosko (2003) explain Borderline psychodynamics from more than one perspective:

> Dutton and colleagues' linking of Borderline Personality Organization with anxious attachment, early life recollections of shaming, and abusive behaviors is consistent with the notion that for many abusers, violence is a manifestation of a shame-based personality, in which shame, or an experience of self as inherently defective, is masked in a defensive script. In this scenario, shame and the anger-rage continuum are co-assembled and linked to scripts governing assumptions about the insecure nature of relationships. The result is an investment in "Attack Other" defensive strategies, which protect the individual from the painful experience of seeing self as defective and, therefore, unlovable. In this respect, anger and violence become a means of ensuring that the other does not leave the orbit of the self through real or feared separation. This argument provides a bridge to attachment theory, which posits

TABLE 4.2 Signs of Drug Use and Their Dependency Potential

General early signs: (1) Reduced competence at school or work, (2) Difficulty paying attention, (3) Lessened concern about physical appearance/dress, (4) Appears distracted, irritable, (5) Loss of interest in usual pursuits, (6) Need for money, borrowing from family, friends, employers, coworkers, (7) Changes in friendships

Drug type	Active use	Between use	Psycho-logical	Physical
CNS depressants Alcohol, barbiturates, benzodiazepines, hypnotic sedatives, misc. tranquilizers	Drowsiness, slurred speech, impairment of motor skills, altered perceptions and judgment, poor concentration	Anxiety, insomnia, agitation, tension, anger, chronic heartburn	Alc: 4 Other: 2–4	Alc: 4 Other: 2–4
Narcotics Opium, heroin, codeine, morphine, Demerol, Percodan, Darvon, designer analogues: China white, MPPP	Sleepiness and drowsiness, scratching, constipation	Watery eyes, constricted pupils, needle marks, anxiety	3–4	3–4
Stimulants Caffeine, tobacco, diet pills, amphetamines, cocaine, designer analogues: methamphetamine "ice"	Increased alertness and sexual performance, hyperactivity, impulsive behavior, anger, weight loss, lack of sleep, poor concentration, speech "pressured," blurred vision, dilated pupils (snorting cocaine: nasal stuffiness, runny nose)	Fatigue, sleep for long periods, depression; paranoia and (sometimes) hallucinations	Tob: 3–4 Amp: 4 Cocaine: 5	Tob: 3 Amp: 2 Cocaine: 2
Cannabinoids Marijuana, hashish; dronabinol, nabilone	Dreamy state, distorted sense of time/place, lack of motivation, increased appetite, red eyes, dry mouth, facial pallor	Anxiety, irritation, memory loss	2–3	1
Hallucinogens Mescaline, peyote, LSD, psilocybin, phencyclidine (PCP), amphetamine variants, designer analogues: ecstasy, XTC, Adam; Eve, Love Drug; PMA	Odd behavior, exaggerated sense of well-being, panic, hallucinations, identity loss, difficulty communicating (PCP: hyperactivity, mood disturbance, impulsiveness/violence)	Depression, flashbacks (sometimes)	2	PCP: 1 Other: 0
Inhalants/volatile solvents	Odd behavior, difficulty concentrating, coughing, sneezing, nosebleeds		2	0–1

Source: B. Stimmel (1993), *The Facts About Drug Use.*

that the function of anger "is to dissuade the attachment figure from carrying out the threat of abandonment" (Bowlby, 1988, p. 30). For the insecurely attached individual, anger thus becomes the means of repairing the interpersonal bridge that is always put in jeopardy by the experience of shame. On this basis, we believe that there is a strong link between shame, which is at the heart of the fear of abandonment, and the anger accompanying it. [p. 53]

PSYCHOPATHY

An individual who fits Holtzworth-Munroe's category of *generally violent/anti-social* is likely to satisfy the diagnosis for Antisocial Personality Disorder, but may not necessarily be a psychopath. Psychopathy is a more profound personality disturbance and is essentially untreatable (Hare, 1993). Like antisocial types, psychopaths violate the rights of others and are nonconforming, deceitful, impulsive, irresponsible, and exhibit no remorse for their actions. The common assumption that psychopaths come from abusive homes is only partly true: as many grew up in loving homes as in dysfunctional ones. Psychopathy is highly associated with criminal behavior. About 20 percent of female and male prison inmates are psychopaths, and psychopaths commit 50 percent of all serious crimes. In one study, Robert Hare (1993) found that 25 percent of male batterers who were court mandated to complete a domestic violence treatment program were psychopaths. According to Hare, when these individuals go into a batterer intervention group, they "are likely to attend . . . simply to appease the courts rather than to change their behavior, and they may do little more than occupy a seat that could be better used by someone else. . . . But perhaps the most disturbing consequence . . . is the false sense of security it can engender in the assaulter's wife" (p. 94).

As conceptualized by Hare, psychopathy symptoms fall into two categories (Table 4.3). Many nonpsychopathic individuals will exhibit some of these symptoms. The counselor who suspects that a client may be a psychopath should consult a qualified, registered forensic psychologist or psychiatrist before rendering a final diagnosis. For more information, read *Without Conscience: The Disturbing World of the Psychopaths Among Us* (1993), by Robert Hare.

DOMESTIC VIOLENCE LETHALITY ASSESSMENTS

No method currently exists to predict lethality with a high degree of accuracy. Some researchers have expressed skepticism about the possibility of identifying the precise

TABLE 4.3 Psychopathy Symptoms

Emotional-Interpersonal	Socially Deviant
glib and superficial	impulsive
egocentric and grandiose	poor behavior controls
lack of remorse or guilt	need for excitement
lack of empathy	lack of responsibility
deceitful and manipulative	early behavior problems
shallow emotions	adult antisocial behavior

risk markers for spousal homicide. Murder is a rare event, and the majority of individuals who perpetrate the most serious abuse never kill their partners. There are also factors outside the control of either perpetrator or victim, such as availability of police and medical emergency services and their response capabilities. Finally, most of the study samples have focused on female victims and male perpetrators. Thus, although most of the same risk factors that apply in cases of female victims undoubtedly apply to male victims as well, the research is lacking. This does not mean that lethality assessments are not useful. They highlight the seriousness of the threat, and help service providers motivate victims to better help themselves.

The most reliable checklist for identifying factors associated with increased risk of homicide in women has been developed by Jacqueline Campbell (1986, 1995). It has been extensively used in both research and in clinical settings. The newest version is included among the assessment instruments in this volume (see page 186) and is also incorporated in the oral interview. Recent research on 220 female partner abuse murder victims, and a control group of 343 abused women (Campbell et al., 2003) has highlighted additional risk factors, including perpetrator's unemployed status, stepchild living in the home, and victim leaving after having lived with the perpetrator. Three of the most salient risk factors for spousal homicide and severe battering, cited by Campbell and elsewhere in the literature, are generalized aggression, antisocial tendencies, and, most significantly, past use of violence. In general, the more numerous the risk factors, the more likely the danger threat.

CHILD ABUSE RISK ASSESSMENT

Individuals assessed for partner abuse should always be questioned about their relationships with their children, because of the strong correlation between partner abuse and child abuse. Listed below (Table 4.4) are the major risk factors for perpetration of physical child abuse.

TABLE 4.4   Risk Factors for Physical Child Abuse

Demographic and Social	Biological	Personality	Behavioral
Nonbiological parent	Neuropsychological and psychophysiological health problems	Poor ego strength and low self-esteem	Use of alcohol and drugs
Single parent	Physical disabilities and health problems	External locus of control	Poor parenting practices: authoritarian style; harsh discipline and corporal punishment; using less reasoning/explaining, and less praise
Young parent	Attention Deficit Disorder	Inadequate child development knowledge	Poor interaction with adults and antisocial tendencies
Lower education level	Hyperresponsiveness to stimuli	Inappropriate expectations of children's behavior	Frequent marital discord
Large number of children		Negative perceptions/evaluations of children's behavior	
Social isolation		Misattributions of children's responsibility for behavior, including hostile intent	
Parent was mistreated in childhood		Negative affect—e.g., anxiety, anger, depression, loneliness	
Lower socioeconomic status			

Source: J. S. Milner & C. Chilamkurti (1991), "Physical Child Abuse Perpetrator Characteristics: A Review of the Literature." *Journal of Interpersonal Violence, 6,* 345–366.

II

Treatment

5

General Features

AN ECLECTIC APPROACH

Interventions in domestic violence can be categorized into three types. The following chart (Table 5.1) illustrates the features of each.

The treatment approach outlined in this manual can be considered eclectic, utilizing a variety of modalities and based on current knowledge regarding etiological/risk factors for partner violence. Of the three intervention types outlined below, we primarily draw from the second and third. We recognize that the feminist ap-

TABLE 5.1   Types of Intervention

Feminist	Family Systems	Psychological/Behavioral
In this perspective, partner violence is caused by a patriarchal society that sanctions male violence against women. Perpetrators are average men who are merely exercising their "male privilege" through the use of power and control tactics.	This approach identifies interpersonal conflict and dysfunctional relationship patterns as the cause of partner violence. Perpetrators can be men or women who are motivated to meet their individual and relationship needs but lack the tools with which to do so.	The cause of partner violence is assumed to reside either within the individual, in the form of emotional and mental disturbance, and/or in unhealthy reinforcement contingencies. Abusive individuals are motivated by impulses beyond their control, and/or to obtain rewards and avoid punishment.
Interventions seek to change misogynist, patriarchal beliefs, typically through psychoeducational groups, such as the "Duluth" or "Emerge" models.	Interventions seek to educate couples and families regarding interaction dynamics and to improve the couple's anger management, communication and conflict resolution skills, so as to arrive at a healthier functioning equilibrium, through conjoint therapy or multi-couples groups.	Interventions can be carried out in various modalities, but typically through individual counseling. Treatment goals include improved self-esteem and self-awareness, and greater impulse control.

proach is useful to some extent, with certain subgroups of male offenders. However, in light of shifting gender roles, women's strides toward greater social equality, the phenomenon of gay and lesbian violence, and the fact that patriarchal beliefs do not discriminate violent from nonviolent men (Sugarman & Frankel, 1996), the feminist paradigm is rapidly approaching obsolescence. Systems interventions will be discussed in a separate section of this volume. Among the psychological/behavioral explanations for partner violence, there are psychodynamic models, including object-relations theory, that provide sophisticated accounts of pathological phenomena, but can be arcane and speculative, insufficiently grounded in empirical data. Far more useful are social learning, attachment, and trauma theory.

Social learning theory, based on the behavioral principles of observational learning and reinforcement contingencies, gives us an elegant, empirically derived, easily understandable framework for understanding and treating domestic violence. As formulated by O'Leary (1988), it explains a number of the key risk factors in partner violence, including stress, violence in one's family of origin, personality, and substance abuse, and illuminates the mechanisms by which each factor operates and their relationship to one another. Because it also takes into account marital conflict and negative interchanges between partners, it fits quite nicely with systemic models. As comprehensive as it may be, however, social learning theory cannot, by itself, adequately explain the full spectrum of domestic violence problems. For instance, although having experienced violence in one's childhood significantly increases the risk for perpetrating violence in adult partner relationships, most violent individuals did not experience such abuse (Sommer, 1994; Straus et al., 1990).

Attachment and Trauma Theories

For a more complete understanding of domestic violence phenomena, we need to draw from attachment theory, which looks at disturbed patterns of child–parent relationships and their effects on adult functioning (see also pages 133–138). The trauma model is also concerned with attachment phenomena but takes a combined developmental and psychobiological perspective.

Research by Daniel Siegel (1999) and Allan Schore (1994) has shed greater light on the specific mechanisms by which early childhood experiences affect adult relationship functioning in batterers. Infants depend on a stable relationship with a nurturing, attentive caregiver, and the opportunity to fully participate in the complex "dance" between them, in order to feel soothed and safe, and to develop normally. This mutual, intersubjective regulation process allows for the acquisition of self-regulatory and social skills, and the ability to differentiate oneself from the other. When attachment is disturbed, because the child has been physically abused; has witnessed domestic violence; or has been abandoned, rejected, or harshly criticized, that child experiences elevated levels of anxiety. This anxiety causes the production of stress chemicals and hormones which, if unabated, lead to physical changes in the frontal occipital lobe and the limbic system. It is these areas of the brain that regulate a healthy sense of self and the ability to manage emotion and interact successfully with others by correctly interpreting social cues and recognizing nonverbal communication.

In her doctoral thesis, Kerstin Gutierrez (2000) investigated male-perpetrated battering in the context of this recent research. The following excerpts are from an article she wrote for the *FAVTEA Bulletin,* the newsletter of the Family Violence Treatment and Education Association (2003):

> Without such interactive soothing between the infant and the caretaker, the child is more likely to be unable to learn to self-soothe; and as the infant grows into childhood, this inability to self-soothe may develop into a way of relating to others which is based on a non-verbal level of anxiety. Such a child, finds it difficult to engage in tasks that require attention for extended lengths of time, and may find it difficult to control his/her temper.

> These children have . . . what psychologists call an anxiety-based style of relatedness to others. The development of this type of interpersonal style seems to depend on the ability of the child to turn to his caretakers for emotionally rewarding interactions: the child naturally seeks out praise and recognition from those adults whom he values in his life. If the results of these interactions are humiliating or emotionally harmful, research tells us that the child is more likely to have difficulty learning ways to cope with emotions in general, but especially with embarrassment, shame or loss. Such negative emotions tend to leave the child physiologically overwhelmed by neurological chemicals that cause the body to prepare for action or flight. Without the benefit of learned regulation or modulation, the child is more likely to appear to others as though he is suddenly out of control: the child may lash out at others, explode verbally or physically, and then feel remorse or shame afterwards. As this pattern of coping solidifies, and the child becomes a young adult, those interactions with others that tend to elicit such impulsive and negative reactions become linked with emotionally vulnerable exchanges, such as those experienced in intimate relationships.

> Psychologically, such an individual is most vulnerable to feelings of shame, loss and self-doubt when in relationship to another. When such feelings are triggered by the other, the individual who has not had the benefit of early nurturing caretaking is more likely to have difficulty regulating the physiologically powerful chemistry, which is designed to promote action or flight. These, then, are often men who batter, and the violence may look to others as though they are trying to exert control over the other; but in many cases . . . the batterer is unconsciously trying to find a physiological balance internally, through external and violent means. [Guitierrez, 2003, p. 3]*

Teaching emotion regulation and self-soothing (e.g., in the form of anger management and relaxation techniques) is covered in the following section, as well as in the section on group interventions.

ELEMENTS OF TREATMENT

Before discussing treatment plans, it is useful to identify the basic goals and tasks of treatment, regardless of the treatment modalities used. The primary goal is the elimination of violence and other abusive behaviors. Secondary goals may be to build healthy relationships and increase autonomy and self-esteem. In order for these goals to be achieved, the counselor assists each client with certain tasks.

Overcome Stress

Stress is a major cause of chronic and immediate violence. For this reason, treatment ought to provide the resources with which to reduce the sources of stress in everyday

---

*From Transmission of violent coping by Kerstin Guitierrez, 1998, *FAVTEA Bulletin, 1*(1), 3. Reprinted with permission of Kerstin Guitierrez.

life. External stressors, such as financial difficulties, job demands, or acting-out children, can be addressed through a combination of problem-solving, self-soothing, and relaxation techniques. At John Hamel & Associates, we teach skills didactically, with a white erase board, handouts, and audiotapes, and help clients apply the material to their own particular situation. Internal stressors originate from the way individuals view stressors in the environment—whether they believe they have any control, and the extent to which they make cognitive errors that exacerbate stress, as in magnification (exaggerating a danger) or mind-reading (making unwarranted assumptions about the other's thoughts or intent). This type of stress can be addressed using a cognitive-behavioral approach that helps clients identify and challenge distorted thinking styles. Our clients are presented lectures on this approach, and are asked to share with the therapist and/or the group the anger episodes recorded in their workbook, in which such episodes are scrutinized for evidence of cognitive distortions.

Challenge Irrational and Pro-Violent Beliefs

Distorted thinking styles and irrational, pro-violent beliefs cause and maintain anger and aggression. Albert Ellis and others held that such beliefs lead to stress and general relationship dysfunction, which in turn contribute to the use of verbal and physical violence.

Beliefs specifically supportive of violence are acquired in one's family of origin, in previous adult relationships, or through the broader influence of society and cultural norms. Helping clients abandon such beliefs is therefore a major task of treatment. This involves two steps:

Identification

The client must learn to identify the cognitive distortions that trigger and maintain aggressive behavior, such as mind-reading, labeling (having thoughts such as "idiot," "bitch," "lazy," etc.), magnification, and absolutizing (rigid thinking and expectations). Examples of underlying irrational beliefs are: "I must obtain love and approval from peers, family and friends," and "I must be perfect and unfailingly competent in all that I undertake."

Clients must also be educated about the connection between socialization factors and domestic violence, and helped to recognize beliefs that cause and maintain violence. Beliefs vary, and may include male beliefs about having to be in charge of the household, female beliefs that minimize the seriousness of their own violence and exclude men from having a say in child-rearing, and beliefs by both sexes that violence is an acceptable means for resolving conflicts under certain circumstances. (e.g., a misbehaving child, an unfaithful partner).

Disputing

Both types of irrational beliefs, general and pro-violent, need to be challenged before change can occur. Traditional cognitive therapy methods utilize a process of logical analysis, in which clients systematically and rationally dispute each distorted idea or belief. The process may be helpful with some violent individuals; others may not be amenable to this approach. For some clients, the process is too alien and their defenses too deeply entrenched. Pro-violent beliefs do not seem illogical to them; their beliefs have been reinforced by a society that conveys mixed messages about violence. However, clients can comprehend how such beliefs are detrimental to their own interests.

Most clients feel justified in the use of aggression, even when they acknowledge that they have overreacted. A social-psychological review by Frodi and colleagues (1977) found that rates of aggression by women are comparable to men when women feel justified, which tends to lessen aggression anxiety normally associated with feminine social roles. For both sexes, to behave according to whether anger is effective in resolving problems, rather than whether it is justified, is infinitely more productive. To assist clients in overcoming the thoughts that maintain justified anger, we suggest that the counselor do the following:

- *Cycle of violence:* Explain the reinforcement contingencies for anger and aggression, how violence seems to work in the short run but not in the long term, and how tension relief and the renewed intimacy that often result from violence are merely fleeting phenomena, inevitably followed by more assaults and the perpetuation of an endless cycle of violence.
- *Payback:* Explain how victims of violence either respond with violence or respond in passive-aggressive ways, engaging in sabotaging behaviors.
- *Impact on children:* Even the most bitter, resentful clients can be reached if the counselor helps them see the effect of their abuse on their children.

Identify Unhealthy and Abusive Interaction Patterns

The dynamics of domestic violence can take many forms, depending on the nature of the relationship. The extent of power imbalance is an important variable. In a majority of violent relationships, the abuse is mutual. Others involve a dominant aggressor and a victim, each characterized by particular dynamics. Thus, in addition to the traumatic bonding of severe unilateral battering relationships (Dutton & Painter, 1993), abusive couples engage in various negative reciprocity, demand–withdraw and attack–defend patterns (Babcock et al., 1993; Burman et al., 1992; Cordova et al., 1993; Jacobsen, Gottman, Waltz, Rushe, Babcock, Holtzworth-Monroe, 1994; Margolin, 1988). Paul and Paul (1983) identified the following dynamics in high-conflict couples: control-control, control-compliance; and control-indifference. Interaction patterns that maintain a cycle of abusive behavior, whether mutual or unilateral, must be identified and altered. Because the proper modality of treatment is conjoint therapy, these interaction issues will be discussed in a later section, on family interventions.

Acquire Pro-Social Interpersonal Skills

To provide the client with a rationale for change the counselor presents the benefits of an equalitarian approach to decision-making and a willingness to work through conflicts. He/she assists in identifying a client's individual and relationship needs, and in fostering self-awareness and insights into emotions, motives, and defenses, with a focus on increased empathy. The counselor presents alternative means with which the client can achieve legitimate goals within the relationship, including anger management, communication, empathy, and conflict resolution skills.

Adopting an Equalitarian Decision-Making Model

The National Family Violence Surveys (Straus et al., 1990) made it clear that relationships characterized by joint decision-making, in which neither partner dominates, experience the fewest conflicts and the lowest rates of spousal abuse.

Willingness to Work Through Conflicts

As described by Paul and Paul (1983), the conflict resolution process can be demanding and frightening. But individuals who are open to resolving problems, as opposed to maintaining a closed, defensive stance, benefit in a variety of ways. Even when conflicts are not completely resolved, the partners achieve intimacy, build trust, and grow individually and as a couple.

Identifying Individual and Relationship Needs

The hierarchy of needs, as described by Abraham Maslow, is an excellent tool to identify the basic needs all human beings have in common. We stress the importance of trust-building, and the steps required to actively nurture the relationship, using the "emotional bank account" concept described on page 228 (Gottman, 1999). A relationship is akin to a three-legged stool, in which the first leg represents the needs of one partner; the second leg, the needs of the other; and the third the needs of the couple. All three must be strong in order for the stool to remain upright.

Self-awareness

Violence is overcome and relationships are healed when there is a change in *behavior*. To a large extent, however, people want to understand the reasons for their actions. Understanding the connection between internal processes and behavior allows them to *own* the behavior. In addition, clients need to identify and express the vulnerable feelings that often lead to anger and aggression. Attention is directed toward how feelings of embarrassment, pride, hurt, betrayal, and various defense mechanisms sabotage accountability. Clients identify and overcome

- Denial, minimization, and blame
- Projection (ascribing one's own feelings and motives to the other)
- Undoing (assuming that merely apologizing will make up for abuse)
- Displacement (directing anger or other strong feelings about something or someone on another, innocent person)

Empathy

Empathy allows individuals to identify their own vulnerabilities within others, and thus find a common basis for humane treatment of their fellow human beings. Those clients who have, or can develop, empathy, are far more likely to cease abusive behavior. Helping clients build empathy is a process that can be conducted in a variety of modalities, but most effectively in conjoint sessions. Clients are asked to imagine (or are directly told by the victim) how the victim may have felt when being abused. They are then asked to compare the experience to a similar one of their own. Empathy involves reframing the other's motives, so that the other's best intentions are acknowledged. Clients who assume malicious motives on the part of their victims are asked to determine what their own motives might be if the situation were reversed.

Anger Management

In research by Averil (1983), subjects were asked to keep an anger log over several months. Results indicate that 76% of the targets of the subjects' expressed anger viewed the experience positively, and came to realize their own faults as a result. Also, 48% of these targets reported that it strengthened, rather than weakened, their relationship. Anger, then, can contribute positively to relationships when properly expressed. The danger, of course, is that it can be misused in the form of abusive and controlling behaviors. Once clients understand how the misuse of anger is detrimental to their personal and relationship needs, they can seek effective ways of managing it.

Cycle: Thoughts → Feelings → Behavior

- Recognize anger at lower levels, before it escalates.
- Identify the triggers, both internal (e.g., thoughts, other feelings) and external, that lead to anger escalation and aggression.
- Use anger-reduction techniques such as *self coaching*, in which the client talks him/herself through the anger, replacing irrational and negative self-talk with empowering messages (e.g., "I can handle this," "I don't have to react," etc.). With *time out and creative time outs* the client either leaves the house for at least an hour (in situations of intense anger and high violence potential), or finds a way to temporarily withdraw (e.g., gets a drink of water, changes rooms, washes the car, digs in the garden, goes for a run, etc.). *Relaxation techniques* involve the client taking several deep breaths during the interaction, or sitting down and relaxing the body posture, unclenching fists, and engaging in a brief meditation during a time out.

Communication Skills

High-conflict and violent individuals don't always lack proper communication skills. In fact, highly controlling individuals may be extremely verbal and may use this ability to dominate their partners. These individuals need to recognize the internal forces that drive them and the consequences of their behavior. For many, basic communication skills are either lacking or improperly used. Good communication requires *active listening*, listening in such a way that the other person actually feels heard. There are two psychological obstacles to listening. Clients must learn that: (1) Listening does not equal agreeing: Listening is simply a process that allows the transmission of information. Individuals always have a chance to disagree when it's their turn to speak. (2) Listening isn't a favor to be granted: The belief that listening should only be granted to someone who "deserves" it is wrong. The counselor explains how listening is a necessary part of communication and essential for relationship functioning.

Respectful expression is another important communication skill. Thoughts and feelings need to be expressed in a clear, honest, and nonthreatening way. The client learns an *assertive*, rather than *aggressive*, manner of setting limits and presenting grievances. The three steps of presenting an assertive message are (1) State the problem *behavior* (make an *observation* rather than blame or criticize), (2) state how that behavior is *affecting* you, and (3) *request* a change in behavior.

No one likes to be criticized, or reminded of a failure or wrongdoing. But presenting the message as detailed above can help lessen resistance. Focusing on the other person's behavior rather than character, and making a request rather than a demand demonstrate respect, and stating the effects of the behavior (e.g., how it makes one feel) fosters empathy in the other person and provides a *reason* to change abusive behavior.

When an individual finds another person's behavior a problem, his/her goal is to get the other person to change. This goal, however, will not be realized unless the assertive message is heard. Being heard is therefore the more immediate consideration. There is no guarantee that being heard will automatically lead to compliance—the other person may accept or reject the request—but listening increases the odds in the speaker's favor. A useful way for helping clients understand this principle is to use the "spotlight" analogy. Clients are asked imagine a bright spotlight. When they are assertive, they are able to keep the spotlight where it should be—on the other person. However, when they are aggressive, their anger now becomes the central issue, negating whatever point they have been trying to make. Thus, the imaginary spotlight is turned back on them.

Positive communication is characteristically lacking in high-conflict relationships. An important component of trust-building is increasing the frequency of positive communication, relative to negative and neutral statements. Positive communication includes:

- Praise and compliment: Example: "You're great at getting the kids' attention."
- Expressions of appreciation: Example: "I like how you reorganized the closet."
- Encouragement and support: Example: "You'll do great on the interview."
- Expressions of empathy: Example: "I can imagine how sad you must feel."

Meta-communication means the individual *observes* the communication, and delivers messages in a non-blaming way. In either the role of speaker or listener the client monitors the communication carefully and promptly addresses communication problems as they arise. The goal is mutual and not an attempt to gain the upper hand. By alerting the partner to impediments in the flow of information, the communication can get back on track. Meta-communicative observations may concern one's own internal process or behavior, the other person's behavior, or mutual behaviors. Communication can be used to clarify misunderstandings, set limits, or point out dysfunction. Examples of meta-communication statements:

"I'm getting kind of worked up here. I'm taking a time out."

"You're raising your voice, and I'm uncomfortable with that."

"We seem to keep going back and forth, just attacking each other."

"You look angry. Did I say something to offend you?"

"I'm not sure I understand what you said. What did you mean by that?"

Conflict Resolution

Conflict resolution begins with conflict containment. A client who learns how to manage anger will be better able to keep conflicts from escalating. Although it only takes one person to keep a conflict from escalating, it requires two people to resolve a conflict. Conflict resolution involves *identifying the conflict escalation process.* One helpful tool (found in the section on group curriculum) is a chart depicting the three levels of conflict. It begins with the issue level itself, where the problem may potentially be resolved, then proceeds to the personality and relationship levels, where individuals engage in behaviors that have no chance of resolving the problem. Conflict escalation can also be understood in terms of attentional focus. Conflicts can easily escalate when an individual is preoccupied with the partner's external self (i.e., what the partner is saying and doing, and how he/she appears). With little access to one's internal state (self-awareness), an individual is likely to misinterpret and exaggerate verbal and nonverbal messages and simply react impulsively, based on unconscious relationship "scripts," as anger rapidly escalates. The counselor instructs clients to maintain focus on their inner selves (e.g., monitor their anger level, identify their needs and wants), as well as on the partner's internal self (what the partner might be feeling, also known as empathy).

Adopting the proper attitude is vital. Clients discover that no conflict can be resolved if either party intends to "win." A more productive alternative is to seek understanding, and make this the number one priority. With understanding come safety and commitment, and the possibility of mutual and satisfactory resolution to problems. Partners must also have *reasonable expectations.* Not all conflicts can be resolved. Some involve temperament, personal habits, ingrained personality characteristics, or core values that are inherently resistant to change.

> Lena complains that her husband, Roger, "doesn't get excited about anything." Roger thinks that Lena is "too nervous" (temperament).

> Wyatt is ready to divorce Pam, his wife of 7 years, because she "refuses to pick up after herself" (personal habits).

> Samuel wishes that his partner, Tom, wouldn't "intellectualize" so much (personality).

> Gail occasionally spanks her children, and once washed her daughter's mouth out with soap. Her husband, Drew, who came from an abusive family, is adamantly opposed to any type of corporal punishment (core values).

Couples can learn to live with such problems by developing tolerance and acceptance. When mutual respect and understanding are a priority, even the most intractable problems seem less important.

Partners can *learn useful techniques.* Conflict resolution is a process that takes on a life of its own. When the partners assume a win–lose posture and fail to address disagreements with meta-communication techniques, conflicts negatively spiral. On the other hand, with a win–win attitude, anger is curtailed and careful communication monitoring creates a positive spiral. A technique for generating forward, positive movement is an approach known as S.O.L.V.E. (Weisinger, 1985). It may be done formally, with pen and paper, or in a less structured manner, where the individuals utilize the principles inherent in the approach. Done correctly, the technique builds confidence and trust and reduces defensiveness and blame. Neither partner gives up anything or loses face because the process is entirely driven by what is *effective*, rather than what is *better* or *right*.

SOLVE:

S—*State the problem behavior.* Clients are directed to describe the problem in neutral, non-blaming terms. "The problem is that you are being unreasonable" violates this principle because blame is imbedded in the problem description. "The problem is that we disagree on how to deal with our son's behavior" is a description both parties can agree to. Agreement by both individuals on what the problem is means they are 20% closer to a resolution.

O—*Outline previous solutions.* In this step, each party thinks of previous instances of the problem, and tries to identify any solutions that may have worked. Once a consensus is reached, the next step is to implement that solution again, and the problem is resolved. If all previous solutions are found wanting, then the couple is 40% closer to a solution, having agreed on what *doesn't* work.

L—*List alternative solutions.* Here the parties brainstorm. Both partners write down as many possible solutions as they can imagine. Even the most outlandish, seemingly unworkable solutions should be written down, and it is forbidden for either one to prematurely discuss any of his/her partner's suggestions. This frees each party to think of solutions creatively. With the completion of this step, the parties are 60% closer to a solution.

V—*Visualize the consequences of each solution.* Each possible solution is seriously considered. The two parties imagine what would happen if it were implemented. How would it affect each person? What might be other consequences? Would it cause more problems than it would solve? By a process of elimination, the couple should be able to narrow the list to a few possible solutions acceptable to both. It is now simply a matter of presenting each one, alternating between the suggestions of one partner and the other. At this point, the couple is 80% closer to a solution.

E—*Execute the best solution(s).* The last step is straightforward in that possible solutions are tried until one of them works. If none of the solutions appear workable, yet all steps were carried out properly, the couple has engaged in a cooperative process that built trust and confidence in their ability to manage conflict, and established emotional connection and intimacy.

Overcome Emotional/Mental Disorders and Childhood Trauma

Treatment modality depends on the severity of pathology, degree of power and control exercised, and whether genuine remorse is present. At one end of the continuum are those individuals without any serious *DSM-IV* psychopathology, and whose problems would generally be diagnosed under V-codes or Adjustment Disorders. Generally, these individuals engage in only minor violence, usually in response to stress or heat-of-passion conflicts, and represent the majority of abusive individuals. At the other end are those with serious emotional problems, such as Major Depression or Bipolar Disorder, and individuals with personality disorders, primarily Anti-social and Borderline, who use violence for the purpose of dominating their partners. For clients on this end of the continuum, intensive, insight-oriented psychotherapy is normally required before, or in conjunction with, group or conjoint therapy. Individuals with Borderline personality traits typically must overcome childhood attachment disturbance and trauma, and the subsequent constellation of adult traits, most notably intense dependency needs accompanied by rage and self-loathing.

Based on her review of neurobiological/developmental research linking childhood trauma and attachment disturbance to altered brain development and subsequent cognitive, social and emotion regulation problems in adulthood, Gutierrez (2000) concludes:

> Of primary importance . . . is an individual treatment program (perhaps in conjunction with current group therapy approaches) which addresses issues of narcissistic wounding and regulation. The goal of treatment . . . is to bring his emotions into alignment or attunement with his sensory (internal and external) input. This integration of emotion and sensory states must be achieved through orbitofrontal integration which requires intensive therapeutic interventions. [p. 100]

According to Gutierrez, successful outcomes are enhanced when the following tasks are incorporated into the overall treatment plan:

1. *Integrate emotion and sensory states:* The therapist uses a calm voice and maintains direct visual contact, while helping the client recognize facial expressions and how to link those expressions to emotions of self and other. In addition, the therapist uses body posture modeling and naming, and assists the client in naming and articulating feelings states.

2. *Rebuild object relations and reconfigure regulatory mechanisms:* Through the use of exercises such as role-modeling, the therapist helps the client acquire skills in nonverbal communication and in articulating feelings in self and others. It is especially important for the client to participate in interactive sequences in which his/her needs can be addressed. In the course of therapy, issues of dependency and intimacy may bring up intense anxiety for the client, triggering old patterns of shame-based coping responses.

The acceptance, "holding," and emotion regulation and limit-setting that the therapist and setting provide allow the client to work though such responses. This approach "depends on the gradual pacing of regulatory interactions, much as a toddler receives as he explores his world with the help of an expanding emotional repertoire" (Gutierrez, 2000, p. 101).

Change Reinforcement Contingencies

When clients learn pro-social communication and conflict resolution skills, they have the tools to change the pattern of interpersonal rewards within the relationship. Aggression tends to be repeated because it works. But aggression can only be maintained when the aggressor is able to secure the reward that consciously or unconsciously motivates him/her. Aggressive behavior that is no longer reinforced becomes extinct. The aggressor makes "I" statements, takes a time-out, and new, healthier reinforcement contingencies are strengthened even further. Through the use of listening skills, praise, and so forth, the recipient of the aggression can also reinforce prosocial behaviors.

The specific reinforcement that maintains a particular negative behavior can be difficult to identify. A woman yells at her husband to get him to wash the dishes. He not only shoves her, but still refuses to do the chore. A man confronts his wife about her failure to pay their mortgage on time. After ignoring him, he throws the bills all over the kitchen and calls her a "stupid bitch." She cries, packs a suitcase, leaves to go live with her sister, and returns several weeks later. These are examples of the repeated cycles of aggressive couple interaction. How do aggressors benefit from these behaviors? Why would they repeat behaviors if they don't work? A complete behavior analysis provides some answers. Two possible rewards for aggressive behavior include (1) *maintaining a belief system or self-image:* Wife beating, for a man who is repeatedly sent to jail, is partially rewarded by fulfilling his role as a dominant male. The punishment of prison is offset by the inherent reward of solidifying a cohesive self-identity by protecting a fragile, shame-based ego. (2) *continued interaction and intimacy:* Couples continue to assault, emotionally abuse, and control because it is the only way they know how to relate to each other. Fighting means connection, and connection means love.

More than one explanation is sometimes needed to understand a particular phenomenon. In the examples cited, a psychodynamic view adds to the behavioral one. This is a major reason for adopting an eclectic treatment approach. Human behaviors are complex, under the influence of many forces, and executed for a variety of reasons. One constant we have found is the universal need for individuals to master their environment and feel good about themselves. Whether a particular client's motivation for violence stems from a need to dominate (feminist theory), to meet individual and interpersonal needs (family systems theory), or from poor impulse control (psychological theory), *perpetrators are far more likely to abandon the violence when they are shown that they can.* Resource theory (Goode, 1971) tells us that most people are so fearful of losing their partner's respect and affection that the exercise of physical violence is typically used as a last resort. Violent individuals, for the most part, feel powerless. When they are not lashing out in a desperate, misguided attempt to secure their interpersonal needs, they lash out in spite and retribution, out of sheer hopelessness. By providing support and the proper tools to negotiate their needs, treatment can instill a measure of the self-confidence necessary to overcome their unhealthy dependencies.

WORKING WITH VICTIMS: COMPONENTS OF INTERVENTION

In a broad sense, everyone involved in domestic violence is a victim, including the batterer, who may be repeating a cycle of abuse learned in childhood. It is equally true that in most domestic violence relationships the abuse is mutual, and the differences between perpetrators and victims are not always easily distinguishable. Having said this, a great number of men and women experience severe abuse at the hands of a dominant aggressor. Because of their relative lack of power, victims require special assistance. Here are the essential tasks in working with victims.

Gather Information

The information-gathering assessment process provides the opportunity to build a trusting, workable relationship with the client. The counselor should conduct a thorough psychosocial history, and question each client at length regarding domestic violence histories, both as a perpetrator and as a victim of abuse. Three crucial areas to assess when working with victims are (1) time-span of abuse, (2) extent of outside support and resources, and (3) lethality potential.

Provide Reassurance/Establish a Therapeutic Alliance

The counselor builds a supportive relationship with the victim as data is gathered. The questioning cannot in any way blame the victim for the abuse. Respectful, businesslike interviews do not exacerbate the problem. Victims often feel responsible for what happened because the abuser has convinced them that it's their fault, and their guilt masks feelings of powerlessness. The victim unconsciously decides, if I blame myself, then maybe I can fix the problem. The counselor may have to explicitly assure victims that they are not to blame for the abuse, that the information-gathering process is intended to help them overcome their problems, and that the counselor is there to support them in all possible ways.

Self blame is not empowering, but taking responsibility is. No matter how powerless victims may feel, only they hold power over their own lives. Although difficult for some clients to accept, the message of empowerment may need to be repeated throughout the course of treatment.

Provide Outside Resources and a Safety Plan

Victim safety is of paramount importance. The counselor can increase clients' ability to protect themselves by providing the necessary resources and helping them construct a safe, workable plan. A sample client safety plan handout can be found in Appendix B, and a list of resources can be found in Appendix D.

A vital resource for domestic violence victims is the local battered women's shelter, where one may obtain counseling, housing, and legal assistance. Victim groups are usually available to provide encouragement, understanding, and support. Such shelters were initially set up to help battered women and their children. Other than the Valley Oasis Shelter in Lancaster, California, there are at present no shelters that provide living arrangements for abused men. In addition, local shelters do not reach out to male victims. Shelter operators maintain a focus on female victims because of fear that efforts to help men would dilute services for women. However, some battered women shelters will assist male victims. Along with legal help and counseling, shelters provide referrals to support services, child care, housing, and so forth. Male victims who need immediate lodging can obtain shelter in traditional homeless shelters, if necessary.

Male Victims: Should They Fend for Themselves?

Because men are socialized to present a brave façade and rarely seek help, it is difficult to imagine men as domestic violence victims. When men are victims, the assumption is that because they are generally in less physical danger, and are often the primary breadwinners, they are in lesser need of assistance than women. Women suffer two to three times the number of injuries in spousal assaults, and are the victims in up to 78% of spousal homicides. However, male victims are at the receiving end of equally intense emotional abuse and highly controlling behaviors, and suffer a significant proportion of serious injury. Men have every reason to fear the unpredictable violent assaults of a pathological female batterer, even if they don't always admit to this fear. A substantial number of male victims are stalked and terrorized when they attempt to leave their partners. They experience crippling levels of emotional distress as a result.

Even when able to defend themselves, men cannot always protect their children from mom's abuse, and Child Protective Services will deny parental rights to someone who fails to protect the children. But men who need to leave their batterer often lack the financial resources to do so, and fear losing children in a custody dispute or from false allegations of spousal abuse. Feeling as powerless as women victims, these men are in dire need of assistance. Male victims and their children can benefit from financial and legal resources, housing, and emotional support.

Educate Victim About Battering Dymanics

An integral part of any intervention is to teach victims about the nature of their abusive relationships. Severely abused clients must understand the phenomenon of traumatic bonding, the cycle of violence, and the victim's dependency on the abuser. Without blaming the clients, the counselor shows them examples from their relationship of how they unwittingly contributed to their own victimization. By working closely with clients to formulate the agenda for treatment and by demonstrating concern, empathy, and respect, the counselor provides a model for equalitarian decision-making.

Develop a Consensus for Change

As they attempt to help victims escape abuse, counselors will sometimes find themselves in a power struggle with victims who, because of their dependency needs, insist on staying in the relationship and/or are not willing to cooperate with police after their abuser is arrested. In such cases, the counselor is faced with a terrible dilemma. On the one hand counselors can recognize a self-defeating and dangerous situation far better than the client can. On the other hand, if counselors vigorously pursue their own personal agenda, they will lose the client's trust and the opportunity to exert any positive influence. Once counselors have helped clients better understand their motives and have educated them about the dynamics of abuse, counselors are obliged to honor victims' choices. The recent book by Linda Mills (2003) eloquently describes the sometimes dangerous consequences of mandatory arrest policies that deny victims a choice.

Table 5.2 from Peled and colleagues (2000), which follows, outlines a model for empowering female victims who have chosen to stay in their relationship. There is every reason to believe that this model, liberated from its gender-specific references, would be equally useful in working with male victims.

TABLE 5.2   Honoring a Victim's Choices: Ecological Levels

Planes of construction	Societal-cultural	Institutional-organizational	Interpersonal	Individual
Reality perception	Intimate violence can be stopped from within the relationship. Heterogeneous and idiosyncratic choices of women influenced by contextual/situational variables and their own subjective interpretations of their decisions.	Accountability is for the woman's well-being and safety. Separating victim and perpetrator cannot be equated with lowering of the violence or enhancing women's well-being.	Women's staying is a choice that reflects an attempt to stop violence from within the relationship, rather than an attempt to come to terms with it.	Staying is a legitimate choice to be supported on the woman's terms.
Meaning creation	Women's staying in intimate violence is a legitimate choice.	Reassess whether and how rules, ideologies, and operations, as well as hidden agendas, foster or inhibit battered women's own desired intervention outcomes and criteria for success.	If violence continues, the woman may decide to leave just as she decided to stay.	Staying does not preclude leaving in the future, just as leaving does not preclude returning.
Operational implications	Alter social expectations concerning women's choice to stay. Encourage and support, both socially and institutionally, the decision to stay as well as to leave.	Formulate policies and practices that allow for and support a wide range of choices for women coping with violence from within the relationship.	Assume that the woman is not weak and easy prey, but rather strong and competent; her decisions are to be respected.	Realistically assess the sources of and responsibility for the violence, as well as realistically evaluate individual resources available for stopping it.

Guide the Client Toward Growth and Autonomy

Change may not be rapid or dramatic, but if the counselor has gained the victim's trust, change will be genuine and long-lasting. As the relationship develops throughout the course of therapy, the counselor acts as a container for the client, providing structure and safety to overcome old dependencies. The counselor encourages the client to grow and take risks, while allowing the client to set the pace. During this process, the counselor allows the client to transfer some dependence onto the counselor in order to provide a continued sense of safety while slowly guiding the client toward autonomy.

Ending the Intergenerational Cycle of Violence

Many victims of domestic violence repeat childhood cycles of abuse in their adult relationships. Clients begin to recognize and work through complex feelings, inner conflicts, and defenses. As victims begin to recover from trauma, past and present, they can also begin to assume responsibility for any abuse they may have perpetrated, including verbal and physical assaults against their children. Not all victims displace anger and stress on loved ones, but when they do, the damage can be severe, with long-lasting consequences. When individuals cease becoming victims *and* perpetrators, the intergenerational cycle of abuse finally comes to an end.

6

The Treatment Plan

SAFETY CONSIDERATIONS AND CHOOSING THE RIGHT MODALITY

The five primary goals of a viable domestic violence treatment program are (1) help clients find more effective ways to respond to stress, (2) identify and replace the irrational beliefs that cause and exacerbate violent behavior, (3) identify unhealthy and abusive interaction patterns, (4) teach clients to adopt pro-social interpersonal skills, and (5) help clients overcome childhood trauma and emotional disorders. The question remains—What might be the best treatment modality for a given client?

Individual Therapy

With two exceptions, individual therapy is not the preferred option for most violent individuals:

- Individual treatment may be more personal, expeditious, and rewarding than participation in group for the individual with less severe problems, who has a strong support system, and a partner willing to participate in couples work.
- In depth one-on-one therapy is necessary for individuals with severe personality disorders, mood disorders, or other mental illness, who would be unable to benefit from group. In many cases, individual therapy sessions can be an adjunct to treatment, concurrent with couples work or group.

Irrespective of the insight gained in individual therapy, most individuals with a serious anger management and/or domestic violence problem *must* also learn basic relationship skills. A long-standing practice of therapists, social service organizations, probation, and diversion programs has been to recommend anger management/ domestic violence educational programs for abusive men, but supportive and/or psychodynamic therapy for abusive women. In some localities, female perpetrators are referred to victims' groups, due to a lack of appropriate resources. These practices overly pathologize women, absolving them of their responsibilities and denying them the full range of resources they need to overcome their problems.

Group

Couples therapy is not possible when one or both partners refuse to participate, and contraindicated when there are safety concerns. When the level of the violence is serious or there is a dominant perpetrator, it may be necessary for couples therapy to be deferred until the perpetrator has demonstrated the ability to control his or her behavior. Self-control can effectively be learned in group. Through the mechanism of identification (particularly in same-sex groups), participants secure a degree of support and understanding not found elsewhere. The peer group assists the individual with accountability by confronting resistance to treatment, and by challenging unhealthy conduct while encouraging healthy behaviors and modeling success. A valuable contribution by social learning theorists in the field of domestic violence is the concept of *efficacy expectations* (O'Leary, 1988), which addresses the problem of motivation. The concept can be easily adapted to a group format:

> A client or patient may believe that a given behavior produces certain outcomes but doubts whether he could perform the behavior in question. People's beliefs in their ability to perform important behaviors (efficacy expectations) determine whether they will engage in those behaviors. The stronger our efficacy expectations, the greater the efforts we will make in trying to overcome obstacles. Therapeutic efforts to alter efficacy expectations may focus on changing our accomplishments by providing us with vicarious experiences in which we see others perform anxiety-provoking behavior without adverse consequences, by verbally persuading us that we can perform certain behaviors, and by reducing emotional arousal that often debilitates performance. [p. 35]

Among men's treatment programs, three kinds of group approaches have been utilized. Traditional models, such as the Domestic Abuse Intervention Project in Minnesota (Brygger & Edleson, 1987; Pence & Paymar, 1993), also known as the "Duluth" model, view men's violence as instrumental in all cases, with its root cause in a patriarchal system that supports men's violence toward women:

> In intimate heterosexual relationships where violence is occurring, the primary aggressors are typically men, and the victims are women. Every source of data, from police reports to hospital emergency rooms, from counseling centers to divorce courts, points to an enormous gender disparity in who is initiating the violence, who is more physically harmed, and who is seeking safety from the violence. . . . Violence in the family is directly linked to status in the family and to socialization. Men are culturally prepared for their role of master of the home even though they must often physically enforce the "right" to exercise this role. They are socialized to be dominant and women to be subordinate. [E. Pence & Paymar, 1993, p. 5]

In the Duluth Model, participants are challenged to take responsibility for their abusive and controlling behaviors and to learn appropriate alternatives. The 26-week curriculum teaches eight such alternatives: (1) nonviolence, (2) nonthreatening behavior, (3) respect, (4) trust and support, (5) honesty and accountability, (6) sexual respect, (7) partnership, and (8) negotiation and fairness. In light of recent structural changes in society reflecting a greater (yet hardly complete) acceptance of the rights of women, the model has become increasingly outdated. But it remains unrivaled in its emphasis on perpetrator accountability, and is appropriate for many batterers with rigid gender biases but without serious psychopathology.

Cognitive-behavioral models (Faulkner et al., 1992) are more sophisticated, viewing men's violence as partly expressive, a problem of poor impulse control and distorted cognitions. Finally, eclectic approaches, such as those used by Rosenbaum and Maiuro (1989), view battering as both expressive and instrumental, and incorporate communication and relationship dynamics as important parts of assessment and treatment. In light of research indicating that violence by women is perpetrated at rates approximate to those of men, and that the dynamics of female battering are similar to those of men, there is no question that group work can benefit individuals of either sex.

Conjoint Therapy

Although controversial, conjoint work with violent couples has been shown to be at least as effective and safe as group interventions (Greene & Bongo, 2002). Carefully conceived outcome studies, using experimental designs that included random assignment to treatment condition, have found this to be true in a variety of cases where the man's violence was the initial focus of treatment. Multi-family couples counseling has been shown to be effective among voluntary civilian couples (O'Leary, Heyman, & Neidig, 1999), military couples (Dunford, 2000), couples who are court-referred (Brannen & Rubin, 1996; Stith, Rosen, McCollum, & Thomsen, 2004), and among couples in which the perpetrator also was treated for chemical dependency (Fals-Stewart, Kashdan, O'Farrell, & Birchler, 2002). This format also appears to be effective for a variety of ethnic groups, including Latinos (Brannen & Rubin, 1996) and African-Americans (Stith, Rosen, & McCollum, 2004).

One of the first domestic abuse programs to successfully utilize couples counseling was the Family Preservation Project, which treated court-mandated male batterers and their wives at the East Texas Crisis Center, a battered women's shelter in Tyler, Texas (Geffner et al., 1989). The program was initiated after discovering that many of the women refused to leave their partners, as the staff recommended, and instead sought assistance in working on the relationship. Also, counselors in the men's treatment program were concerned about the limitations of working only with perpetrators, who routinely reported continued problems at home, even as they made efforts to change. The wives sometimes resisted their partners' new behavior (i.e., misinterpreting time outs as evidence of abandonment and blocking the door to keep the men from leaving), and would sabotage their partners' progress in other ways. Many of these problems are overcome when couples are introduced to the same materials and treated conjointly. Working conjointly reduces much of the mistrust that exists when the individuals go to separate counseling.

Other Benefits

Couples therapy may be the most desirable treatment option for a majority of violent and abusive individuals. A comprehensive review (National Research Council, 1998) found that men who complete traditional batterer groups benefit only slightly more than those who drop out or never attend. Well-designed and operated programs may fare much better. However, Neidig and Friedman (1984) explain why conjoint therapy may in some cases be more effective:

We assume that when violence occurs within the context of an ongoing relationship, the behavior of each individual within the relationship is contingent on the behavior of the other, and that the behavior of each can be thought of as both a cause and an effect depending on how the interactional sequence is punctuated. . . . The interpersonal perspective fosters a sense of personal responsibility and suggests the possibility of positive intervention strategies. The unilateral view of spouse abuse, with its emphasis on societal factors as causing males to be abusive, may reduce the husband and wife's sense of guilt and responsibility while increasing their feelings of helplessness. Additionally, treatment that takes the unilateral view of violence encounters the following problems that can be avoided if the interpersonal perspective is maintained. First, there is the implication that there are fixed "victim" and "perpetrator" roles. Victims may assume that they can legitimately seek retribution or punishment, which can in turn lead to additional violent attempts to settle the score. Second, if the violence sequence is punctuated too narrowly, if either party only views the incident from his own perspective, and if interactional variables are not attended to, the violence may appear as if it erupted spontaneously and is beyond the influence of both parties. This perception is a therapeutic dead end. Third, when positive relationship factors and the contribution of both spouses to the conflict escalation process are ignored, women tend to be viewed as helpless, childlike victims, thus perpetuating conditions that may contribute to additional violence. Ultimately, it is no favor to be defined as a victim. [pp. 3–4]

The Physical Aggression Couples Treatment program in New York (Heyman & Schlee, 2003), incorporates the major elements of Neidig and Friedman's program, with its emphasis on practical skills building and immediate cessation of violence. It also views partner violence within a systemic framework, and recognizes the circular and mutual causality inherent in couples conflict. However, the program departs from Neidig and Friedman to some degree by eschewing an entirely gender-neutral approach and instead emphasizes men's greater ability to cause physical damage. According to Heyman and Schlee, the couples program has been shown to be as, and in some ways more, effective in treating violent men than traditional same-sex batterer groups. In addition, they have found that couples treatment is more palatable for the average couple, who view their relationship problems as more problematic than the violence itself. It is also palatable to domestic violence treatment providers, who want to see the violence treated right away.

When conducted properly, couples therapy is the most direct vehicle for achieving the five treatment goals mentioned earlier. Whether the violence is mutual or unidirectional, partner dynamics are a central target of intervention. Research indicates high levels of negative interaction in violent relationships, even those dominated by a male aggressor. Anger, hostility, negative conversational start-ups and negative responses, attack–defend and demand–withdraw patterns—all of these can be directly observed in the couples format. The immediacy of the experience enhances learning so that it is more likely to be incorporated into one's behavioral repertoire. It is through couples therapy that the defenses of denial, projection, repression, and displacement can best be overcome, and a sense of empathy encouraged and developed. Role-play, useful in same-sex groups to teach empathy, is even more useful in couples work. As suggested by resource-exchange theory, individuals act out when they believe they are not getting out of the relationship what they put in. Couples therapy can identify these deficits, and provide a forum in which grievances can be discussed and negotiated.

Finally, couples therapy helps individuals see the effect of their behavior on the cycle of violence in the relationship. In a study of college couples (Vivian &

Langhinrichsen-Rohling, 1994), the subjects expressed far more concern about their negative communication and interaction patterns than about the physical assaults.

In some relationships, especially when violence is severe, there can be such an imbalance of power that couples work is clearly contraindicated. The therapist's goal is to support the victim in leaving the relationship. In many cases of unilateral violence, couples work may be possible if the aggressor is motivated to change and expresses contrition for the behavior, and if the partner feels safe. Without condoning the violence or suggesting that the victim is responsible, the therapist helps both partners assert their needs, and reach an understanding on how unhealthy communication contributes to the relationship unhappiness and the escalation process. Ultimately this is what clients need, and what they want.

Systemic Perspectives: Pro and Con

Systemic perspectives reduce blame by eschewing rigid victim/perpetrator categories. Using the Locus of Control Scale (Nowicki & Marshall, 1974), Neidig and Friedman found that both husbands and wives scored high on external locus of control prior to treatment, and that following treatment, both subsequently developed a higher internal locus of control. An external locus of control serves to render one powerless and leads to blaming, a major obstacle to change (Ganley, 1989). Neidig and Friedman (1984) write:

> To avoid blaming either party, couples must think of the causes of violence in a circular feedback model rather than a linear one. When people think in linear terms of A causing B causing C causing d, they will likely attribute blame depending on how they punctuate the sequence (Watzlawick, Beavin, & Jackson, 1967). However, by adopting the feedback model, clients can assess their participation in a process where they are both abuser and victim. For example: when she begins to raise an issue of importance to her, he begins to feel defensive and retreat; she in turn speaks more loudly to break through, and he retreats further to avoid the unpleasantness; she becomes more insistent and moves closer, while he begins to signal that he needs space and time to cool off; she experiences this as additional rejection and a lack of concern, and so on. Circular feedback, as opposed to linear interpretations ("Her nagging made me retreat" or "His retreat made me nag"), lends itself to constructive interventions in the escalation process, permitting each partner to accept a portion of the responsibility. [p. 40]

Bograd (1984) cautions us about the limitations of systemic approaches. As a feminist, Bograd is exclusively concerned about violence perpetrated by men, and her analysis presupposes patriarchal "realities" that either don't exist or are far less important than she would have us believe. She voices the usual feminist outrage about terminology (i.e., that neutral terms like *couples violence* or *battering system* obscure the fact that victims of battering are "always" women). Nevertheless, Bograd makes a number of important points that cannot be dismissed. Whether the violence is seen as only one of several systems problems, a symptom of more important problems, or as a homeostatic mechanism for maintaining system equilibrium, the experiential, emotional, and physical realities of being victimized are minimized. In addition, systems formulations imply that both parties are accountable, even when one person is clearly the dominant aggressor. Systems theory too readily dismisses personality variables. Although causality is supposed to be circular, some clinicians put too much emphasis on transactional sequences prior to the violence, which subtly blames victims for provoking the abuse.

> A wife reminds her husband to fix a broken window. He feels infantile and withdraws: She impatiently reminds him; he feels inadequate; she demands that he do as he promised; he angrily lashes out and slaps her. In this "neutral" description, the woman is described as demanding and aggressive, which are conventionally undesirable female qualities. Her behavior is framed as provocation or nagging, and not as the legitimate right of a wife to voice dissatisfaction. The husband's role is downplayed through the more sympathetic portrayal of his insecurity. The violence is almost normalized as an understandable attempt to regain his "rightful" place in the marriage.
>
> Similar formulations are further biased against women because they 1) imply that the battered woman could and should control her husband's feelings and actions; 2) attenuate the man's responsibility for his violence; 3) ignore physical size differences between men and women; and 4) deny that violence may be linked to preexisting personality characteristics of the abusive husband and not only to transactional variables that developed over the course of the relationship. [p. 561]

Bograd finds couples therapy problematic, for several reasons. First, when the batterer is not ready to relinquish his violent ways, conjoint sessions can put the woman at risk. Second, allowing the couple to meet in the same room gives the subtle message that both parties are responsible for the abuse. Third, couples therapists often focus on the violence as the primary problem only when it is severe, thus implying that "minor" violence is permissible. And last, therapists often put too much emphasis on the couples staying together, to "work things out." The abusive husband, who is most responsive during periods of separation from his wife, has no motivation to change, and the wife is denied an opportunity to establish her own independent power base.

Notwithstanding Bograd's focus on men-as-batterers, some of her criticisms are valid. Although women are generally as assaultive as men, and many relationships are either mutually violent or characterized by unilateral female-perpetrated battering, her criticisms are valid for the severe, dominant perpetrator type of abuse she has chosen to discuss. The key to responsible treatment is careful assessment, an evaluation based on all the facts of the case. Systems formulations have their drawbacks, but are useful when properly applied. The neutral descriptions, for instance, are indeed only functional descriptions and not moral assessments of accountability. But that is also the value and strength of the systems approach. The astute clinician can be objective about processes, and yet hold the perpetrator accountable for his or her actions. Systems theory can aid clients in better understanding couple interaction, without making a moral equivalency of, say, a wife's nagging to her husband's response of breaking her jaw.

Safety Considerations

Acknowledging the value of non-blaming, conjoint models, safety issues are nonetheless paramount (O'Leary & Murphy, 1999; Ziegler & Hiller, 2002). Margolin and Burman (1993) recommend conjoint therapy only when violence is designated as the primary problem. It is contraindicated, according to Jennings and Jennings

(1991), when the violence is instrumental and severe. Rosenbaum and O'Leary (1986) have formulated sound guidelines on how to proceed with treatment in cases of male battering. The guidelines would be equally applicable in cases of female battering. Conjoint therapy may be implemented when the following considerations are answered affirmatively:

1. Is the wife aware of resources and shelter services if needed in the future?
2. Does the couple wish to remain together?
3. Are both spouses willing to participate?
4. Is remediation reasonable?
5. Can violence be controlled?

Such guidelines have been successfully implemented in numerous programs, including those utilizing the multi-family couples format mentioned at the beginning of this section. Each of the programs were careful to select only those couples who had experienced relatively minor incidents of violence, leading to no or minimal injuries. Consequently, as reported in the O'Leary et al. (1999) New York study, "wives in the conjoint treatment were not fearful of participating with their husbands; were not fearful during the sessions; did not blame themselves for the violence; and were not put at an increased risk for violence during the program" (p. 498). And at the Family Preservation Project in East Texas, there were no reported incidents of battering as a result of treatment, over the seven years prior to the publication of their outcome studies.

As Goldner (1998) points out, therapists cannot impose their will on victims who wish to include their spouses in couples work. Furthermore, she argues, the immediacy of this modality actually *promotes* safety.

> Since many couples do not physically separate even though that may be the safest choice to make, it strains common sense to argue that separating them in treatment necessarily promotes safety. After their respective sessions, the two end up at home together anyway, often not any more enlightened about the specifics of their escalating process, and its dangerous moments.
>
> *It is one thing, for example, to tell a violent man that he must leave the situation before he "gets too angry." It's another to be in the room with the couple and ask the man whether he is aware that he has begun to interrupt his partner* [italics added]. Once his attention has been captured, his wife can then be asked whether she is beginning to feel the first signs of tension and fear. Having seized the moment, it now becomes possible to say to the man, "This is the moment you should say to yourself, 'It's time to go.'" [p. 266]

Generally, men have the potential to inflict more serious damage if the conflict escalates into hand-to-hand combat. But we also recognize that women assault vulnerable mates (e.g., an intoxicated or sleeping partner) and are capable of inflicting serious damage with the use of weapons. Concerns about potential use of violence are guided by the facts of each case, rather than by preconceived bias about gender roles. Clients are given realistic goals, such as the initial reduction, rather than the elimination of verbal and emotional abuse. Throughout treatment all clients are admonished that physical assaults are unacceptable and inexcusable.

Improving communication and resolving relationship issues can only be achieved with the cooperation of both partners. Controlling anger and preventing violence is the perpetrator's responsibility, irrespective of how obnoxious the behavior of the partner might be. We maintain our policy for both sexes. Male victims may laugh off a partner's assaults, and fail to call police out of a fear of appearing weak. But acceptance of violence by either sex leads to more violence, and renders treatment ineffective. Table 6.1 presents the criteria and guidelines for choosing a treatment modality, based on the chart on page 18.

A THREE-PHASE APPROACH TO TREATMENT

To provide for the safety of all parties, and to ensure a successful outcome, treatment must be appropriately structured regardless of the treatment modality. This is particu-

TABLE 6.1   Treatment Options According to Type of Violence

Perpetrator Characteristics and Nature of Violence	Recommended Modalities
Quadrant 1: Unilateral Severe Battering Serious and very serious violence with extreme use of control. Highly asymmetrical power structure. Severe, multiple injuries. Perpetrator often has a criminal history. Little or no remorse. High level of psychopathology.	Mandatory same-sex batterer group for perpetrator. Also, intensive individual psychotherapy with a clinician specializing in both domestic violence and in treating personality disorders. Supportive counseling for victim. Priority on helping him/her leave. Conjoint therapy contraindicated.
Quadrant 2: Mutual Severe Battering Characteristics are as above, except that violence is mutual and power structure more symmetrical.	Separate same-sex batterer groups for each partner. Intensive individual psychotherapy. Couples counseling after each party has acquired anger management/conflict resolution skills.
Quadrant 3: Unilateral Common Battering/High-Conflict Violence Range of violence, from minor to severe. Mild to moderate injuries. Low to moderate use of control. Moderate to high asymmetry in power structure. Remorse. Less severe psychopathology.	Batterer or anger management group for perpetrator, depending on severity of violence, extent of power/control. Supportive therapy for victim. Structured couples program, or traditional couples counseling after cessation of violence and perpetrator shows sufficient treatment progress.
Quadrant 4: Mutual Common Battering/High-Conflict Violence Characteristics are as above, except for greater symmetry in power structure.	More severe cases: Separate same-sex batterer groups, or structured, multifamily couples group. Less severe cases: Separate anger management groups, or traditional couples work w/ clinician experienced in partner violence dynamics.

larly the case when conducting conjoint sessions. Treatment at our center regardless of modality is conducted in phases, as shown in Table 6.2.

The first phase is mainly psychoeducational, with an emphasis on establishing trust, and stimulating motivation and opportunities for success. Clients are taught the difference between *primary* problems, which are the initial focus of conflict, and *secondary* problems, which represent the fallout from ineffective attempts to resolve issues. The priority, in this phase, is to avoid creating more secondary problems. Clients are given basic information about the mechanisms of anger and aggression, including the dynamics of conflict escalation; and are presented with anger, stress, and conflict management techniques, including effective communication skills. Clients are introduced to the *control scale*, which reminds them that they have more effective control over their own external and internal states (behavior, emotions, thoughts, desires) as opposed to the external and internal states of others. Attention is directed toward monitoring existing behaviors. The relationship undergoes "first order change," in family systems parlance. Only the most proximate causal factors are explored. These include behaviors that initiate or maintain conflict, such as critical, blaming statements, as well as the internal self-talk associated with those statements. Geffner and colleagues (1989) write:

> The counselors do not discourage couples from expressing their feelings or from being emotional. In fact, clinicians consider this expression to be vital. However, we have found

TABLE 6.2   Phases of Treatment

I	II	III
Overall approach	*Overall approach*	*Overall approach*
Psychoeducational	Psychoeducational/cognitive	Cognitive/insight-oriented
Goals	*Goals*	*Goals*
Eliminate physical aggression. Avoid secondary problems. Minimum ventilation of affect. Build confidence and trust. Focus on content. Learn how anger works, conflict escalation dynamics, role of stress, impact of control and "dirty fighting" tactics, and equalitarian decision-making. Acquire basic anger management, communication, and conflict containment skills.	Begin to reduce verbal/psychological aggression. Continue avoiding secondary problems, but begin addressing lesser primary problems. More ventilation of affect. Continue trust and confidence building. Continue focus on content; limited discussion of process. Identify and challenge "self-talk." Expand communication skills and learn conflict resolution and problem solving techniques. Assertiveness training.	Eliminate verbal/psychological aggression. Begin addressing core issues. Encourage full expression of affect. Greater attention to process. Identify belief systems underlying distorted self-talk. Begin addressing and working through childhood-of-origin issues.
Type of change sought	*Type of change sought*	*Type of change sought*
First-order, behavioral, immediate	First-order, behavioral, some internal	Second order, systems level, internal

that the unchecked ventilation of emotion through several counseling sessions is generally ineffective in achieving the long-term goal of helping the couple change. In order to believe that counseling is effective, the couple must see that change is occurring, that skills are being learned, and that the relationship is improving. In general, we have found that the couples seem to be better able to tolerate high levels of emotional expression later in counseling, after they have learned certain communication techniques, RET [Rational Emotive Therapy], and other cognitive intervention principles. . . . As the couple use these methods and the anger and violence subsides, the program shifts to an exploration of personal, relationship, and family-of-origin issues. The focus is then upon the communication patterns in the relationship and underlying assumptions about communication rules. [pp. 115–117]

We have found it useful to include an intermediate stage between the first and third, in which the couple acquires more skills and practices these along with those previously acquired, both in session and at home. Only in the last phase are clients encouraged to address the core issues of their relationship. It is at this point that second order change occurs, in which the relationship system itself is altered, and there is an increased possibility that the changes will be long lasting.

For anyone working in the field of partner violence, a solid knowledge base of treatment options increases the odds that the intervention selected will be effective. Whatever modality is selected, the therapist's particular choice of treatment ought to be empirically derived, based on the literature and sound clinical considerations, rather than on political ideology or personal experience. Individuals involved in partner violence are among the most wounded and desperate therapists will encounter in their practices. Work with such clients can be extremely rewarding, but it can also be problematic, triggering dangerous feelings that may severely hinder treatment progress. Such feelings include contempt for some or pity for others. Clinicians must avoid taking sides, and resist the urge to demonize one party or the other. The clinician provides a healthy dose of competence and self-esteem to those hardened by arrogance and false pride, as well as those mired in helpless confusion. A sensible approach neither pathologizes nor infantilizes victims, nor does it humiliate perpetrators. In the end, there must be a renewed sense of dignity for everyone. Above all, there must be hope.

INITIATING PHASE I

Coordinating Treatment

Certain problems, such as substance abuse, medical conditions, or serious mental disorders beyond the counselor's expertise, may need to be treated separately, either concurrent with or prior to the domestic violence interventions. Alcoholics and drug addicts, in particular, are unlikely to benefit from treatment unless they have achieved sobriety and the tools and support systems to maintain it. They have their own issues and needs, which can be fully addressed only in specialized programs, such as A.A. In these cases, the domestic violence counselor can incorporate all treatment goals into one plan, but will need to make the necessary referrals and function as a case manager, verifying participation in outside treatment (e.g., drug/alcohol treatment) and coordinating with all treatment resources along the way.

Personal Goals

Clients bring to therapy their own unique strengths and deficiencies, which counselors will consider as they help them attend to the more salient deficiencies. Some of the questionnaires previously described can be useful, such as the Staxi-2. At our center near San Francisco, we find the Assessment of Self and Partner's Relationship Functioning (page 170) particularly useful. We go over the most problematic areas with the client, and then read together the characteristics that describe excellent functioning for that category. From this list, we help clients select those areas most in need of improvement, and set their corresponding goals:

1. Take personal responsibility
2. Manage anger
3. Cope with stress
4. Communicate in an effective and healthy way
5. Resolve conflict successfully
6. Let go of the need to control and accept equalitarian decision-making
7. Obtain support outside the relationship

Setting Priorities and Introduction to the Progress Log

At our center, clients are given written information on the basic Phase I tasks of taking responsibility, ceasing all physical acts of violence, and beginning to take control of their anger. They are also given a packet of log sheets, to keep track of their progress throughout the course of treatment. Individuals entering group can find this material in the introduction section of their client workbook (pages 195–204). These materials are intended to empower clients by giving them concrete, useful information right from the start. They serve to bridge the gap between assessment and the start of formal treatment and, later, between treatment sessions.

7

Group Work

GROUP COMPOSITION AND FOCUS

Our center uses an eclectic approach for the effective treatment of most clients. Not every group can be exactly the same. Outcome studies on the effectiveness of domestic violence treatment groups indicate that effectiveness is diluted when assessment and treatment rely too heavily on an overly rigid "one-size fits all" model (National Research Council, 1998). Programs should be tailored to client characteristics. Clients benefit from the same core material, but need a choice of groups. This choice should be determined based on the composition of the group's members, the content that is emphasized, what is supplemented, the proportion of time devoted to open discussion/process compared with didactic presentation, and the extent of process work that is encouraged. Certain populations require either special attention and/ or segregation into homogeneous groups. These populations include women, severe batterers, gays and lesbians, and ethnic minority clients.

Women

Our center has successfully conducted mixed-sex groups for individuals on the "high-conflict violent" end of the DV spectrum. As a practical matter, court-mandated clients must be segregated by sex according to California law. However, even with self-referred clients, it is often preferable to treat men and women in separate groups, to allow for greater group cohesion and identification, and to address gender-specific issues.

At the University of Massachusetts, the women's offender groups follow a curriculum that is in many respects the same as the men's program (Leisring, Dowd, & Rosenbaum, 2003). Like the men, the women are taught (1) to take responsibility for their violence, (2) to recognize anger signs and the use of time outs, (3) to learn about the consequences of their violence (especially how it affects their children), (4) to acknowledge the feelings that come with anger (what they term the *anger suitcase*), (5) communication and stress reduction skills, (6) how to change irrational beliefs, and (7) ways to overcome problems related to substance abuse. The women's program differs from the men's, however, in its increased emphasis on basic economic issues, personal safety, parenting, PTSD, the conditions that may undermine mood stability (e.g., depression and PMS), and in its decreased emphasis on issues of power and control. Some of these modifications make sense. For instance, the woman's physical safety will generally be more severely compromised in a violent relationship than the man's. Unfortunately, the program minimizes the consequences of partner violence on male victims, and its assumption that women cannot be considered batterers because of their lesser ability to physically intimidate is simply without merit. Power and control come in many forms, and research indicates they are utilized by both sexes.

The Institute for Counseling in San Diego, in conjunction with Robert Geffner and The Family Violence and Sexual Assault Institute, offers a treatment manual for their female offenders group (Koonin, Cabarcas, & Geffner, 2002). Topics include: family of origin, communication, family issues, intimacy, relapse prevention, and self-management, which includes anger control.

The authors point out that abusive women often have strong caretaker tendencies and will neglect to take care of themselves. This leads them to experience distress and anger, and is a set-up to eventually lash out with abuse. Learning to validate one's anger and differentiate it from depression, and finding ways to set appropriate boundaries and limits are key treatment goals.

In the family issues component of the program, participants are asked to bring to group photographs of their families. This innovative exercise is designed to help group members develop empathy by helping them connect their violent behavior to a loved person, and by making the abuse they have perpetrated more real. Another outstanding feature of the program, used to help participants take responsibility for their abuse, is the Female Aggression Wheel, an illustrated summary of the kinds of tactics typically used by violent females (e.g., physically attacking the partner's genitals, threatening to have him fired, making false accusations, not letting him have access to the children, and making fun of his sexual performance).

Laura Petracek (2004) supplements the standard cognitive-behavioral techniques used in men's programs with narrative, music, and art therapy. In one exercise, the women are asked to draw a picture of their anger and share this experience with the group. In another, they bring in some music that reflects how they are feeling. Our center offers women the same basic curriculum as men, although facilitators will emphasize certain material in accordance with client needs. We have found that the issues of concern to men and those of importance to women are quite similar. Both genders present with similar motives for their violence and use similar defense mechanisms. Whereas women more willingly admit to having been violent, they tend to minimize and dismiss their violence with humor. In addition, there are some practical differences in the way male and female groups are conducted. Women find role-play less threatening, and can more readily discuss process issues, such as feelings about other group members. Because men are less emotionally expressive than women, the facilitator needs to structure groups accordingly.

Severe Batterers

Our center places less abusive and first time offenders in separate groups from those with severe, chronic histories. This is partly because of the different issues involved, and partly because first-time offenders and family-type batterers, whose violence is more related to poor impulse control and stress, do not identify with Jacobsen and Gottman's Cobras and Pit Bulls. Although the program content is the same in each group, there is a greater emphasis with severe batterers on power and control and the ways they were socialized to become violent.

Of the two primary severe batterers, the antisocial and psychopathic type are the least likely to benefit from therapy because of lack of remorse and inability to empathize with their victims (Hare, 1993; Jacobsen & Gottman, 1998). Because the literature has little to offer in terms of treatment strategies for these groups, the remainder of this section will focus on clients with Borderline Personality Disorder. Individuals with BPD have frustrated therapists for decades. High dropout rates stem from their difficulty in effectively utilizing the therapeutic relationship. Due to early life experiences with abusive or neglectful caregivers, Borderlines develop a fragile, shame-based ego, and have problems trusting mental health professionals. Their poor self-image is projected onto the therapist, who is regarded as all-powerful, rejecting, and withholding. The Borderline in treatment becomes needy, demanding, and belligerent. In working with Borderlines, counselors can experience anxiety and anger, and must be careful to closely monitor countertransference reactions.

Borderlines also manifest cognitive errors, such as black-and-white thinking (e.g., splitting of intimate other and splitting of self-concept), personalization (tendency to self-blame and attribute external occurrences to the self), and the inability to differentiate others' wishes from demands (Arndt, 1994). A cognitive-behavioral approach challenges such errors, as well as the borderlines' irrational belief that they are powerless, vulnerable, and inherently bad or defective, and that others are dangerous and malevolent. Dutton (1998) found that Borderlines benefit from other components of a psychoeducational group program. For instance, stress management exercises can help reduce the feelings experienced during the tension-building phase of the abuse cycle.

Dutton cautions providers about the use of confrontational tactics. He encourages his clients to discuss, within the safety of the group, their most abusive behaviors—a confessional process that helps them overcome their shame through a process of "vicarious detoxification" (Wallace & Nosko, 2003). However, "in-your-face" confrontations, which are usually effective in helping clients relinquish rigid gender roles of "male privilege," are too threatening to Borderlines. They add further shame, and tend to entrench defense structures, rather than motivate change. Marziali and Munroe-Blum (1994) agree and advocate a process group for Borderlines, rather than a psychoeducational one. Unlike many psychodynamic approaches, their model is modified for this population. They found that direct interpretations cause intense emotional reactions that can block self-awareness and hinder the learning process. Instead of using definitive interpretations about motivations and meanings, they recommend that counselors make tentative observations, particularly on how a client's emotional reaction may be inappropriate to the situation, and how erroneous assumptions are made about self and others. Marziali (2002) writes:

> The therapists' primary stance is that of affable, neutral observers who demonstrate an unwavering interest in each client's dialogue. The therapist's therapeutic responses consist of acknowledgment, reflection, and affirmation of the clients' propositions. Most therapist statements are tentatively phrased and communicate doubt and uncertainty. In fact, the therapists know neither the causes nor the solutions to the clients' dilemmas. An uncertain

response is an honest response and is more likely to resonate with the client's own responses. In this model, the clients have control over the dialogue by choosing whether or not to respond, and the therapists communicate uncertainty and confusion while maintaining an acute interest in each client's narrative. [p. 362]

We have found that many individuals with Borderline traits can function well in an eclectic psychoeducational group that combines open discussion with didactic presentations that observe the guidelines suggested by Dutton and Marziali. These individuals benefit from the group structure, and from being exposed to material that is presented in a non-demanding, "take what you can use" manner. The more severely afflicted Borderlines, however, may not be able to function in any type of structured domestic violence group, and will need a purely process group, or to be referred to intensive one-on-one therapy.

Gays and Lesbians

Although rates of partner violence among gay and lesbian populations are somewhat higher than among heterosexuals, the violence takes the same form. Because of homophobia, and the fact that gays and lesbians have issues and dynamics specific to their populations, they generally benefit more when treated in separate programs from heterosexual clients. West (1998a) outlines some of the differences between same-sex and opposite sex relationships, and the implications for treatment.

- *Homophobic control:* Gay men and women experience the same stresses as hetero-sexuals do, but with the added problems of homophobia and societal discrimi-nation. Gay and lesbian batterers often use homophobia as a control tactic. In a survey of 100 lesbian victims, (Renzetti, 1992) 21% indicated that their partners had threatened to "out" them.
- *HIV status:* It is not uncommon among gay couples for the perpetrator to use his HIV status against his partner. This may include threatening to infect the partner, using one's failing health to instill guilt in the victim, or manipulating others into believing he/she is not the aggressor. Noninfected aggressors may threaten to reveal their partner's HIV status.
- *Mutual battering defense:* Because combatants in same-sex relationships are pre-sumed to be physically equal, the myth persists that gay and lesbian partner violence is always mutual. Although there's a high degree of mutual battering in all types of relationships, gay and straight, many gay and lesbian relationships are characterized by a dominant aggressor. The use of power and control often includes physical intimidation. In fact, dominant females can more effectively utilize this particular type of control in lesbian relationships than in heterosex-ual ones, because the victim, being female, is usually less able to defend herself. Perpetrators use the myth to their advantage in order to minimize abusive behavior and avoid responsibility.
- *Internalized homophobia, social isolation and dependency:* The discrimination suf-fered by gays and lesbians is often internalized, causing stress, poor self-esteem, and difficulties establishing committed relationships. Furthermore, because this population is marginalized by society, intimate partners tend to be more dependent on one another, leading to the phenomenon of fusion. Moves

toward autonomy by one partner may be interpreted by the other as rejection, and can lead to violence.

- *Avoidance of help-seeking:* Gays and lesbians involved in violent relationships seek help at a far lower rate than do heterosexual couples. This may partly be due to the perception of homophobic societal attitudes. These attitudes are especially prevalent among law enforcement workers, who often dismiss gay and lesbian battering as mutual, posing no great physical danger, and therefore, less important than battering among heterosexuals. Well-intended mental health professionals may lack sufficient understanding of gay and lesbian issues, or may perceive themselves (correctly or not) as unable to help. As Coleman (2002) points out, the lesbian batterer sometimes may reinforce her victim's fear of help-seeking by telling her that the police will not believe her because she's a "dyke."

As previously discussed, "Duluth"-type models of treatment, based on feminist sociopolitical theories of patriarchy, are appropriate for only a subtype of male batterer. These models are even less appropriate for gay or lesbian clients. Patrick Letellier (1994) writes:

> Obviously, battered gay and bisexual men do not have that single quality that has been the focus of the domestic violence movement: They are not female. By definition, they cannot adhere to the profile of the passive or submissive woman who is in a powerless position in relation to men in society. Sexism and misogyny cannot be the root cause of violence against these men. Their sexual orientation and gender may influence the reaction to the violence and their ability to escape from it, but they are not battered because they are men, nor because they are fulfilling a feminine sex-role stereotype. . . . Although there are similarities between battered men and women, under this more inclusive theoretical model, battered gay and bisexual men do not have to be examined as mere versions of battered women. [p. 98]

Coleman (2002) finds group treatment beneficial for many lesbian batterers. "Not only is the isolation common in battering eliminated," she writes, "but new norms for recognizing and expressing emotions are established" (p. 194). Among the interventions her program utilizes are instructions on time out, having clients keep power and control logs, and the Iceberg Exercise.

> The visible tip of the iceberg is the expressed or "visible" anger. Beneath the surface are the underlying and hidden feelings. The diagram of an iceberg is drawn, with anger and its synonyms written in the tip (e.g., rage). A line is drawn to separate the visible emotions in the tip of the iceberg from those "hidden" underneath the water line. The patient is then encouraged to identify those feelings underlying her/his anger, such as hurt, fear, powerlessness, helplessness, confusion, vulnerability, shame, etc. These are then written under the waterline. Phrases that capture these feelings—such as "I felt like a fool" or "I felt she deserved it . . . she shouldn't have said that"—are placed to the side of the iceberg under the heading of "thoughts." Thus patients are helped to separate their thoughts from their feelings. This step also helps them learn to identify and exert more control over the negative self-talk that frequently escalates batterers' aggression. [p. 195]

Ethnic Minorities

Asians

Some ethnic minority clients will resist the group format. For example, many Asians tend to fear disclosure about couple/family violence within a group of strangers.

They may be helped only in individual or conjoint therapy. In some cases, such as the EMERGE program groups for Cambodian batters (Haley et al., 1998), clients are counseled individually for several weeks until sufficient trust has been established between client and counselor. Afterwards, the clients are referred to a small group of no more than three or four men.

For the group format to work, the facilitator may need to employ alternative approaches. Asians will be more forthcoming, especially about sensitive issues, when questioned indirectly. Metaphors are sometimes useful, or the counselor may frame the problem as belonging to a third party, either a hypothetical case or someone whom the client knows and is concerned about. Facilitators are also advised to reframe the cultural belief that help-seeking and disclosure of feelings will cause "loss of face," as a courageous effort to help the family. Asian clients will generally prefer a psychoeducational format, in which practical information, relevant to their own lives, can be quietly utilized without their feeling put on the spot. The Asian man's reluctance to express feelings stems from traditional Confucian values, which regard such displays as an infringement on the rights of others and a disturbance of their harmony. This reticence may be exacerbated by experiences with discrimination in a white-dominated society. Mun Wah (1998) offers this personal perspective:

> My father taught me that the world was not a safe place to compete with the White man or to show him anger. Standing up to the White man could mean your job, your chances of promotion, and, in many cases, even your life. He told me never to offend White people or to share any family secrets with them because Whites could not be trusted and might someday use that information against me or our family. My father also told me to use my education and my wealth as a way of telling Whites that I was better than they were. What he was indirectly saying to me was that I should keep my anger and my hurt to myself. My wealth and my position would be my revenge and my sword. [p. 136]

Because of the identification and sense of safety provided by a shared ancestry and experience, the participants in Mun Wah's Asian men's group are not limited to a psychoeducational format. Using psychodrama, for instance, they address and work through a number of important issues, such as racism and their relationships their fathers. In one role-play, the participants act out a scenario in which an Asian man is double-parked on a street and a white man jumps out of his car, yelling and using racial epithets. Taking the part of the more powerful white man, a participant is free to express himself and to let go of his own buried anger. In another exercise, each participant is asked to come to group wearing his father's clothes and to assume his father's role. The others question the "father" about his feelings toward his son (himself), as well as his experiences growing up. At the end of the role play, the "father" is asked to share some words of wisdom he wished *his* father might have said to him. In this exercise, the men are able to articulate, without fear of rejection, what they have needed and wanted from their fathers.

African Americans

African Americans, who have long suffered discrimination at the hands of the dominant culture, are sometimes uncomfortable in a racially mixed group. Facilitators can foster greater trust by acknowledging the existence of the discrimination and racism that can contribute to stress and tension in the home. Racially mixed groups ought to have, at a minimum, two African-American participants, in order that each "may validate the experiences of the other, both for themselves and for the others in the group" (Williams, 1994, p. 6). Of course, problems of abuse and violence cut across racial and ethnic lines, and it is the counselor's job to help clients overcome such problems, not to eradicate racism. Still, facilitators are advised to avoid a rigid "color-blind" approach when conducting mixed-race groups. In a well-meaning effort to avoid the appearance of discrimination, counselors can make the mistake of treating minority clients as though they were white, overlooking real differences between the races. Unless such differences are acknowledged, the formation of a strong therapeutic alliance will be impeded, and the effectiveness of group will be limited. According to Williams (1994), African-American men may benefit from participation in either homogeneous or heterogeneous groups, as long as the groups provide a culturally sensitive environment.

> In treatment groups for men who batter, the primary purpose of the group is to stop members' physical and emotional abuse of intimate partners. All domestic violence programs must focus on this issue. But these groups implicitly or explicitly have secondary purposes as well, such as the broader socialization and education of their members, upon which success in achieving their primary goal may depend. Thus, workers and clients address issues other than the abusive behavior with an intimate partner. . . . Among the themes that will emerge with these men are their experiences with racism, both personal and institutional. This content, which may be intimately linked to their abusive behavior as a result of economic deprivation, frustration, and so on . . . will be discussed only if there is an atmosphere of trust. . . . Denial or even nonrecognition of African American social realities by other group members as well as by the worker can lead to reduced trust, openness, and participation by African American clients. [pp. 2–3]

Latinos

Depending on the level of acculturation, a Latino client may benefit from either a mixed group among non-Latinos, or from a homogeneous group, perhaps conducted in Spanish. Two related issues that must be addressed with Latino batterers, whether Cuban, Puerto Rican, Mexican, or Central or South American, are the issues of family and machismo. Although Latino men overall are no more misogynistic than other men (West, 1998b), they come from highly patriarchal traditions in which gender roles are more sharply delineated than in the white culture. Divided power arrangements are not inherently dysfunctional, nor do they necessarily lend themselves to conflict or violence (Coleman & Straus, 1990). Still, men with a propensity for violence will seek support where they can. In this respect, certain patriarchal traditions will be misinterpreted to justify abuse (Dutton, 1994). Research indicates that rates of intimate partner violence, by men and by women, are highest among acculturated Latinos (Malley-Morrison & Hines, 2004). A central task of the group intervention program offered by Carrillo and Goubaud-Reyna (1998) is to help the men reclaim the positive aspects of machismo, which have been distorted by racism and the stressful, highly dangerous conditions associated with immigration and acculturation:

> When the men are asked, what is a macho? They respond in the following manner: "El macho is violent, arrogant, savage, rebellious, stubborn, a womanizer, one who makes decisions on his own without consulting anyone." The Latino media are filled with images that in fact

reinforce this blatant character of el macho. However, when the discussion is directed toward the learning of masculine behaviors in the native countries the men are from, el macho, in contrast, is portrayed in a completely different manner: "El macho is a man of his word, a responsible man, a provider, honest, respectful, admirable, humble, faithful, loyal to friends, family, and community, a man of integrity." Most men in treatment will agree that in the countries of origin, the previously described values are reflective of "macho" men. [p. 61]

The men are asked to consider both sets of characteristics, and to determine for themselves where they are on the continuum between "violent and arrogant" macho and "humble and noble" macho. Through a cognitive-behavioral approach and various interactive exercises, the facilitator guides the men to choose the latter description as representative of a truly responsible man. The following dialogue well illustrates this approach:

> Manuel and the other men in the group are asked the following question: "If your partner wants to go to work, do you let her, or does it not matter to you?"
> Manuel responds, "I won't let her go to work." Other men reply, "I'll let her go to work." "I will give her permission to do so." The facilitator asks, "Who gave the right to determine her actions? Where's the ownership title?" The facilitator reflects to the group that their responses are indicative of their oppressive attitude toward their partner and toward women in general. After all, states the facilitator, "Is not the prerogative of the hacendado (plantation owner) to let his peons (slaves) work for him?" Manuel begins to contemplate this perspective. [p. 62]

GROUP CURRICULUM[1]

Taking into account the needs of specific populations, as outlined in the previous section, counselors will find the domestic violence treatment program as presented in the following pages suitable for a majority of violent and abusive individuals. The topics for each of the 52 weekly sessions follow. An asterisk indicates that there is a workbook exercise for that session (see Appendix C, pages 205–253).

1. Basics of anger management
2. Basics of anger management
3. *Basics of anger management
4. The cycle of abuse
5. Alternatives to time outs
6. *Stress basics
7. *Managing stress
8. *Managing stress
9. Identifying distorted self-talk
10. *Challenging and replacing distorted self-talk
11. *Identifying and expressing vulnerable feelings
12. *Anger management review
13. *Socialization of violence: Gender roles and aggression

---

[1]The complete facilitator's guide, including specific program content and materials used for each of the 52 weekly sessions, is available for treatment professionals who enroll in the 8-hour workshop. Please contact John Hamel, LCSW, for details at (415) 472-3275 or angercounseling@aol.com

14.   *Power and control tactics
15.   *Building healthy relationships
16.   *Learning from conflicts
17.   *Basics of parenting/helping children with their anger
18.   *Gender roles: Childhood socialization
19.   *Communication: Basic principles
20.   *Active listening
21.   *Positive communication/Emotional bank account
22.   Identifying and expressing needs/Assertiveness
23.   *Assertiveness
24.   *The conflict escalation process/Communication skills review
25.   *Resolving conflict
26.   Effects of domestic violence on children
27.   Basics of anger management
28.   Basics of anger management
29.   *Basics of anger management
30.   *Importance of accountability/Legal definitions, statutes
31.   Alternatives to time outs
32.   *Stress Review/Preparing for provocations
33.   *Managing stress
34.   *Managing stress
35.   *Irrational beliefs
36.   *Irrational beliefs
37.   *Developing empathy: Identifying vulnerable emotions in others
38.   *Anger management review
39.   *Socialization of violence: Adult problems from family of origin
40.   *Power and control tactics/Battering dynamics
41.   *Defenses: Overcoming resistance to responsibility
42.   *Effective parenting review
43.   *Gender roles: Impact on adulthood
44.   *Communication: basic principles
45.   Review: Active listening + listening to criticism
46.   *Positive communication
47.   Review: Identifying and expressing needs + assertiveness
48.   *Assertiveness: Responding to blocking maneuvers
49.   Coping with angry people
50.   The conflict escalation process/communication skills summary
51.   *Resolving conflict
52.   *Effects of domestic violence on children: My role in family violence

GUIDELINES FOR FACILITATORS

The domestic violence treatment program at John Hamel & Associates near San Francisco is appropriate for both voluntary and court-mandated clients, including those required to complete a 52-week batterer program. As stipulated under PC 1203.097 (California), the program consists of 52 meetings, each lasting 2 hours, composed of participants of the same sex. The educational program covers gender roles, socialization, the nature of violence, the dynamics of power and control, and the effects of abuse on children and others. Other key program topics include: anger management, coping with stress, communication skills, positive conflict resolution, and effective parenting. The group is formatted like a workshop, with an emphasis on skill-building and mutual support. Group does not substitute for intensive psychotherapy, nor is it structured to be confrontational.

Group Composition and Format

The group is open-ended, which means that clients can join whenever there is an opening. Because each participant is given a workbook containing the essential elements of anger and violence control, a new member need not start at any particular point. A disadvantage of an open-ended group is that it takes time for new members to feel like they belong. However, despite the lack of camaraderie possible from a shared beginning and end, the advantage for a new participant is that he/she doesn't have to wait unnecessarily. In addition, the newcomer benefits from joining a group with "old timers," who are a source of strength and guidance.

Group composition should be based on the clients' domestic violence histories, as indicated in the assessment process, rather than socioeconomic considerations or whether the person is court mandated or appears voluntarily. First time offenders or others who have engaged in less severe forms of violence such as pushing and grabbing, and who have not caused serious injuries, often resist joining a group composed of more pathological clients who have a long history of serious perpetration. In order to foster full participation, groups should ideally be limited to no more than 8–10 clients.

The format consists of an open discussion period during the first hour, followed by a didactic presentation of the course material during the second. The facilitator starts each meeting with a "check-in" period. This is the time when the participants are encouraged to report to the group on how they have been doing the past week. When the group is small enough (4–6 participants), it is possible to go around the room, asking everyone in turn to share. However, if the group is larger (7–10), it is preferable to ask for volunteers. The group leader ought to take note, however, of participants who elect not to share for several weeks in succession. In such cases, the leader ought to show concern, and remind non-participants that they will gain more from their group experience if they speak up more often.

How much time individuals spend during their own "check-in" depends on the number of people in the group and on the nature of their sharing. The group leader is advised to prevent check-ins from going on too long and can do so by using one of the listening skills from the course material, known as "summarizing." An example might be, "Well, Fred, it sounds like you've been quite busy at work, putting in ten-hour days, doing new projects. Hope it gets better for you. All right, now, how about if we hear from Stan?" The leader should be more generous with time and attention with anyone who is in crisis, who shares significant treatment progress, or who demonstrates honesty and depth not seen in earlier sharing. In such cases, the open discussion period can spill over into the second hour. A group leader must be flexible.

In the second hour, the leader presents the course material for that week, using the white erase board. The curriculum material consists of 26 sessions, most of them repeated with some variation for another 26. Individuals committed only to 6 months are thus exposed to the core elements of the program, whereas those enrolled for the full 52 weeks benefit from some repetition, as well as the added material. Most of the handouts and exercises come in pairs, with one part presented during the first 26 weeks, and the second part presented during the next 26. An example is the material on gender roles, presented in weeks 18 and 43. Although the core material is similar in both, the emphasis and written exercise for week 18 is on childhood socialization, whereas week 43 focuses on adult roles.

The leader should not merely lecture, but rather create opportunities for group participation.

- Ask participants to discuss the relevance of the material in their own lives. What problems are they currently having, or have had in the past, that the material might help with?
- For those who have tried these techniques in the past, did they work? If not, why not?
- Encourage participants to be skeptical and to ask questions. Not all the material is immediately useful to everyone. Some of it may seem counterintuitive and needs to be discussed before clients can accept it.
- Bring up several examples of your own, so the group members have a better sense of how the material can be used.
- When appropriate, share how you have benefited from the material yourself, in your own life. By occasionally showing that you're human, you can help make your clients feel more at ease and willing to open up. On the other hand, it is important that you appear in control. The group is not a place for your personal therapy.
- When doing in-class exercises, make sure all group members are completing their handouts or participating in the discussion. Be aware, however, that some material may bring up painful or embarrassing feelings in clients, and that they may not always be eager to talk about certain issues. Remember that this is not a "process" group or an intensive therapy group, but a skills-building workshop. If a client, or the whole group, runs out of time, these exercises can be completed as a "homework" assignment.

Additional Suggestions

Conducting domestic violence groups is challenging. Most of the clients are referred through the court system, which means that they may not be fully motivated. A number of clients have never been in counseling before, and are not very psychologically minded. Clients enter the program because they have committed illegal, destructive, and abusive acts, some of which may seem despicable to the most seasoned group facilitator. Clients come in "hard wired" in patterns of behavior that involve primitive "fight or flight" responses and deeply ingrained learning. Here are some suggestions for conducting domestic violence/anger management groups that may help overcome these challenges:

1.   See to it that the participants observe the group guidelines, which are included in their workbooks. They should have gone over them with the group leader during the assessment. From time to time, briefly go over them in the group.

2.   Treat all clients with respect, no matter how egregious their acts upon their victims, or obnoxious their personalities. You cannot expect people who do not respect themselves or their victims to change for the better unless you can show respect for them. As the group leader, you are a role model.

3.   Keep the discussion focused on relationships, and in particular how each client is currently managing anger and letting go of aggressive, controlling, and abusive behaviors. On the other hand, keep in mind that other problems, including those at work, inflate levels of stress and make conflicts more difficult to deal with. Allow some discussion, therefore, on any serious issue affecting a client's life. A client who feels more empowered in general will be more able to take responsibility in personal relationships.

4.   Showing respect also includes holding clients accountable for their actions. Any confrontation, however, should be carefully made, with gentleness and understanding, and without shaming the person. Criticize the behavior, not the person. Most clients act the way they do because at one time in their life they had been abused or shamed by someone else. Keep in mind that you are modeling the very techniques you are teaching. Examples:

> "Don, you keep saying how much your wife nags you. It does sound like it would be irritating, but what can you do to make things better?"

> "I'm sorry about your marriage problems, Maria. But you've missed quite a few sessions lately, and haven't been completing your progress log. Do you think you could be more consistent?"

5.   Clients are motivated less by what is "right," but by what works or doesn't work in getting their needs met. Therefore, constantly ask about the consequences of behavior. Especially focus on the impact of aggression and abuse on the children. Clients may be bitter and resentful toward their spouses (sometimes for good reason), but have a harder time justifying the damage done to the kids. Examples:

> "What happened after you yelled? Did she listen?"

> "Did the nagging work? I mean, has he become more of a go-getter since then?"

> "Your daughter was in the next room. How do you think she felt about what you did?"

6.   Set the tone for accountability by asking new members to describe the behaviors that got them referred to the program. Remembering what they revealed during the assessment process, be quick to correct attempts to minimize, blame, or leave out crucial information (e.g., such as the victim having to go to the hospital).

7.   Strive to create and maintain an atmosphere of growth and accountability. The leader's role is crucial in setting the tone, providing the material, and keeping things together. But the most fruitful group experience is one in which the members offer each other support and hold each other accountable. You can encourage this by asking others for their input when a client needs support or to be confronted. No personal attacks are allowed and no one is permitted to give unsolicited advice. However, the group leader can directly ask if a client wants any feedback, and the other participants can be encouraged to share from their own experiences. In particular, use the experience of more senior members, who have been in the group longer. Examples:

"Who here thinks Don's yelling doesn't affect his kids?"

"Has anyone gone through these kinds of job problems that Lucas is talking about?"

"Manuel, you've been around the group almost ten months. We all remember when you were doing some of the things Joe is reporting today. How did you turn things around?"

8. Encourage participants to share their successes, and not just their failures.

9. Avoid commenting on group process or making psychodynamic interpretations of behavior. This is not an in-depth therapy group. Obviously, it may be necessary to intervene if one client's behavior or statements are clearly upsetting someone else, and it may be necessary to ask a reluctant client why he/she hasn't shared. With respect to any interpretations, stick to the curriculum material, even if it was presented in a previous session. Otherwise, the comment could be perceived as attacking, and will confuse the client. Examples:

"Nancy says she only slapped her boyfriend, and that he should be able to take it. Has anyone here ever been slapped or hit? Does anyone remember our session on defenses? Does that seem like minimizing to anyone?"

10. Constantly go back to the curriculum in order to make it relevant to each person's learning. Examples:

"Luke grabbed his son by the arm, causing him to cry. Thinking back to our session on parenting, what could he have done differently to get Billy to clean up his toys?"

"Veronica, you managed to avoid reacting to your husband's criticisms this time. What do you think you did right? Any anger management techniques you can share with us?"

11. Facilitators should be aware of their own internal processes. They should be especially aware of countertransference and of projection mechanisms. Did a client's statement make the facilitator unduly angry, fearful, or upset? Past experience with abuse cannot be allowed to interfere with one's ability to do one's job.

8

Family Interventions

RESEARCH ON FAMILY VIOLENCE

At least 10 million children are exposed to marital violence each year (Straus et al., 1980). Most of them, it appears, are fully aware of the fighting (Holden & Ritchie, 1991). Law enforcement agencies report high numbers of child witnesses to domestic violence. For instance, the Sheriff office in Contra Costa County, California, reported that in official spousal abuse cases, covering a period from January 1 through September 30, 2000, children were present 73% of the time (Contra Costa Office of Sheriff, 2000). Research by Fantuzzo and Lindquist (1989) reveals that children raised in homes where the mother has been physically abused by the father are at a 30%–40% higher risk for psychopathology than are children from nonviolent homes. These children are also at higher risk than children who have only been exposed to neighborhood violence (Litrownik, Newton, Hunter, English, & Everson, 2003). Literature reviews suggest that children exposed to marital violence are at risk for exhibiting a host of internalizing and externalizing symptoms, from depression to conduct disorders and school problems (Edleson, 1999; Kolbo et al., 1996; Wolak & Finkelhor, 1998).

Children are differentially affected by their parents' marital violence, depending on their age. Toddlers are generally the most distressed (Jaffe et al., 1990). A gender effect (e.g., whether boys have more externalizing problems and girls have more internalizing problems) has not been clearly established, but overall these symptoms are equally prevalent (Kitzmann, Gaylord, Holt, & Kenny, 2003). We know that witnessing marital violence has a continuous, cumulative effect on all children. Children who have witnessed such violence, especially severe assaults, become sensitized rather than habituated over time, and are retraumatized whenever there is an incidence of *any* marital conflict (Holden, 1998)

For years, the literature on how children are affected by marital violence has been almost exclusively based on interviews with battered women, with the focus on the father as perpetrator. More recently, studies have drawn from broader community samples. In a New York City study by Salzinger, Feldman, Ng-Mak, Mojica, Stockhammer, and Rosario (2002), the mothers were primarily victims of marital violence; whereas in a large Northeast U.S. study (English, Marshall, & Stewart, 2003), the mothers were primarily perpetrators. These and other studies (e.g., Johnston &

Roseby, 1997) indicate that children are adversely affected whether the marital violence is perpetrated by the mother or by the father. A discussion of these effects, including gender differences, can be found on pages 139–141.

Partner Abuse and Child Abuse

Clearly, the effects of partner violence on children should give us cause for alarm. But what about other forms of family violence? We know that intimate partners perpetrate severe assaults upon one another (punch, kick, bite, choke, beat up, use objects or weapons) at a rate of approximately 4–5 per 100 couples. However, assaults by other family members are far more frequent (Straus et al., 1980). Parents perpetrate severe assaults on their children at a rate of 11 per 100. (Mothers hit the most, largely due to the greater amount of time spent at home. Assaults by fathers are more often fatal, but mothers cause the greater number of deaths through neglect.) Siblings perpetrate severe assaults against one another at a rate of 53 per 100, and they punch, kick or bite their parents at a rate of 9 per 100. What are the effects of these other forms of violence, and how do they interact with one another? As the Johnston and Roseby research indicates, we cannot ignore the reciprocal nature of relationships or the fact that events in one part of the system reverberate throughout the whole. A well-known finding, for instance, is that children who witness their parents fight are at high risk of being assaulted themselves, and that parents who physically abuse their children are more likely to perpetrate spousal abuse (Straus et al., 1990). Another consideration is the relationship between family violence and general dysfunction. A review of the literature reveals a number of important trends, but no definitive answers.

Salzinger and colleagues (2002), examining 100 cases of physically abused children in New York City, ages 9–12, determined that the effects of having experienced direct child abuse were greater than having witnessed violence between the parents. In their Northwest study conducted the following year with a cohort of 261 preschool children referred to CPS for child abuse and neglect, English and associates (2003) found similar results. However, according to the most recent, comprehensive meta-analysis of the literature, conducted by Kitzmann and her colleagues (2003), the overall impact, in terms of both internalizing and externalizing symptoms, on a child who has experienced direct parental abuse is no greater than that on a child who has witnessed marital violence.

In a study by Hershorn and Rosenbaum (1985), children from discordant but nonviolent homes were determined to be just as aggressive and oppositional as the children of battered women. And in a study by Grych and Fincham (1990), children from violent and discordant families exhibited similar internalizing and externalizing symptoms. Subsequently, Fantuzzo and colleagues (1991) compared a group of battered women and their children living in a shelter, with battered women and their children still living at home, and a nonviolent control group. Children from both types of violent settings exhibited more externalizing problems than did children from nonviolent homes. However, the shelter children exhibited more internalizing symptoms than the home-violent group:

> The results of our study suggest a direct relationship between interparental conflict and familial disruption and the nature of child adjustment problems for young children. In this

respect, verbal conflict only was associated with a moderate level of conduct problems; verbal plus physical conflict was associated with clinical levels of conduct problems and a moderate level of emotional problems; and verbal plus physical conflict plus temporary shelter residence was associated with clinical levels of conduct problems, higher level of emotional problems, and lower levels of social functioning and perceived maternal acceptance. [p. 263]

According to Wolak and Finkelhor (1998), "Pervasive conflict that takes the form of overt verbal hostility *or* violence harms children by causing stress, impairing effective parent–child relationships, and training children to be aggressive. Overall, children from violent homes appear to be at greater risk for showing clinical-level behavioral and emotional problems, but it is likely that some symptoms are caused by the conflict and not necessarily the violence" (pp. 91–92). The authors propose that the deleterious effects of marital violence may be direct or indirect. Direct effects include physical danger (from being around thrown objects, etc.), and psychological trauma leading to internalizing and externalizing symptoms. Indirect effects include the harsh parenting associated with marital violence and other poor parenting practices such as inconsistency, low positive involvement, and attachment disturbance. They also include the accumulated stress that children take on due to the anxiety and depression experienced by maritally violent parents, as well as the attendant problems of substance abuse, economic difficulties and relationship break-ups.

In fact, even the *possibility* of divorce is traumatic to children. Laumakis and colleagues (1998) examined the differential impact on children of physical marital aggression, negative tone, verbal put-downs, and threats to leave. Seventy-four children listened to staged audio fights between couples. A sophisticated coding system allowed the children to respond in their own words, rather than choose from a list of responses. The most negative emotional reactions were given by children who had listened to couples physically fight or threaten to leave. The finding that threats to leave caused as strong a reaction as physical violence or verbal abuse was significant, according to the authors:

> Why are physical aggression and threats to leave more upsetting than conflicts with name-calling and negative voice qualities? . . . *The key feature of these two scenarios is the implied impact on the child, by virtue of the potential for major disruption and change in the marriage and in family life as the child knows it.* These data lead one to examine more closely the commonly stated assumption that exposure to marital aggression and violence is more upsetting than exposure to other forms of marital conflict. [p. 280]

MEGAN

The reader is asked to read the vignette below, and to put him/herself in the place of the child. This exercise is meant to illustrate some points previously made about the nature of partner violence and its effects on children.

> Megan would usually be in bed when the fighting started. The yelling, the name-calling, the threats—there was so much hatred in that voice, a deep, swelling hatred

that seemed to press upon her, twisting her up inside, making her sick to her stomach. "Shut up!," she'd hear. "I hate you, you worthless drunk! Do you hear me? You're worthless!" Sometimes, there were other noises, too, scary noises, of things being tossed around—like lamps and plates, and things she couldn't identify. Megan would press her hands over her ears, trying desperately to shut out the noises. Sometimes she would stand by her door and listen, waiting for the cling-clang of the kitchen drawer, where the knives were kept. Eventually, she would crawl under her covers, pull them tight over her head as she cried herself to sleep and thought about her baby brother in the next room. Did he hear? Was there anything she could have done to stop this from happening? She didn't know. She was scared, and she was confused. "Me, too," she would think. "I'm worthless."

Who is perpetrating the abuse—mother, father, or both? Is the perpetrator's gender important? From the child's experience, how much does it matter whether the violence consists only of emotional abuse and threats, or actual physical assaults and injuries?

The Role of Stress

Families, by their very nature, produce high levels of conflict. Many tasks need to be carried out, including the generation of income, household chores, and raising children. At the same time, it is within the family that one seeks to meet such basic emotional needs as belonging and self-esteem. However, families are made up of individuals from different generations, at different developmental levels, and with competing needs and interests. This results in high levels of stress. In combination with poor impulse control and insufficient problem-solving skills, family stress can lead to intense conflicts, and sometimes physical violence among the various family relationships—parent to parent, parent to child, child to child, and child to parent. The latter may involve assaults by adolescents on their smaller, weaker parents, or by adult children on their elderly parents (elder abuse):

> An example is that of an 86-year-old woman who lives with her 50-year-old daughter. The daughter is employed and is also a single mother of two teen-aged sons. Because the daughter is pressed for time, she chooses her mother's meals and clothing and restricts her activities so she does not fall and injure herself—as she had the previous year. The mother is resentful, bored, and increasingly passive, placing more pressure on the daughter to make decisions and perform tasks on her behalf. This in turn causes the daughter to feel more stressed and overwhelmed, resulting in escalating household tension, arguments (which may include pushing and slapping), and threats of nursing home placement. [Brownell, 1998, p. 19]

The family, according to researcher Murray Straus and his associates (1990), is "the most violent institution a citizen is likely to encounter." This is largely due to the higher tolerance for violence in families, especially corporal punishment. We know, for instance, that parents who use corporal punishment are at higher risk for crossing the line into physical child abuse (Straus & Donnelly, 2001). And parents who give themselves permission to hit their children are far more likely to turn their aggression against their spouses. Straus writes,

The family has different rules about violence than do other groups. In an academic department, an office, or a factory, the basic rule is that no one can hit anyone else, no matter
what they do wrong. A person can be a pest, an intolerable bore, negligent, incompetent,
selfish, or unwilling to listen to reason. But that still does not give anyone the right to hit
such a person. In the family the situation is different. There, the basic rule is that if someone
does wrong and won't listen to reason, violence is permissible and sometimes even required.
[Straus et al., 1990, p. 184]

Although some types of assaults are more likely to cause physical injury than
others (e.g., husband on wife, parent on child), *any* use of violence is destructive.
Violence inflates stress to higher levels and tends to beget more violence, thus gravely
undermining the family's ability to carry out its functions. Children growing up in
such an environment learn that violence is an acceptable way to resolve problems.
More important, they learn that love and abuse tend to go together. As adults, these
children are far more likely than those from nonviolent homes to become involved
in pathological, dependent relationships and become abusive themselves, thus trans-
ferring the cycle from one generation to the next. Domestic violence, therefore,
cannot be understood outside of a family context.

In Wolak and Finkelhor's (1998) analysis, there was a correlational relationship
between marital violence, family dysfunction, physical child abuse, and the various
internalizing and externalizing symptoms suffered by children. Other researchers
have proposed a direct causal link between these phenomena, with husband-on-wife
battering as the primary cause. Holden and Ritchie (1991) compared 37 battered
women with 37 women from nonabusive households. The battered women were
observed to engage in more conflicted, negative interactions, and were less involved
with their children than were those in the comparison group. Because maternal
stress and paternal irritability were the strongest predictors of child behavior and
emotional problems, the authors concluded that there is a spillover effect from the
marital violence that affects parenting by both parents.

Moore and Pepler (1998) conducted an ambitious study with four groups of
latency-age children and their mothers: 113 in a battered women's shelter, 82 homeless families in temporary housing, 82 single-parent families (mother only) and
100 intact, two-parent, nonviolent families. Mothers were administered the Conflict
Tactics Scale, the General Health Questionnaire, and the Child Behavior Checklist
(measuring children's internalizing, externalizing, and social problems). The children were given the Wide-Ranging Achievement Tests, Revised (WRAT-R) (scholastic
achievement), the Digit Span subscale of the Wechsler Intelligence Scale for Children
(WISC) (memory), and the Children's Locus of Control Scale. The authors found
that low income, less parental education, frequent moves, and poor maternal health
were characteristics of both shelter and homeless families. The shelter and homeless
children scored significantly lower in social competence than did those from two-
parent families, and they also scored much lower on the Digit Span test. The homeless
children scored more than one standard deviation below grade level on the Reading
and Math tests of the WRAT-R. The most telling finding, however, was that the
mother's verbal abuse toward her children was the strongest predictor of poor
adjustment in all groups—more than the father's verbal abuse toward the children or
his violence against the mother. "Mother's verbal aggression," the authors concluded,
"may augment or exacerbate preexisting emotional susceptibility brought about by
witnessing interparental violence. . . . Physically abused mothers may become too

exhausted, distressed, and distracted to provide their children with the necessary attention, discipline, and affection" (p. 179).

Thus, marital abuse is seen by some as the primary source of stress in families of battered women and the ultimate cause of both child abuse and its consequences. Is it possible that in the Moore and Pepler study, none of the mothers had parenting problems prior to the abuse? This is unlikely. But even if this holds for cases of severe, unilateral battering, in most physically abusive relationships the violence is less severe and usually mutual. Furthermore, there is an equal likelihood that marital discord and violence follows, rather than precedes, parent-on-child conflict. Lynch and Cicchetti (1998) determined that the existence of child behavior problems prior to having been exposed to marital violence contributes significantly to overall levels of family stress, which in turn may aggravate both marital and parent–child relationships. We have seen how attitudes favorable to corporal punishment are associated with pro-violent attitudes toward spouses (Straus et al., 1990; Straus & Donnelly, 2001). We should be careful, then, in making unwarranted generalities. In a study of 110 Israeli families, Sternberg and associates (1993) found that children who were both witnesses to marital violence and had experienced physical abuse did not suffer more psychological damage than children who had only witnessed marital violence, or children who had only been directly abused. In their review of the literature, Kitzmann and colleagues found similar results. "Violence *anywhere* in the family," the authors suggested, "may be sufficient to disrupt child development" (p. 346).

The New York City study by the Salzinger group (2002) sought to identify the relative effects of family stress, partner violence, caregiver distress, and child abuse on children's development. Caregiver distress was not found to be a function of partner violence. Partner violence was a mediator of child abuse, not by directly producing poor functioning in children, but rather by increasing the risk of aggression against them. Among all the variables, the authors identified two significant causal paths. In one, family stress increased the risk for partner violence, which increased the possibility of child abuse. In the other, family stress contributed to caregiver distress, which in turn led to child abuse. These findings are impressive, and even more so when we compare them with those of Kitzmann's meta-analysis. In looking at the impact of exposure to marital violence on the children, she found that the effect size in studies that controlled for family stress was smaller than in those that did not. Among the factors hypothesized to impact negatively on child functioning, general family stress stood out as the most significant, the one that can exacerbate any of the other conditions. In this conception, partner violence is merely one, albeit important, factor in family dysfunction.

Effects on Adult Functioning

The effects of intimate partner violence unfortunately persist well into adulthood, when the child grows up and becomes involved in an intimate relationship. We know that children from abusive families are more likely than children from non-abusive families to exhibit aggressive behaviors later in life. The mechanisms by which this behavior is thought to be transmitted fall into two categories. In the first, children learn to become violent through the process of observational learning. For instance, results of the National Family Violence Surveys (Straus & Gelles, 1990) indicate that children who have witnessed marital violence are twice as likely to perpetrate partner violence as adults than those who have never witnessed such violence. For violent women, the assault rates are generally the same whether they had witnessed violence by the father, by the mother, or both. Violent men, however, are more likely to have witnessed violence by the mother upon the father.

The other mechanism involves the effects of child abuse and neglect. Litrownik and his colleagues (2003) found that psychological child abuse at age 4 predicted internalizing symptoms of anxiety and depression later in childhood, whereas a combination of physical and psychological child abuse predicted aggressive behavior. An analysis of the National Violence Against Women Survey (Pimlott-Kubiak & Cortina, 2003) found significant correlations between childhood physical abuse and adult depression and drug use.

Using the Conflict Tactics Scale and a self-report test known as the EMBU, Donald Dutton (1998) investigated the relationship between early parent–child relationships and adult abusiveness in a population of male batterers. The most critical elements of the EMBU were experiences that led a child to feel unloved, guilty, and shamed. Shaming was particularly aversive: personal verbal attacks, public punishment or humiliation, and random punishment—the sort of experiences that lead a child to regard his or her entire self as flawed or "bad."

Dutton found that shame and parental physical abuse in combination had the highest predictive value. Men who had experienced shame without physical abuse were less likely to become physically abusive as adults, but were emotionally abusive instead. A study with 140 male batterers yielded the following correlations (Table 8.1) among the three EMBU subscales and associated features of adult abusiveness.

Current Policy

Violence between intimate partners is a significant social problem, not only because of the physical and emotional harm done to adult victims but also to the children

TABLE 8.1   EMBU Subscales and Adult Abusiveness

	Shame		Guilt		Unloved	
	mother	father	mother	father	mother	father
BPO (Borderline Personality Organization)	.37	.55	.31	.38	.27	.23
Anger	.43	.43	.28	.30	.28	.23
TSC (trauma symptoms checklist)	.27	.38	.26	.37	.25	.19
PMWI 1*	.39	.35	.33	.31	.29	.27
PMWI 2	.34	.33	.32	.30	.10	.08
CTS (man's self-report)	.38	.31	.12	.09	.41	.35
CTS (wife's self-report)	.24	.26	.18	.17	.55	.50

*Psychological Maltreatment of Women Inventory (Tolman, 1989). PMWI 1 is the dominance/isolation subscale; PMWI 2 is the emotional abuse subscale.

who are witnesses to such violence. Although public policy and intervention have focused on the most severe types of domestic violence, by male perpetrators, it appears that children suffer the same kinds of emotional, behavioral, and social symptoms by witnessing the mother hit the father as when the father hits the mother. From this perspective, the gender of the maritally violent parent is not very significant. Nevertheless, women who assault their partners are rarely referred to anger management programs. Only 18% of spousal abuse arrests in California involve female perpetrators, and an even lower percentage of women are mandated to complete a 52-week batterer program. For example, in Judge Craddick's Misdemeanor Domestic Violence Court in Contra Costa County, 95% of defendants mandated to batterer treatment are men. The women are presumably referred to other types of counseling. Traditionally, therapy for violent women, whether voluntary or court-ordered, has consisted of supportive individual therapy. Far too often, they are referred to victim groups.

In contrast to past decades, when it received scant public attention, intimate partner violence now thoroughly dominates public discussion, policy-making, outreach, and intervention strategies on family violence. There seems to be an exponentially increasing number of professional seminars and community forums on the subject of partner violence, but few that address child abuse specifically, or family violence in general. "Family violence" law centers in fact often exclusively address the needs of battered women. Plaintiffs in child custody disputes routinely are granted restraining orders against an ex-spouse on the grounds that they feel "threatened," gaining custody and causing major disruptions in the children's lives, even though those same plaintiffs may be overly punitive, and sometimes physically abusive to their children. Shelters are only recently beginning to offer services for children—this despite the fact that children suffer the greater share of assaults and physical injuries. In addition, children who are verbally or physically abused by their parents are at an equal, if not greater risk, than those exposed to marital abuse for exhibiting short-term and long-term pathology. In California, both spousal abusers and child abusers are legally required to complete a certified 52-week treatment program. Although there are twice as many CFS child abuse reports than spousal abuse arrests, batterer intervention programs far outnumber those targeting child abuse. Within the four Bay Area counties of San Francisco, Marin, Alameda and Contra Costa, there are approximately 50 of the former, and only three of the latter.

Conclusions

The mechanisms by which partner violence and child abuse negatively impact on children are complex, but appear to be mediated by family stress. The cause of child symptomatology is rarely a unitary one. It is, instead, the result of overlapping, reciprocal interactions among the various family members. Physical violence, or even verbal conflict, between any subgroup causes stress throughout the entire family system, which leads to conflict between other subgroups, thus generating additional stress and increasing the probability of further violence. That is not to say that all types of family violence have equal consequences, or that they should be responded to in the same manner. Clearly, severe spousal battering is a greater concern than pushing and grabbing, or mild forms of corporal punishment. However, persistent, high levels of verbal abuse, particularly put-downs and criticism that shame the other, are far more toxic than common types of physical violence. Likewise, emotional abuse and parental rejection of children warrant more attention than nearly all forms of spousal violence. The point is that every family is different. The most damaging forms of abuse will vary from family to family and, often, within the same family over time.

ASSESSING AND TREATING FAMILY VIOLENCE: AN OVERVIEW

- Inquire about possible abuse by both partners, male and female, regardless of physical size or strength. Ask about violence perpetrated *by* them, and *upon* them.
- Determine the extent of verbal and emotional abuse and the use of power and control tactics, using a gender-inclusive questionnaire that includes tactics utilized by both men and women.
- Conduct a thorough assessment of parent–child relations. Ideally, this should include the Parent–Child Conflict Tactics Scale, a measure of corporal punishment and child abuse.
- Look for evidence of sibling violence, as well as violence by children upon their parents—in particular by older, more physically threatening adolescents.
- Treat all members of the family, using individual, couples, family, and group therapy as needed, but adopt a family systems perspective and strive to avoid rigid distinctions between perpetrators and victims. For reasons of treatment and safety, one needs to know when there is a clear, dominant aggressor, and victims of serious violence must be protected. Keep in mind, however, that the victim of one person's violence is often the perpetrator toward another (e.g., the violent man who had once been shamed and physically assaulted by his mother, the battered woman who physically abuses and neglects her children, or the abused teen who assaults younger siblings).
- Refer all maritally abusive partners to an appropriate anger management or batterer intervention program, depending on the nature and severity of the violence. An individual who perpetrates minor assaults and whose violence is more expressive than instrumental may not need to enroll in a batterer program.
- Don't send abusive parents to a short-term generic parenting class, anger management group, or 52-week batterer intervention program, but rather to long-term treatment specifically tailored to their needs—something like the 52-week High-Conflict Family Violence Parent Group offered at our center. In this type of group, parents not only learn how to manage their own anger and acquire nonviolent parenting skills, but also how to prevent their children from acting violently toward other family members and lessen family stress. They are also educated about the systemic nature of family conflict and the intergenerational transmission of violence.
- When there are major disruptions in the caregiver–child relationship, provide conjoint therapy with the affected parties (Van Horn, Best, & Lieberman, 1998). In these cases, the children typically have ceased to view the primary caregiver as a dependable protector from the other parent's abuse, and have

begun to act out in various ways. The caregiver, in turn, often responds with harsh, punitive parenting, or else rebuffs the child's solicitations for attention and nurturing. A good resource for parents is the book by Christina Dalpiaz (2004), *Breaking Free, Starting Over: Parenting in the Aftermath of Family Violence.*

- Send violent adolescents, when appropriate, to a separate anger management program where they can learn how to control their own aggressive impulses, even when they may also have been victims of parental abuse.
- Provide supportive psychotherapy for the children who have been traumatized by the marital violence and/or the abuse directed against them. An excellent treatment model can be found in the book by Johnston and Roseby (1997).

SYSTEMS AND THE RESISTANCE TO CHANGE

The following sections offer methods for conducting children's groups, parenting programs, anger management groups for teens, and strategies to help the entire family. The marital dyad is the central component of any family unit and therefore must be the central focus of any treatment plan. For couples without children, the marriage *is* the family unit. Until the couple/parents cease their abuse/aggression, adopt pro-social communication and conflict resolution skills, and repair the damaged relationship, other family interventions will have little effect. Parents set the example, establish and enforce rules, set limits, and offer support. The parents are responsible, morally and legally, for the health of the whole family.

A traditional view among family therapists is that families are closed systems that tend to resist change (Jackson, 1965). When external and internal stressors exert influence on the system, it becomes unbalanced, causing instability in the marital relationship. Violence serves to correct instability, and return the system to homeostasis. Other systemic models allow for the possibility of a runaway dynamic, which takes the system in a new direction, rather than a self-correcting one. Central to all these perspectives, however, are certain propositions. The first is that each family member influences, and is influenced by, the other family members. The second, as we have previously seen in the section on choosing treatment modalities, is that no relationship behavior has one definite, discrete cause. The systems approach to domestic violence is not a victim-blaming model, nor does it use a victim–victimizer dichotomy.

Violent relationships tend to be self-perpetuating and highly resistant to change. There are a number of reasons this is so:

- *What Is Normal*
  Either because individuals have previously experienced abuse in other relationships and/or their family of origin, the partners see violence as normal. It is therefore more readily accepted.
- *Mutual Dependence*
  Abusive relationships, whether characterized by unilateral or mutual violence, are established and maintained because each partner is benefiting in some way from the arrangement. The benefits may be economic and/or emotional. Research indicates that the relationships of aggressive and distressed couples

are not only characterized by highly negative interactions, but by many positive interactions as well:

> Perhaps in aggressive marriages, spouses attempt to compensate for aggression with more positive interaction that offsets the harm done by the abuse, or the high levels of positive interaction may indicate the presence of intensive marital attachments . . . the results of the present study also hint at the enmeshment of the aggressive-distressed marriage noted by Dutton and Painter (1993). Certainly, the themes of attachment and enmeshment among distressed-aggressive couples bear further scrutiny. [Lloyd, 1996, p. 193]

- *Stress and Change*
  To change means to take on additional stress—something that individuals already overwhelmed with life problems understandably want to avoid. For some, taking an hour to see a marriage counselor may seem like an insurmountable task.
- *Controlling the Familiar*
  A basic human motive is the need to master one's environment. Individuals who have grown up with abuse become proficient at coping with verbal and physical assaults and navigating the turbulent seas of family dysfunction. No matter how maladaptive their behaviors, and seemingly self-defeating the consequences, human beings feel more in control within such relationships than outside of them.
- *Identity Suicide*
  For most people, perpetrating spousal violence is ego-dystonic. What seems like minimizing and rationalizing to a therapist may also be a good prognosticator for treatment outcome. The person who feels remorse after an outburst, or says, "I just lost it," doesn't see him/herself as fundamentally abusive. The more chronic and severe the violence, the more likely it has become part of the perpetrator's core personality. To change would simply be too threatening. It would mean the loss of one's sense of self, and would be akin to committing identity suicide.
- *Correcting the Past*
  Harville Hendrix (1988) popularized the idea that individuals seek out intimate partners who fit an internal image, or *imago*, of crucial caregivers from childhood. The unconscious intent is to work out unresolved childhood issues with their unconsciously selected mate. For instance, a woman who grew up with a domineering mother may find herself dating only strong, assertive men. Naturally, this sets up a dysfunctional dynamic from the outset, almost guaranteeing relationship difficulties. However, once identified, this dynamic can actually be used in therapy to produce growth and healing.

The Three-Phase Treatment Model

The three-phase treatment model (see pages 82–85) was designed to overcome resistance to change and alter rigid, dysfunctional systems that maintain abuse and violence. The first step is for new information to find its way inside the system's boundaries. This happens in the first phase of counseling, when individuals learn about the dynamic of violence and acquire basic relationship skills. The resulting changes in behavior are said to be of the first order type, in family systems parlance. First order changes not only empower clients by providing alternative tools with which to meet their needs, but also elicit a new response from others, thus setting into play alternative interactions that will challenge the system's homeostasis.

Once the other party makes a corresponding change, second order change has occurred and the system establishes a new homeostasis. With violent couples, it is essential that both partners internalize the same learning so that changes can occur in a mutually agreeable fashion and the new homeostasis will be stable and healthy. Change made by one partner is threatening to the other, who may unconsciously sabotage the other's efforts. One example would be the abused husband who complains about his wife's increasing frequency of anger management counseling sessions, threatening to leave the relationship because he feels ignored. In second order change, the system itself is altered. From a systems perspective, couples don't fight over specific issues, but rather over issues of power and control. When power and control begin to shift and change for the better, even the victim can feel anxious. The couple has been doing the same dance with each other for so long that when one changes the steps, the other can feel lost for a while.

When second order change occurs, the relative power bases have shifted. Communication becomes more open and respectful, and decision-making acquires an equalitarian and inclusive character. The parties overcome unhealthy dependencies and begin to individuate. The relationship becomes a choice, maintained by the mutual agreement of two healthy individuals.

Change must proceed in a gradual, nonthreatening way so that the couple does not flee treatment. Clients feel out of control when they first seek help. They don't trust each other and have little confidence in their abilities to improve their situation. Therefore, in first and second phase work, interventions are structured and designed to empower clients and provide a sense of safety and optimism. New, more adaptive ways to perceive and behave in the relationship are front loaded so that by the third phase, the couple has picked up enough momentum to carry through the difficult work of addressing and resolving childhood issues.

COUPLES COUNSELING: PHASES I AND II

General Features

A survey by Hansen and associates (1991) arrived at the disturbing conclusion that a substantial number of marriage and family therapists downplay the significance of violence. Subsequent inquiries by O'Leary and Murphy (1992), and Aldarondo and Straus (1994), indicate that when marriage counselors administer the Conflict Tactics Scales to their clients, they discover additional assaults not previously identified from standard assessment procedures, as much as 75% of the total. A therapist must be well versed in the field of partner violence, including assessment procedures and domestic violence dynamics. The therapist must adhere to the safety guidelines outlined on pages 80–81 and remember that couples counseling can be appropriate in cases of unilateral or mutual abuse, but cases of severe violence should be referred out to a DV specialist. Collaboration is always an option, fruitful in many situations.

Couples therapy should follow the three-phase model, as previously discussed. It may be conducted in the traditional manner, one couple at a time, or in a multicouples format.

1. *Setting Guidelines and Addressing Preliminary Issues*
Couples treatment begins during the assessment process as the counselor establishes a therapeutic alliance with the clients. Early on, the counselor should accomplish the following:

DEFINE VIOLENCE AS THE PRIMARY PROBLEM

Individuals involved in abusive relationships, both victims and perpetrators, tend to minimize the importance of partner violence and often fail to consider it as a crime. One way to quickly establish its importance is to compare it with other types of violence. For instance, perpetrators might be asked what would happen if they slapped a waiter or waitress because of poor service. Victims might be asked if they would go back to a restaurant after being slapped or choked by a waiter or waitress.

HOLD PERPETRATORS ACCOUNTABLE

Teach clients the difference between explanation and excuse. Agree that there may be extenuating circumstances around a perpetrator's violence and assure clients that relationship issues will be addressed, but emphasize that stopping violence takes precedence, and is solely the responsibility of the perpetrator.

ADDRESS THE VICTIM'S DILEMMA

The dilemma, as described by Goldner (1998; pronoun *she* can be viewed as indicating either sex):

> If she expresses herself fully and completely, with all the emotional intensity her concerns warrant, she could put herself at risk after session. But if, out of fear, she minimizes issues to mollify her partner, the therapy is inauthentic and she loses the chance to speak her mind, which is what people come to therapy to do. (pp. 272–273)

Emphasize to the victim the importance of authentic expression for treatment success, but keep in mind that genuine, truthful expression cannot happen unless there is trust, and that trust begins with safety. Continually probe for evidence of fear in the client's responses and body language, as well as signs of control by the perpetrator—such as unwarranted expressions of disapproval or anger, frequent interruptions, mind-reading, and attempts to speak for the victim.

ADDRESS MUTUAL DEPENDENCY

Perpetrators and victims fail to leave high-conflict situations largely because of dependency needs. Without using *mutual dependency* and other psychological terms that sound negative and trendy, the counselor highlights the fact that if they didn't care about one another, they wouldn't fight. Yet abuse undermines any positive feelings they have for one another. Control of violence and victim safety are given higher priority than the relationship. Without safety and an end to violence, there is no self-respect. Victims cannot help their partners if they are unwilling to help themselves.

ASSUME THAT VIOLENCE IS CONTROLLABLE

As indicated in a previous section, perpetrators pretend to have lost control of their anger impulses and use this as an excuse for their violence. Here are some ways to challenge excuses:

- Ask the perpetrator to imagine a situation in which he has had two moving violations. He has just been pulled over by a police officer for speeding. The next ticket will result in a hefty increase in insurance premiums and possibly the loss of driving privileges. Ask the perpetrator to further imagine that the police officer is curt and rude, and when the perpetrator begs the policeman to let him go, the policeman smirks and gives him the ticket anyway. On a scale of 1 to 10, what would the perpetrator's anger level be at that moment? Assuming that there would be a high level of anger, ask what the likelihood is that he would scream at or physically strike the policeman. Then ask why it is that he has been violent at home, toward his spouse or children, when he has experienced similar or even lesser levels of anger.
- Ask the perpetrator how often she feels like engaging in verbal or physical abuse, and how often she restrains herself. Point out the contradiction between a belief that she can't control her anger, and the fact that most of the time she actually does.
- Ask clients if they know any other couples who have relationship problems, such as issues with children, finances, or in-laws. Ask if these couples use violence as a way to resolve their difficulties.
- Ask clients to rephrase vague statements such as, "It got violent, I blew up," with statements that convey responsibility for their actions ("I slapped her," or "I punched him").

2. *Setting Priorities and Presenting Basic Tools for Anger and Violence Control*
Initial success will determine the long-term outcome of couples therapy. Resistant, anxious, and skeptical clients may be initially motivated out of desperation, but will continue to remain motivated if they feel they are moving forward, making progress, and accomplishing their goals. Clients must work on *achievable* goals, and the efforts made must have *immediate* results. For this to happen, the couple must commit to work together as a team:

> Battering couples are in enemy camps. Life is war. They do not cooperate, they are not a team, and there is no mutuality. Whatever opportunity presents itself to pull them together must be capitalized upon. In order for change to take place, there must be bonding. The presentation of mutual goals, feelings and needs will help create a bond between them which will begin to bridge the gulf that divides them. [Geller & Wasserstrom, 1984, p. 39]

The essentials of anger and violence control outlined in pages 195–198 of Appendix C for the group program are equally relevant to couples. In Phase I, couples must:

- Immediately eliminate all physical aggression, and reduce the amount of verbal aggression and emotionally abusive and controlling behaviors.

- Avoid additional secondary problems (hurt, resentment, and distrust from abusive behaviors) instead of trying to resolve their primary problems (what the initial issue may have been, such as the children, money, etc.).
- Increase awareness of inner tension and anger levels.
- View anger as an activated smoke alarm, where there may or may not be an actual fire. The anger alone is not dangerous, does not need to be stuffed and ignored, or allowed to escalate. There are no documented cases of people imploding because they were angry.
- Utilize the *control scale* concept, by recognizing that one has unequivocal control over one's behavior, some control over one's internal state (feelings, thoughts, desires), and no control over the internal state or behavior of others.
- Understand that disengaging from conflict by taking a time out is neither defeat nor surrender, but rather a way to take control of a dangerous, unpredictable situation.

3. *Acquiring Communication and Conflict Resolution Skills*
According to Telch & Lindquist (1984),

> Couples in battering relationships are similar to other couples in treatment. They have low self-esteem; they have greater difficulty with communication; and they experience greater dissatisfaction and disagreement in their marriages than satisfied spouses. Therefore they are likely to need and respond to interventions such as communications training, negotiating, and other skills typically used by marital therapists. Emphasis to V couples that the content of their problems is no different from most married couples seems valuable for their self-esteem and for rapport. . . . Our violent couples were found to exhibit more passive and aggressive behaviors and less assertive behaviors than the comparison couples. This pattern suggests that the V couples have difficulty in expressing wants, needs, and feelings directly, and that instead they operate in a passive-aggressive manner. The violent outburst presumably results in part from the inadequacy of this pattern in terms of getting one's needs and wants met. Assertion skills training would appear to be a fruitful direction to pursue for professionals working in this area. [p. 247]

These skills can be found in a previous section, "Elements of Treatment" (pages 65–68), and in the multicouples curriculum below.

Multicouples Groups

Phases I and II may be conducted in a multicouples group. The model developed by Neidig and Friedman, from which our own program has drawn heavily, uses a psychoeducational format and utilizes male and female co-leaders. Couples are selected on the basis of safety, motivation to change and level of commitment. Our experience, as well as that of others (e.g., Stith, Rosen, & McCollum, 2002), suggests that couples with weak relationship commitments tend to drop out at much higher rates than other couples. Each group should be limited to no more than five or six couples, in order to achieve maximum involvement by each participant. Such a format allows each couple to acquire the skills needed to rebuild trust and commitment, but with the added benefit of group participation. Clients benefit more from didactic material when there are other couples available to provide feedback. The presence of one's partner, as in traditional couples therapy, facilitates integration of what is learned. This format also helps couples overcome the isolation associated with battering relationships, as they are able to identify with others in similar predicaments, and obtain support and encouragement from the other couples.

The Virginia Tech Domestic Violence Focused Couples Treatment Program (Stith et al., 2002) is a 12-week, solution-focused group that works primarily with an African-American clientele, and is limited to couples in which the male has perpetrated mild to moderate violence. Based on feedback from the women following the initial pilot project, the program began to teach anger management skills to both parties. A recent 6-month follow-up study (Stith et al., 2004) found strong support for the multicouple format: 25% of the men treated in this format reoffended, whereas the recidivism rate was 43% of the men who had completed individual couples counseling, and 66% for those in the untreated comparison group. An interesting approach is utilized at Family Violence Prevention Services in North Carolina (Maupin, 2002), where each partner in the relationship is assigned to a separate group prior to joining together in a multicouples group. Deschner (1984) assigns her clients to parallel same-sex groups for five sessions before they come together in a multicouples group, with the respective group leaders now acting as co-facilitators. During the first series, each partner works on acquiring basic anger management skills. Afterwards, they move on to communication, assertiveness, and conflict-resolution skills.

Our program brings the couples together from the beginning for a period of 10 consecutive weeks. Each session lasts two hours, divided between a structured check-in time and presentation of the didactic material. During check-in, couples bring up examples of conflicts they have had in the previous week. The couples are not expected to discuss these problems at length, or try to resolve them during the session. Instead, they are asked to indicate how they dealt with the problem. Ventilation of affect is discouraged. Each couple, upon completion of the assessment process, is asked to become familiar with the list of aggressive, emotionally abusive, controlling, and dirty fighting techniques, and to keep a progress log (pages 198–203). During the group check-in, they are expected to disclose the extent of such behaviors and how these may have undermined their conflict-resolution efforts during the week. At this time, the couples are asked to indicate how successful they may have been in utilizing the skills they had previously learned in group.

The 10-week curriculum is outlined below. Much of the material can be found in more detail in the "Elements of Treatment" section (pages 61–70) and among the group workbook handouts.

Session One

1. INTRODUCTIONS—Couples identify their issues, including the extent of the abuse, and state their personal goals for group.
2. ABUSE/CONTROL SCENARIOS—Group members go over this list (Table 8.2) intended to show how both partners can be abusive, often in gender-specific ways.
3. REVIEW—Anger and violence control priorities (pages 195–198).
4. EXERCISE—Recognizing anger cues
    Participants are asked to identify their anger cues, such as rapid heartbeat, rapid speech, high level or tone of voice, angry thoughts, inability to listen, tightness of stomach, arms or legs. Partners are asked to identify cues from their own perspective.
5. REVIEW—Progress log, definitions of abuse, and dirty fighting.

TABLE 8.2 Abuse/Control Scenarios: Which Is Worse?

Being told you are stupid
Or: Being kept up all night by a partner who insists on having his/her say

Someone threatens to take your children away
Or: Someone threatens you with physical violence

Spouse refuses to give you money for groceries
Or: Spouse ruins your credit by racking up huge debts and forcing you into bankruptcy

Partner isolates you from the family by turning the children against you
Or: Partner isolates you by not letting you work outside the home

For a woman to be called a "slut"
Or: For a man to be called a "loser"

Being ignored and emotionally shut out of your partner's life
Or: Being pressured into having sex

Constantly being questioned about your whereabouts
Or: Partner calls your boss to say that you are abusive and an alcoholic

Your ex calls you 20 times a day and shows up at your job site to verbally harass you
Or: On the road, you and your new boyfriend are followed by your ex

Session Two

1. EXERCISE—Comparing progress log entries.
    Couples compare log entries to provide a reality check for those who may be minimizing their behavior.
2. TIME OUTS—Couples are asked to discuss their progress in disengaging from conflicts. Their resistance to taking time outs is explored (e.g., not wanting to back down, thinking it's the partner's fault, etc.), as well as their resistance to allowing the partner to take time outs (e.g., want the last word, worried the problem will never get dealt with).
3. ADDITIONAL INFORMATION ON ANGER AND AGGRESSION

    *   What you can do with anger: You can't prevent yourself from ever feeling angry, nor would you want to, because anger is a normal and sometimes useful emotion. Once you feel angry, you can escalate (blow up) or stuff the anger, or else choose one of the two productive alternatives—direct it or let it go. When you direct your anger, you are using it to solve a problem or assert your needs. When you let it go, you recognize that there is no immediate solution to the problem and that staying angry will do you no good. Unlike stuffing, you acknowledge and own your anger, are willing to revisit the problem at a later time, and are willing to seek support and counsel if necessary.
    *   Positive functions of anger: Internal cue that something is wrong, motivator and energizer for taking constructive action.
    *   Negative functions of anger: Stuffed anger leads to stress-related physical problems; escalated anger can lead to abuse and violence; high levels of anger overwhelm an individual, making it impossible to listen attentively or express oneself in an articulate and respectful manner.

- Anger/aggression as a default mechanism: You blow up and/or control others because you have never learned, or are unwilling to use, prosocial alternatives.

Session Three

1. CREATIVE TIME OUTS—With a full time out, one leaves the situation for an hour or more. When anger is less intense, when danger of violence is not an issue but the conflict is escalating, a shorter time out may be useful. The idea is to stop the conflict for a few minutes to give all parties a chance to calm down, collect their thoughts, and commit to a healthy, productive discussion. Like regular time outs, creative time outs should always be done with respect for the partner, without placing blame or taking parting shots. The person taking the time out should never make "you" statements, but should either use an "I" statement ("I'd like to cool off for a few minutes; let me get a drink of water"), or preface the suggestion with a "we" or a "this" statement ("Maybe we should take five" or "This situation is getting tense; why don't we meet up in the living room."). Examples:

   - Go to another part of the house.
   - Go to a larger room. In small spaces, such as the kitchen or bathroom, a person may feel closed in, which can trigger primitive, old-brain flight-or-fight responses.
   - Get a drink of water, juice, or something non-alcoholic and caffeine-free.
   - Go to the bathroom and splash water on your face.
   - (when driving) Pull over, or count to 60 before reacting.

2. COPING WITH STRESS

   - Explain the mechanism of flight-or-fight response, and how stress can lead to anger, depression, and/or anxiety.
   - Identify the physical, behavioral, and psychological symptoms of stress (workbook exercise, session 6).
   - Identify the external causes of stress (workbook exercise, session 6).
   - Identify the psychological mediators of stress, such as having options, or feeling in control.
   - Teach the body–mind connection: By willing the body to relax by sitting down, unclenching the fists, or leaning back, one can actually feel more relaxed and reduce angry and aggressive thoughts. Example: Try smiling when depressed, running when anxious. See what happens to your mood.

3. MISUSES OF ANGER—Explain that trying to control, punish, cover-up vulnerable feelings, maintain a negative connection to partner, and so on, are not legitimate functions of anger, and that they are ultimately self-defeating.

4. EXERCISE—"Did it work?"
   Couples are asked to think of times when they have been aggressive and identify their motives (e.g., be heard, win an argument). Then they are asked about the consequences:

- Was it effective? Did it work? Did the behavior achieve the desired outcome?
- Did it work in the long run? What was the negative fallout from the behavior?

5. JUMP-STARTING CHANGE—Overcoming dysfunctional behaviors is difficult because alternatives, such as taking time outs or active listening, don't always feel right. We cannot unlearn old tendencies, but we can learn new behaviors that, if repeated enough over time, gradually feel more natural, and replace the old, negative ones. New behaviors feel uncomfortable because they don't match one's self-image. But this resistance can be overcome by adopting a "fake it until you make it" attitude, and knowing that feelings and thoughts often follow behavior change, rather than the other way around. Individuals can "act as if" they have already changed and, in so doing, actually bring about the changes they are seeking.

Session Four

1. EXERCISES

- Do grounding meditation (workbook exercise, session 7).
- Do the Jacobsen progressive relaxation exercise (workbook exercise, session 8).

2. ALTERNATIVES (workbook exercises, sessions 33 & 34)

- Jacobsen, short version.
- Breath-counting meditation.
- Visualization exercises.

3. THE THREE-LEGGED STOOL—Think of your relationship like a three-legged stool. One leg represents you, another represents your partner, and the third represents your life together. All three legs of the stool have to be strong in order for the relationship to stand up. You must nurture yourselves as individuals in order to bring something of value to the relationship. But you must also nurture the relationship itself.

4. LIFESTYLE BALANCE—Stress is exacerbated when one's life is out of balance. One must seek balance and avoid extremes in the following areas:

- Work vs. play
- Time alone vs. time with family
- Time with spouse vs. time with family
- Quiet time vs. activity time

Session Five

1. IDENTIFYING DISTORTED SELF-TALK (workbook exercise, session 10)

- Provocations and anger: Situations don't cause feelings, such as anger; rather, what we tell ourselves about a situation determines how we feel.
- Problems with self-talk: What we tell ourselves is automatic and private; no one can detect it. It catches us by surprise, and there's no one to tell us

if it is distorted. We tend to believe our internal self-talk simply because it is *ours.*

2. CHALLENGING DISTORTED SELF TALK (workbook exercise, session 10)
3. META-COMMUNICATION (page 66, also, workbook exercise, session 44)
4. EXERCISES

   • Messages sent and received exercise (workbook exercise, session 19)
   • Participants imagine situations in which self-talk could lead to an escalated conflict. How does self-talk become a self-fulfilling prophecy? (See Table 8.3.)

Session Six

1. FEELINGS BENEATH ANGER—Remind couples that anger, as a powerful emotion, can mask vulnerable feelings. For example, we feel powerful, strong, and invincible when angry, but weak, exposed, and vulnerable when sad.
2. EXERCISES

   • Feelings inside oneself (workbook exercise, session 11)
   • Developing empathy (workbook exercise, session 37). It is hard to maintain high levels of anger for someone you want to understand. Batterers tend to demonize their partners, by projecting their own negative behaviors on them. By looking for the vulnerable feelings batterers can relate to their partners in a more realistic and more positive way.

3. LISTENING SKILLS—It is not enough to hear your partner; you must *show* that you are actually listening, so that your partner *feels* heard and understood:

   • Be ready and willing (not tired, distracted, etc.)
   • Make appropriate eye contact
   • Let your partner know you're paying attention and listening by using nonverbal cues, such as nodding or leaning forward, or by interjecting ("Go on" "I see") statements.

TABLE 8.3   Distorted Self-Talk

Partner does this . . .	And your self talk is . . .
Keeps chatting about a lunch date, which you care nothing about	*What a stupid jerk.* (labeling)
Is friendly with a member of the opposite sex	*She/he doesn't care about my feelings.* (mind reading)
Won't agree with your point of view	*I have to get through. She/he has got to listen to me.* (absolutes)
Once again, comes home an hour late	*He/she will never be on time.* (futurizing)
Cancels a dinner engagement at the last minute	*This is horrible. The evening's ruined* (magnification).

- Ask questions. Your partner will know you are interested if you ask for clarification or more information.
- Paraphrase your partner's content. Don't parrot, but rather put into your own words what you believe your partner has said.
- Paraphrase feelings. If a particular feeling is evident from your partner's words, tone of voice, or body language, include this in your paraphrase. Present this tentatively, from your direct observation. "It sounds like you're angry," or "You seem sad."

4. EXERCISES—Feeling heard

- Couples practice paraphrasing (workbook exercises, session 20, part C)
- In a minute or less, one partner presents how the day went, while the other partner practices listening skills. With higher-functioning couples, when safe to do so, partners can be asked to present and listen to a specific complaint.

Session Seven

1. IDENTIFYING NEEDS—To overcome their mutual dependency and begin to individuate, it is necessary that violent couples—perpetrators, co-perpetrators, or victims—can identify their needs, separate from each other's.

- Maslow's hierarchy of needs: (1) basic needs (e.g., food, air), (2) relationship, competency, and self-esteem needs, and (3) growth needs (e.g., meaning, spirituality).
- As indicated under fair fighting advice, each individual is responsible for getting personal needs met. Relationship needs, however, involve interdependence, and one must effectively communicate those needs to enlist a partner's cooperation. One cannot communicate needs if one cannot identify them.
- When couples engage in abusive behavior and dirty fighting, it can be over basic needs (job, money, housing) but is more often related to self-esteem, competency, and relationship needs. When the anger smoke alarm goes off, one question to ask is, "What need/want of mine is being threatened, or do I imagine might be threatened?"
- Needs vs. wants: Basic needs are universal and fundamental to most human beings or human relationships. Although we can usually find a variety of ways to get our needs met, needs are less negotiable than wants. Wants are preferences that human beings can live reasonably without. Wants are specific desires. One way to resolve conflict is to find alternative ways to meet our needs by pursuing alternative wants.

2. EXPRESSING NEEDS AND WANTS

- Make "I" statements ("I'm tired. I need to sleep.").
- Include your partner. Don't simply present what *you* want. This could be interpreted as selfishness or lack of consideration. Instead, state: "I'd like _____. What would *you* like?"

3. EXERCISE: Wants and Needs
    The group leader presents hypothetical situations and asks for volunteers to identify what the person may want and the need behind it. They are asked what might be the alternative ways for the same need to be met. For example:

    - Robert feels criticized by Julie.
    - Although Samantha doesn't want Italian food again, Tina insists.
    - Tim is disappointed that Janice has been sulking and is emotionally unavailable.

Couples are asked to identify their own particular wants and needs. Identifying and expressing needs is the first step away from dependency and toward autonomy.

4. ASSERTIVENESS, PART I—When someone's behavior is a problem for you, your goal is to persuade that person to stop the behavior. This cannot happen unless you are heard. You cannot be heard, if, due to fear of conflict, rejection, or abandonment, or out of a determination to "win," you (1) don't speak up, or (2) present yourself aggressively. The first step in effective communication is a clear, assertive message. An assertive message reduces the likelihood of a defensive response when it is clear, direct, and respectful.

    - State the problem *behavior*. If you can't say exactly what your partner did, don't say anything and avoid attacking his/her character.
    - State how the behavior affects you. When applicable, include feelings. "When you interrupt me, it's hard to stay focused," or "That comment really hurt."
    - *Request* a change in behavior. Demanding a change does not make a message stronger, but will likely cause the other person to stop listening. If you succeed by intimidation and threats, the other person will resent you and perhaps get even by behaving in a passive-aggressive way. The relationship will suffer greatly.

Session Eight

1. ASSERTIVENESS, PART II—Delivering a textbook assertive request does not guarantee that you will be heard. Compliance is even less likely if you lecture. Keep communication as simple and brief as possible. But under the best of circumstance, humans become defensive when they are criticized or limits are set on their behavior. Maintain a consistently assertive approach, but expect that others will sometimes deliberately avoid hearing you. A partner can appear or claim to not understand. An assertive communicator must recognize the difference between understanding and caring. People may not care to listen, cooperate, or change behavior, but that doesn't mean they don't understand.

2. EXERCISES

    - Countering blocking maneuvers (workbook exercises, session 48)
    - Couples are asked to role-play an assertive statement, a blocking maneuver, and then an appropriate counterresponse.

3. THE EMOTIONAL BANK ACCOUNT—Research by Gottman (1999) indicates that couples are more able to resolve conflicts peacefully if there is trust

and goodwill in the relationship. One way to think about such goodwill is to imagine an "emotional bank account" in which abusive, controlling, and dirty fighting behaviors are withdrawals and positive behaviors are deposits. There must be a high preponderance of deposits for there to be trust and goodwill. (list of positive behaviors in workbook exercise, session 46)

4. EXERCISE—Checking the emotional bank account
   Couples complete the workbook exercise, session 21, and discuss.

Session Nine

1. CONFLICT CONTAINMENT—Conflicts cannot be resolved unless they are first contained. Managing anger is primary. Also useful is being aware of the mechanisms by which conflicts can escalate:

   - Outward focus vs. inward focus: When in conflict, individuals tend to focus on what their partner is saying and doing. This invites an escalation, because negative statements, body posture, and facial expressions are often reacted to defensively, with similarly negative words and physical expressions. By focusing on your own internal process, you have more control over your behavior, and by trying to imagine what your partner might feel, you develop empathy rather than anger and aggression.
   - Conflict levels (workbook exercise, session 25): Conflicts usually begin at the issue level. At this level, opinions and feelings are freely exchanged. There may be agreement or disagreement. The problem may or may not be resolved. If a person insists on winning the argument, and his/her partner refuses to agree, he/she will then attack at the personality level. At this level, individuals engage in aggressive, abusive, controlling, and dirty fighting behaviors. If the partner still doesn't get his/her way, the conflict may then escalate to the relationship level, where the very relationship is questioned (threats of leaving, taking the children, divorce, finding a new relationship).

2. CONFLICT RESOLUTION, PART I

   - Bringing it back: As soon as the conflict goes to the personality level, it is up to either partner to point this out, calmly and without blame, and to say something like, "Let's bring it back to the issue, please. This is not helpful."
   - Setting limits with love: When your partner is being aggressive or abusive, you can simultaneously set limits while indicating that you are still open to listening if your partner will stop the offending behavior. For example:

     "I could hear you a lot better if you lowered your voice."

     "I know you're frustrated, and I do want to discuss this, but not when you speak to me like that."

   - Forcing a request: When one's partner refuses to stay at the issue level, piles on the criticism and blame, and seems more interested in venting anger than working out the problem, a simple approach can end the harassment. While allowing the partner to feel heard, you can ask, "What is it you would like me to do?" or "Tell me what you want, exactly what you want." If the partner continues the diatribe, immediately disengage. If your partner answers the question, you may be able to respond and engage in a more productive discussion. Or you can say something like, "I hear you. Let me think about it. We'll talk more later."

- Conflict resolution skills are discussed (workbook exercise, session 25).

3. HOMEWORK: Relationship Vision
As homework, couples are asked to complete the Relationship Vision exercise from the book *Getting the Love You Want* (Hendrix, 1988, pp. 247–248). In the assignment, the couples are asked to list what they ideally want for the relationship. First they write separate lists, and rank-order each item according to importance. All items begin with "We," and are to be written in the present tense, as if it were already happening (e.g., "We feel safe with each other"). Afterwards, they come together and create a master list. The items that both indicated were very important are at the top. At the bottom are items that are not shared, and that are deemed not very important.

Session Ten

1. FAIR FIGHTING ADVICE—Participants discuss the handout (see box below).
2. CONFLICT RESOLUTION, PART II—Problem solving steps (pages 67–68).
3. EXERCISE:Each couple sits down with pen and paper, and uses the S.O.L.V.E. problem-solving format to resolve a real-life problem. The problem should be a relatively simple one and not involve core issues that may bring up overly intense, acrimonious feelings.
4. RELATIONSHIP DECISION-MAKING—The group leader reviews the advantages of having an egalitarian, or divided-power, approach to decision-making, rather than one in which either partner dominates (workbook exercise, session 13 A).
5. EXERCISE:Couples are asked to identify their own relationship on the chart, and then to complete the questions in part B. The group leader points out that the communication and conflict-resolution skills the couples have learned can help them move toward a more egalitarian system, should they choose to do so.
6. RELATIONSHIP VISION—The couples share with the group their vision of an ideal relationship. The program ends on a note of optimism and goodwill.

FAIR FIGHTING ADVICE

It takes two people to resolve a conflict, and two to escalate.

It takes only one person to stop a conflict. If one person refuses to argue, and the other continues, there is no longer a conflict but rather a tantrum.

Stop trying to win. When conflicts escalate, there are no winners, only losers.

Stop trying to score points. No one but you cares if you are right or if you won a debating point. There is no hidden jury, no judge, and no verdict. There are, however, victims of your fighting—especially your children.

Forget about "who started it." You both started it when you decided to become a couple. The chain of causality ultimately goes back to your upbringing and your gene pool. Focus instead on what is in front of you and go from there.

Stop complaining about what is unfair. Life is unfair.

Focus on the *consequences* of your actions, rather than your *rights.*

Negotiation is not surrender.

You have a right to ask for whatever you want, but don't expect to get it. Your partner can ask for whatever he/she wants, and you don't have to provide it.

Your partner has a right to be wrong, ignorant, irrational, etc.

The first rule of therapy: If it doesn't work, stop doing it.

When you blame others for your actions, you give them power over you. If they are the cause of your behavior, then they are the solution.

You have free will.

You, and only you, are responsible for meeting your needs. Period.

COUPLES COUNSELING: PHASE III

The goals of phases I and II are to build confidence and trust by teaching couples alternative ways to resolve relationship conflicts. In phase III, couples are assisted in transforming their relationship further by gaining insight into their behavior and using the insight to make long-lasting, second order change. Insight encompasses awareness of dysfunctional beliefs; recognizing and overcoming unhealthy, abusive interaction patterns; and working through core issues from the families of origin.

Phase III work can be done in conjoint sessions or in a multicouples group format. In this phase of treatment, the therapist provides a much less structured environment. Clients are reminded to use previously learned skills, and are didactically presented new information about common belief systems and gender role expectations. The format is primarily open discussion and the overall approach is process-oriented. Rather than simply avoiding creating secondary problems, clients are given permission to tackle any problem. In fact, they are encouraged to take risks by expressing long-suppressed views, becoming more vulnerable with their partner, and uncovering painful, shaming memories. The free expression of emotion is encouraged because insights gained within the crucible of emotion are more likely to be internalized and bring change. An overarching goal is to help clients sort out individual issues from relationship issues so that they may individuate and take full responsibility for their lives. Throughout this phase, the therapist

- Makes neutral observations.
- Refrains from *blaming* either partner, but instead assigns *responsibility*.
- Attempts to elicit the clients' own interpretations about problems and their own solutions before suggesting alternatives. Client-generated insights and solutions are far more likely to be internalized.
- Corrects exaggerated views of an incident (e.g., a few suggestions by one's partner can be viewed as a "harangue," or a few negative comments over a 5-minute period can become "hours of criticism").
- Observes and comments on communication styles (e.g., interrupting and jumping to unwarranted conclusions). Gives couples reality checks regarding mind reading and mistaken assumptions about the partner's motives by asking for clarification of intent. One troubling phenomenon in abusive relationships is for victims to see abuse when no abuse exists. A woman, for instance, may accuse her husband of yelling when he merely made an emphatic statement. This may cause the husband to become angry and defensive, thus reinforcing the woman's image of him as aggressive and dangerous.
- Points out abusive, controlling behaviors, and incidents of dirty fighting.
- Continually reminds couples that they are a team, and that their individual and collective efforts will be suitably rewarded. Reminds them of their goals.
- Carefully watches for episodes of regression and sudden flights into health. The latter phenomenon occurs when Phase I and II couples have quickly ceased the worst of their abuse, and begun to communicate in some mutually satisfactory ways, but have yet to experience long lasting, second order change. Having gratified their dependency needs in the short run, and consciously or unconsciously fearing the implications of further change, they are at risk to prematurely terminate counseling. Couples are reminded about the long-term, incremental nature of change.
- Helps couples adjust to sudden power shifts, which typically occur when victims begin to feel there is a pendulum effect, in which they start expressing themselves aggressively, often with the same abuse as the perpetrator.

Dysfunctional Beliefs

Two main categories of dysfunctional beliefs maintain abusive behavior—general ones, and those related to sex roles. A major task of Phase III work is helping clients identify and change these beliefs. This can be done to some extent didactically, by giving relevant handouts from time to time, but the therapist is advised to find ways to identify these beliefs as they emerge in the natural course of conversation.

Beliefs Related to Sex-Roles and Violence

Ours is a violent society, with one of the highest rates of violent crime in the world. From a young age, we are bombarded with media images of violence. Males in particular are given permission to be aggressive, from the rough and tumble play as small children, through competitive sports, to entering the competitive work world with all the responsibility of primary breadwinners. In times of war, men are drafted into combat, and during peacetime they hold down the most dangerous and physically demanding jobs. And still, society expects men to be emotionally strong and in control.

Women are raised to avoid direct expressions of aggression. However, they learn indirect methods of control, such as ostracism, gossip, and passive-aggressive behavior. More importantly, society grants women considerably more leeway in the expression of physical violence against intimate partners than it does men. Society gives men and women mixed messages about who should be in charge of the home. Many men justify the use of power and control on the premise that "a man's home is his castle." However, women have traditionally assumed de facto control in many homes. This natural rivalry, together with societal messages about violence, creates tension that can easily erupt into verbal or physical assaults. Examples of dysfunctional sex role beliefs, and functional alternatives are:

DYSFUNCTIONAL: *I'm the man. This is my home. I need to be in charge here.*

FUNCTIONAL: *This is our home. I may want to be in charge, but I don't have to be. There are serious consequences to me, and to the relationship, if I persist in thinking this way.*

DYSFUNCTIONAL: *I can hit him because I'm only a woman and he should be able to take it.*

FUNCTIONAL: *I can hit him, but not without undermining our relationship. He may be able to handle it physically, but anyone who is assaulted suffers emotional hurt and resentment.*

The therapist's task is not to give a political/sociology lesson, but to help clients understand how sex-role beliefs affect their relationship. In this endeavor, the therapist may want to use the material from workbook exercises for sessions 13, 18, and 43 from the 52-week group program. For homework, suggested readings might include, *You Just Don't Understand* (Tannen, 1990), and *Why Men Are the Way They Are* (Farrell, 1988).

General Irrational Beliefs

Albert Ellis identified a number of irrational beliefs that contribute to human misery and relationship dysfunction. The therapist can find these in the workbook exercises, sessions 35 and 36. Here are two examples of irrational beliefs, and how they can lead to spousal abuse:

BELIEF: *It is an absolute necessity that I have love and approval from peers, family and friends.*

CONSEQUENCE: I feel rejected/abandoned when my partner wants to be alone, is emotionally unavailable, or has a disagreement with me. I use control, emotional abuse, and/or physical violence to secure the love and approval I so desperately need.

BELIEF: *It is horrible when people and things are not the way I would like.*

CONSEQUENCE: When my partner does not meet my expectations, or won't let me have my way, I lash out.

Abusive Interaction Patterns

A number of interaction patterns have been observed in abusive intimate relationships. It is the therapist's obligation to point out these patterns to couples throughout
the course of Phase III. The alternative communication and conflict resolution skills
acquired in Phases I and II, which initially served to empower couples and provoke
optimism about treatment, are now crucial in helping them eliminate old patterns
and institute long-lasting change.

The various interaction patterns listed here are not mutually exclusive. More than
one pattern may be observed in a couple, operating on different levels.

Overall Pattern: Symmetrical or Complementary

Lane and Russell (1989) argue that when clinicians distinguish between perpetrator
and victim, they are simply looking at two halves of a process without taking the
relational context into account. Using a metaphor from Gregory Bateson, they point
out that the aggression exhibited by a lion when it stalks a zebra is different from
the aggressive behavior of two lions competing for territory or for females. In stalking
a zebra, the lion moves very slowly, remaining as unobtrusive as possible. However,

> When two male lions are vying for territory or females, they act in an opposite manner.
> Each lion tends to make itself extremely large and expends a tremendous amount of energy
> in attempting to back the other lion down. This becomes a pattern of mutual exhibitionism,
> with the most common result being one lion's retreating without having to shed blood. Both
> of these stories show lions being "aggressive," however, the behaviors shown by the lion in
> relation to the zebra are the exact opposite from the story of the two lions vying for territory.
> In a linear sense, both stories describe aggression; however, when one shifts to the systemic
> view, one can see in the first relational context that the lion and zebra were in a complemen-
> tary dance of predator/prey. In the second relational context, the lions were in a symmetrical
> struggle, with each attempting to control the relationship . . .
>
> The couples we see with severe, repetitive, one-sided violence generally show extremely rigid
> dominant-submissive complementarity. . . . In our experience, couples whose relationship
> has evolved into a symmetrical pattern of violence often have more episodes of fighting than
> couples in a complementary pattern; however, there are less severe outcomes. The couple
> is constantly in opposition to each other and only shift to brief moments of complementarity
> after an incidence of violence. The act of hitting serves the function in these couples of de-
> escalating the arguments and triggering the ritual of making up . . . [pp. 138–139]

Level of Control

BUILD UP, BLOW UP, CONTRITION: This is the classic battering cycle as described
by Walker (1983), seen in cases of severe, unilateral violence. Although most of the
research on this cycle has focused on female victims, other research (Johnston &
Campbell, 1993) and clinical experience suggest it applies to many cases of female-
on-male battering as well:

> *First Phase:* Tension building. Batterer is moody, sullen, and tends to criticize. He/
> she withdraws affection, and tries to isolate partner. Yells, puts partner down,
> threatens, begins to break things. Agreeable and passive, the victim tries to calm

the aggressor, but feels as though walking on eggshells. Tries to be nurturing, reasonable. Sometimes withdraws.

Second Phase: Battering event. Batterer pushes, punches, chokes or beats up partner. In extreme cases, will use weapons, rape, or take partner hostage. Victim tries to protect self any way possible. Attempts to calm partner. Sometimes responds in self-defense or leaves. Often, someone else will call the police.

Third Phase: Contrition. Batterer apologizes, promises never to do it again, begs forgiveness. Promises to seek counseling, go to church, or get clean and sober. Brings gifts, professes love, wants to make love. Enlists support of family. Victim agrees to stay, takes partner back. Stops legal proceedings. Obtains counseling for partner. Feels happier and more hopeful.

Unless major changes are instituted in the relationship, either from the batterer (stopping the violence) or from the victim (leaving), this cycle is doomed to repeat itself and will often get progressively worse. A useful intervention is for the therapist to ask the victim if, after forgiving the batterer in the contrition phase, the batterer actually changed as promised. The therapist asks the victim if he/she truly loves the perpetrator, and whether allowing the perpetrator to repeat the behavior helped the perpetrator-partner discontinue the behavior, or was enabling. Also helpful is for the therapist to inquire about the apparent forgiveness, and if any underlying anger or resentments may be present. Victims who can understand and express their own anger will be more empowered to confront their perpetrator.

In a CONTROL-CONTROL situation, one person dominates the other by using physical aggression, psychological manipulation, dirty fighting tactics, and emotionally abusive and controlling behaviors. The partner responds with his or her own control tactics. Example:

> Andrea wants to buy a new set of drapes for the living room. Len says they can't afford it. Andrea calls him a jerk, and Len responds by telling her to shut up. Andrea brown bags—listing several complaints at once, unrelated to the issue at hand (i.e., his drinking, his family). Len pushes a lamp to the floor. Andrea takes the lamp and throws it at Len.

In contrast to the classic battering cycle, in which the abuse is perpetrated by a dominant aggressor, mutually abusive couples do not typically make up after a violent episode, but rather continue their negative interactions and remain hostile to one another (Lloyd, 1996; Stacey et al., 1994).

CONTROL-COMPLIANCE is a less serious version of the classic battering cycle. When one person attempts to control, the other complies out of a fear of upsetting the partner further, or from the discomfort of asserting his/her point of view. The therapist points out that discomfort and tension are a normal part of conflict resolution, and asks if the victim's silence is better than continued frustration, hurt, self-doubt, and loss of self-esteem. Because discomfort is inevitable, why not choose a path that leads to solutions and change, rather than more hurt, abuse, and dysfunction? Inquiring about the compliant partner's anger is an additional intervention. What happens with the anger when the compliant partner gives in? The therapist inquires about passive-aggressive behavior or displaced aggression directed at the children or others. The counselor points out that until a problem is properly addressed it is likely to coexist with the controlling partner's behavior.

Level of Communication

Control and communication often go hand in hand. According to Cahn (1996), there are three goals to interpersonal communication. Communication with an *instrumental* goal is intended to resolve a problem or accomplish a task. *Relationship* goals are concerned with maintaining the couple's relationship, and *identity* goals are concerned with establishing or solidifying a desired image with one's partner or others. Attempts to dominate and control one's partner may involve all three goals, not only the instrumental ones. In a systemic perspective, violence and abuse are seen by some couples as a sign of love and commitment, and thus serve to perpetuate the dysfunctional relationship. In addition, highly controlling individuals may use violence to reinforce their status as the dominant ones in relationships, sending the nonverbal message that "I am in charge, and you're not."

NEGATIVE RECIPROCITY occurs when negative statements from one person are met with negative statements from the other and conflict quickly escalates. In a study by Burman and colleagues (1992), wives of abusive husbands responded to both negative-offensive statements (e.g., criticism, insults) and negative-defensive statements (disagreement, "yes, but") with negative-offensive statements of their own. The husbands, however, typically responded to negative-offensive statements with negative-defensive ones. Abusive couples thus engage in attack/defend cycles. In some cases, such as the couples in the Burman study, men become more despairing and tend to withdraw as the conflict escalates.

DEMAND–WITHDRAW is a communication dynamic that Babcock and associates (1993) identified among couples with a violent husband, in which one person issues a complaint or asks for something in a demanding fashion. Rather than respond, the partner withdraws. Men and women are capable of assuming either role, but men more often withdraw because of poorer verbal skills. If demands continue, the withdrawing partner may abusively lash out. Over many years of providing treatment to abusive couples, Neidig and Friedman (1984) have observed that a very common dynamic that precedes violence

> is for one party, usually the man, to withdraw by refusing to communicate further. In many cases, husbands report that they cannot keep up with their wives, who seem to think and speak faster and generally seem to have the advantage in any verbal conflict. . . . The husband may signal that he fears he is about to "lose it" and demand that his wife "back off." She, in turn, experiences this withdrawal as a sign that he doesn't care or is not taking her concerns seriously, and this misunderstanding is likely to increase her efforts to break through to him by moving closer, speaking more loudly, or physically preventing him from leaving. The conflict escalates through this pattern of circular feedback as each partner misunderstands the intentions and behavior of the other. [pp. 62–63]

Demand–withdraw patterns are characteristic of couples in which one partner has fears of abandonment and the other has fears of intimacy. These dynamics can be understood more fully within the perspective of attachment theory. We will revisit these in an upcoming section, and suggest appropriate intervention strategies.

Resource Exchange

Resource exchange theory offers another perspective on the communication and control dynamics of violent relationships, as follows.

Resource-Exchange Theory

Resource-exchange theory (Bagarozzi & Wordarski, 1977; Gelles, 1983) postulates that the health and stability of relationships depend on the balance, or perceived balance, of interpersonal resources—also known as "rewards" in behavioral terminology. If the distribution of rewards from one party is not adequately reciprocated by the other, the principle of "distributive justice" is thereby violated, and the result can be anger, conflict escalation, and violence. Anger, in this scheme, serves as an inner warning, alerting the individual that something is amiss in the distribution of resources. Individuals verbally and physically abuse one another in order to restore the actual or imagined imbalance. Social controls, such as laws and ethical norms about the use of violence, limit the extent of the abuse and how it is carried out. The abuser must factor into his/her decisions the costs of being abusive, such as the possibility of being arrested, losing a partner's love and respect, or violating his/her personal sense of right and wrong. In intimate relationships, however, social controls may be weak, due to the private nature of families and the fact that nothing less than the fulfillment of core needs (e.g., love and belonging) is at stake.

Teichman and Teichman (1989) identified the interpersonal resources (rewards) exchanged in relationships as the following: love, status, information, money, goods, and services, and classified these according to how universal or particular each one might be. Love is a significant resource partly because of its highly particular nature (love from one's partner can only be gotten from that partner). The person allocating this resource thus maintains a position of power over the other.

The use of aggression to restore "distributive justice" is fraught with consequences, which the perpetrator may not be able to recognize until later. Efforts to restore equity often lead to increased control by the aggressor over resources controlled and provided by the partner. This forces a new balance of resources in favor of the aggressor, which the other will inevitably seek to change, leading to further conflict escalation. An important intervention is to help clients understand the effects of their behavior, through a cost–benefit ratio analysis. Threats of incarceration hanging over the heads of perpetrators in treatment diversion programs have proven to be quite effective in suppressing violence, but clients can be persuaded to change based on other costs, such as the potential loss of a partner's love and the damage done to one's self-esteem. The skilled therapist helps foster appropriate guilt, and helps the client understand how violence contributes to a cycle of resentment, retribution, and further violence, and how it is ultimately self-defeating. Expectations about who should command what resources, and under what conditions, whether they come from society-wide norms or from the individuals' own unique perspective, need to be identified and challenged.

According to Teichman and Teichman,

> Changes in the provision of interpersonal resources and in the relative need for resources of each family member alone produce only short-term effects. If core attitudes and beliefs about the relationships between men and women are unchanged, if mutual expectations are unrealistically biased, if the communication difficulties between the spouses persist, and if behavioral (e.g., social skills) deficits remain unchanged, the actual or imaginative resource-deficit will reappear and violence may erupt again. Thus, without changing spouses' cognitions . . . and the modification of resource-exchange relationships, no long-lasting effects can be expected. [pp. 140–141)

Childhood of Origin Issues

Social learning, trauma, and attachment theories suggest different mechanisms by which early childhood experiences influence adult personality and behavior. Whether described as *imagoes*, or *cognitive templates*, we all bring to our intimate partnerships a knowledge of relationships based on our childhood. From a social learning perspective, individuals who observed or experienced violence in their homes are at higher risk of internalizing this behavior and exhibiting similar abuse within their intimate adult relationships. Too often, the abuse perpetrated in adulthood is grossly out of proportion to the precipitating event. But the internalization of violence involves more than observational learning. In a separate mechanism, having experienced or witnessed family violence causes psychic trauma in the children, which may lead to shame-based coping in adult intimate relationships. Shame-based coping may also emerge from childhood neglect and attachment disturbance, in the absence of family violence. Whatever its origins, shame-based coping strategies are associated with intense, destructive emotions, including rage and, ultimately, physical assaults. Third phase work cannot be completed until the therapist helps clients recognize these internal mechanisms and how they lead to abusive behaviors. This is not faulting the past to exonerate perpetrators from responsibility; rather, the intent of treatment is to help clients make more functional decisions, based on an appraisal of current realities.

The following is a good example of insight-oriented work, with a male perpetrator, Richie, and his female partner, Sarah:

Richie:	My background is very difficult. Especially when it comes to women. Abusive women. I have a very hard time with hostility from women.
Tx: (*therapist*)	When you just said to me "I have a hard time," it's in my "background," what was in your mind? What's the image that gets on to her at a moment like that and suddenly you feel, "I'm entitled?" (Pause) You superimpose something on her.
Richie:	(long pause) . . . (slowly) I sure do . . . (haltingly) The hostility registers in me. I see that. That's clear. . . . But it's interesting you say I superimpose a picture on her. In thinking about it, you're right, I *do*. At that particular instance (gets choked up) . . .
Tx:	(softly): Take your time.
Richie:	I see a person. From my past.
Tx:	Do you see the person now as you are talking?
Richie:	(holding back tears) I see the face of a woman that is—bearing down on me in a very hostile manner. And it's a person from my past, a person who's abused me as a child.
Tx:	Who is it?
Richie:	A foster parent.
Tx:	How did she bear down on you? How old were you?
Richie:	Six and seven. She would accuse me of things. She would tell me I'm doing things that I'm not doing! To justify the punishments she would dish out to me.
Tx:	So she really wanted to hurt you.
Richie:	Yes. *This* woman, yes.

Note how Richie begins to internalize his experience of hostility. What he had initially framed as "tension" located in the environment and then as "abuse" emanating from the foster mother now becomes "hostility that registers in me. I see that." Moreover, he takes a giant first step in separating his projection of the sadistic foster mother of childhood from his current experience of the angry Sarah when he elects to clarify the therapist's phrase, "she really wanted to hurt you," by specifying, "*This* woman" (the foster mother), yes."

Tx:	She was almost looking for excuses to hurt you.
Richie:	Yes. And whether I intended to or not, I always managed to accommodate her. Very similar to this relationship.
Sarah:	But she did these terrible things to you! I never did those terrible things to you!
Tx:	That's part of what I think Richie is sensing now.
Richie:	I would try to run away, but she would be sitting in the kitchen in the middle of the night, and the kitchen window was the only way out. And besides, the window was too high up for me to jump out. There was very little I could do.
Tx:	So she *really* terrorized you.
Richie:	Yes
Tx:	(softly) And she still haunts you today.
Richie:	Yes.
Tx:	And that's when it gets very confusing with Sarah . . . the image starts to wobble there.
Richie:	Only when there's hostility.
Sarah:	But anything can set him off! The littlest question can set him off!
Tx:	Well, Richie, we have this side of Sarah. The side that's very forceful—that really wants to express herself, that is not going to be silenced. And when she is that part of herself, this is the part that clicks in for you. Maybe the thing the therapy can do is that, as we bring forth Sarah's feelings and experiences and history, you will be able to separate her from these ghosts. [Goldner, 1998, pp. 276–277]*

Attachment Dynamics

Problems in any of the developmental stages of childhood, if not adequately resolved, may carry through into adulthood, as "unfinished business." For instance, an adolescent whose authoritarian parents overly restrict his or her movements may rebel, and subsequently manifest an antagonistic or controlling style of relating to intimate partners.

> Michael was a likeable, well-behaved, somewhat unassuming child. He maintained a B+ average throughout middle-school, until he discovered girls in ninth grade and his grades began to slip. In an attempt to "get him back on the right track," his father grounded him for the remaining 5 months of the school year, making it impossible for him to have a social

*From Interpersonal violence and its treatment, by Virginia Goldner, 1998, *Family Process, 37*(3), 276–277. Reprinted with permission of Blackwell Publishing Ltd.

life with peers. Michael at first tried to reason with his father, sometimes loudly, pleading with him to reconsider, but this only made his father angry, and led to further punishment. Until he left home at the age of 18 to attend college, Michael became entangled in a series of similarly tense, usually losing, battles for autonomy. At 26, he married Jill, a bubbly, highly confident first-year trial attorney. Currently, he and Jill are in marital therapy in an attempt to resolve their ongoing power struggles. "She's always telling me what to do," he complains. "Whatever I say," she counters, "he takes it the wrong way."

Attachment disturbance in early childhood may have the most chronic, damaging consequences. Citing previous research by John Bowlby, Sonkin, and Dutton (2003) points out that the aggression of batterers is akin to anger displayed by infants when faced with separation from their caregiver. "Anger," writes Sonkin, "is thus an attempt to recapture the object that can soothe tension and anxiety at a developmental stage where the child cannot yet self soothe through signaling the mother that she is wanted and/or needed. Anger is an emotion 'born of fear' of loss" (p. 106).

Significant life events subsequent to infancy, both negative and positive, have a sufficient impact on individual development so that one can hardly assume a perfect correspondence between infant and adult personality. Nonetheless, there is now some evidence that child–parent attachments dynamics, as categorized by Ainsworth from her famous "strange situation" experiments, are to some extent re-created in adulthood in the way a parent relates to his or her child, and how that child responds (Hesse, 1999) as well as how one relates to intimate partners (Bartholomew & Shaver, 1998).

Individuals whose mothers were inconsistently responsive to their needs develop an ambivalent attachment, characterized by repeated attempts to reunite. Conditioned in this sort of intermittent reinforcement schedule, they are at risk of exhibiting a *preoccupied*, clinging style in intimate partner relationships. Those whose mothers were highly unresponsive to their needs learn that attempts to reunite are futile, and typically develop an avoidant strategy. In adulthood, they exhibit a *dismissing style*, maintaining superficial relationships, often based on sex. Intimate partner abuse has been associated with both the preoccupied and the dismissing styles, as well as a fourth category known as *fearful-disorganized* (Holtzworth-Munroe et al., 1997), a consequence of severe childhood trauma. Anxiety around abandonment and intimacy is central to insecure attachment. Preoccupied individuals fear abandonment, dismissing individuals fear intimacy, and those with a fearful-disorganized style fear both. (See Table 8.4. See also pages 60–61 of this volume for discussion of attachment theory in light of recent developmental/psychobiological research.)

Fears of abandonment and intimacy are key components of Borderline Personality Disorder. These fears lead to severe identity disturbance, and deeper expressions of rage.

> With abusive parents, the child is in a situation where he is locked into forming an attachment to his primary caregiver, who is also a source of pain and injury. The rage that is experienced with such a parent is repressed. . . . The underlying personality will remain dormant until an intimate attachment, later in life, triggers the emotional template developed in the original attachment experience. Abusive males who experienced physical violence in their family of origin, often a dysfunctional, unstable family, were also at risk for ambivalent attachment. Although study of this "intergenerational transmission" of violence initially focused on behavior modeling, attachment theory and research suggest that something more is going on. That something more involves the development of faulty internal schemata,

TABLE 8.4 Dimensions of Intimate Partner Attachment

Attachment Type	Intimacy/abandonment orientation	Views of self and partner	DV type
Secure	Low anxiety over abandonment Low avoidance of intimacy/low discomfort with closeness	Positive view of self Positive view of partner	Family only
Preoccupied	High anxiety over abandonment Low avoidance of intimacy/low discomfort with closeness	Negative view of self Positive view of partner	Family only
Dismissing	Low anxiety over abandonment High avoidance of intimacy/high discomfort with closeness	Positive view of self Negative view of partner	Generally— violent/antisocial
Fearful	High anxiety over abandonment High avoidance of intimacy/high discomfort with closeness	Negative view of self Negative view of partner	Borderline

particularly self-concepts and expectations of attachment to others fraught with fear and rage. The groundwork for abusiveness is set. In other words, abusive childhood experiences produce something more than just learned behavior patterns. They produce avoidant-ambivalent bonding styles that generate tendencies to be both overly demanding and angry in adult romantic attachments, a profile often reported by battered women about their husbands, and again consistent with the descriptors of borderline males' pathology. [Dutton, 1998, p. 128]

These men, who most closely resemble the fearful-disorganized adult attachment pattern, are the same types of batterers that Lenore Walker (1979, 1983) has written about, whose violence characterizes the three-phase cycle of the "battered woman syndrome." They are also akin to the "Pit Bulls" described by Jacobsen and Gottman (1998)—extremely controlling and violent men who perpetrate the kind of violence that could best be described as "violence from within." That is, the tension build-up, battering event, and contrition phases of Walker's cycle are fueled primarily by anxiety and "faulty internal schemata," in Dutton's words, rather than by a mutually escalating conflict in which the spouse's behavior contributes to the ensuing aggression. The violence perpetrated by anti-social batterers, whom Jacobsen and Gottman (1998) have labeled "Cobras," is fueled by internal dynamics different from those of Borderlines/Pit Bulls, and their attachment type is dismissing, rather than fearful-disorganized. Like the Borderline/Pit Bulls, they are highly controlling, severely abusive individuals, and their violence also arises primarily from within.

Most researchers have focused on male-perpetrated violence. However, women perpetrate approximately half of all intimate partner violence (Straus, 1990) and cause roughly one-third of injuries (Archer, 2000; Tjaden & Thoennes, 1998). In light of these realities, and the fact that most partner abuse is mutual, it would be wise to investigate the attachment styles of both men and women. Bartholomew and colleagues (2001) found that

> Across studies, for both genders, preoccupied attachment was quite consistently associated with both the perpetration of abuse in relationships and the receipt of abuse (or the inclination to return to an abusive relationship). For women, there were few consistent associations between fearfulness and abuse, although fearfulness was common in women who had left abusive relationships. In contrast, the degree of fearfulness was strongly associated for men with the perpetration and receipt of abuse in all the studies but one. [p. 56]

It would be wise to determine how attachment styles play themselves out in the context of violent relationships. For instance, abandonment fears cause individuals to be clingy and tolerate abuse. But are these individuals always victims?

> Samantha's father, a violent alcoholic, left the family when she was ten. In her current marriage to Donovan, an introverted writer, she alternates between being a caretaker, and lashing out with anger when she feels ignored. When they fight, Donovan often tries to leave and take a time out. Samantha cannot tolerate this, and will follow him out the front door, sometimes hitting him, and demanding that he "work things out."

It is well known among psychotherapists that individuals with intimacy fears resist closeness rather than seek it compulsively, and find superficial ways to relate. This provokes strong feelings in their partners, who feel unloved and abandoned. The partner may become angry, and attempt to connect with aggressive and abusive behaviors. Fear of intimacy and fear of abandonment meld together in a pathological dance.

Attachment theory is therefore of greatest benefit when the violence is viewed from a systemic framework. Among the first researchers to investigate the interactional possibilities of the "dance" were Roberts and Noller (1998), who measured attachment along two dimensions: Discomfort with Closeness (the extent to which one feels uncomfortable in intimate partner relationships) and Anxiety over Abandonment (the extent to which one fears abandonment from one's intimate partner). These two underlying dimensions correspond with other models, such as the one by Brennan and colleagues (1998), in which the two underlying dimensions are Anxiety and Avoidance (see Table 8.4, page 135), around which their Experiences in Close Relationships Questionnaire was constructed (pp. 180–183). Individuals high on the dimension of Anxiety have a need for approval and fear abandonment; those high in Avoidance are uncomfortable with intimacy and resist closeness. For the sake of simplicity, the Roberts and Noller terminology will be used, and abbreviated to D/C (Discomfort with Closeness) and A/A (Anxiety over Abandonment).

Using a community sample consisting of university students and clients at various counseling centers in Queensland, Australia, Roberts and Noller investigated how attachment style, relationship satisfaction, and communication affect couples violence, and the way that these variables interact with each other. The subjects and their partners were administered standardized tests to measure these variables and to provide information about their relationship. In contrast to securely attached subjects, relationship conflict caused anxiety for both high D/C and high A/A subjects, but especially the latter. High D/C individuals experienced anxiety because their partner's attempts to resolve problems led to discussions involving difficult issues which, if acknowledged, might bring up painful childhood memories of abuse and abandonment. Individuals high in A/A would, on the one hand, want to continue the interaction, in hopes of connecting to the love object that continues to elude them, and on the other hand, worry that the disagreements might undermine their relationship and lead to rejection.

The researchers speculated that faced with high levels of anxiety, high A/A subjects would have three basic options: (1) submit to their partner's wishes, and achieve a sort of pseudo-closeness, (2) avoid abandonment by making aggressive, hostile demands, thus intensifying the conflict and prolonging the interaction, albeit negatively, or (3) withdraw. High D/C individuals would have the same options, but would exercise them for other reasons. That is to say, avoiders might submit to avoid prolonging a discussion that might lead to a more intimate subject matter, or use aggression to push their partner away.

The choices these subjects made in times of conflict, and their partners' subsequent responses, were of particular interest to the research team. How would the couple's communication moderate, or intensify the level of conflict? Would violence be a function primarily of attachment style, as in Dutton's Borderline men, or rather of couples communication and interaction dynamics? And would any particular pairing of attachment styles correlate with higher levels of violence? Among the findings:

- A/As were more emotionally expressive than D/Cs, who tended to suppress their feelings, but A/As were also hypervigilant to negative affect in their partners.
- Although the communication skills of both groups were good outside the relationship, A/As displayed poor assertiveness skills around their intimate partners, and D/Cs had poor overall communication. Both exhibited poor problem-solving skills and were resistant to productive negotiation or compromise.
- Attachment predicted violence by women but not by men.
- Men and women both were more likely use violence against their partners when they, the perpetrators, feared abandonment. Women also tended to perpetrate violence upon partners high in abandonment anxiety.
- For both sexes, the association between abandonment anxiety and the use of violence was significant only when the partner was uncomfortable with closeness.
- Couple interaction and communication was found to be a mediating variable between attachment and violence, supporting a systemic interpretation of partner violence.

Attachment security may interact with couple communication to create an environment in which violence is more likely to occur. For example, individuals who are anxious over abandonment may perceive their partner's withdrawal from conflict as highly threatening (relative to those who are securely attached), because withdrawal is interpreted as an act of emotional abandonment. Violence may then be used as a means of preventing the distancing behavior of partners. Alternatively, a person using withdrawal to escape a distressing conflict interaction may be pursued by the partner (i.e., the demand-withdraw pattern of interaction). In this case, a person who is insecurely attached may be so distressed by this "pursuit" that he or she uses violence as a means of halting the partner's pursuit. However, in both cases, it is the interaction between individuals' attachment and couple communication patterns that predicts the occurrence of violence. [Roberts & Noller, 1998, p. 327]

A subsequent study of dating couples by Bookwala (2002) echoed the findings of Roberts and Noller, that the most violent pairings consist of a fearful or dismissing attachment type and a preoccupied attachment type. In many cases, such pairs fall along gender lines (refer to Neidig's observations in the previous section on "demand–withdraw" patterns), with the man taking the D/C role and the woman taking the A/A role. But these roles are often reversed. Partner violence is multidetermined, and cannot entirely be explained by either an attachment paradigm or gender role socialization.

Bookwala also found that propensity for violence was high when a preoccupied attachment style was paired with another preoccupied attachment type. Even securely attached individuals became aggressive when frustrated by a dismissive partner. Of course, violence perpetrated by either partner, whatever the underlying reason, dramatically increases stress in the relationship, and that stress is highly correlated with intimate partner violence. We know that the use of violence by an individual is predictive of future violence by that same individual or by that person's partner (Straus, 1990).

Treatment

In addition to the recommendations by Gutierrez (see pp. 68–69), the counselor working with couples from an attachment perspective might make the following interventions:

- Identify the particular adult attachment styles of each partner, using the Experiences in Close Relationships Questionnaire (see appendix, pp. 180–183). Explain how they interact to produce misunderstandings, hurt feelings, and conflict escalation.
- Act as a safe and stable container for expression of emotion—what Sonkin and Dutton (2003) call a "secure base." Unlike the original parental figures, the counselor must be consistently available to the couple, demonstrating acceptance and concern, while carefully monitoring their communication. Recommend the book, *Do I Have to Give Up Me to Be Loved by You?* (Paul & Paul, 1983), and/or review group workbook exercise number 16.
- Help the couple establish clear, reasonable interpersonal boundaries, within which closeness and independence can both be pursued. Remind them that a mutually satisfying, nonabusive relationship is like the "three legged stool" mentioned earlier—one where the partners are strong and emotionally secure as individuals, yet work in concert to sustain a healthy, viable relationship. Review the communications skills of listening, assertiveness, and meta-communication, so the clients can better understand each other's legitimate needs and find ways to better accommodate one another.
- Inquire about each partner's early attachment figures. As a child, did the clients feel close to or distant from their primary caregivers? Were those caregivers responsive to their needs? If not, how did the clients cope? Separate, one-on-one therapy may be required for clients who find it too difficult or painful to access these memories.
- Point out from examples of the couple's dysfunctional interactions how they confuse the "external reality" of the present with the "internal reality" of the past. Explain that fears of abandonment and fears of intimacy make one feel

vulnerable, and that other, more powerful emotions such as anger, jealousy, and a need for revenge merely mask underlying insecurities. For example:

> "Vicky wanted to spend some time with her friends. When your mom went to the clubs, sometimes she didn't come back until the next day. But Vicky's not like that. You have no need to be jealous."

> "Jim is taking that time out in order to control his own anger. It means he cares about you, that he doesn't want you to get hurt."

> "When Clarisse tells you about her feelings, it's to help the two of you get closer, so you can have a better, more secure relationship. You resist because, deep down, you're afraid it won't last. But you're not a helpless child. You've got a 50% say-so in your relationship."

- Identify relevant irrational beliefs. Do either partner have unrealistic expectations for themselves or others (refer to the group workbook exercises on pages 238–240)? What, if any, are their distorted beliefs about the opposite sex? These include, for example, male beliefs that dismiss women's anger as irrational, or when women justify their abuse on the premise that their male partners should be "man enough" to take it.

These interventions can be used in all treatment modalities, not just in working with couples. For instance, the Compassion Workshop of Prince George's County, Maryland, founded by Steven Stosny, offers a 12-week mixed sex program for men and women convicted of spousal abuse (Stosny, 2004). A core assumption is that abuse begins with inappropriate reactions to a perceived emotional threat from the victim. The program teaches the abusers that if they can learn to value themselves and appropriately care for their needs, they may then become more positively attached to others by building trust, intimacy, and commitment.

OTHER FAMILY VIOLENCE INTERVENTIONS

Beyond the Marriage: Repairing a Broken Family

Couples with children must do more than cease their violence. In addition to changing their abusive relationships into safe, healthy ones, they must also help restructure and repair the family unit. This begins by acting as appropriate role models. First and foremost, the parents must cease any violence directed against the children, and employ the same nonviolent communication and conflict resolution skills with the family that they have learned through the domestic violence program. Depending on the level of family pathology, marital therapy may need to be supplemented with family therapy and parent education programs. The children may benefit from individual therapy or participation in either a victim group or an anger management group in order to learn how to control aggressive impulses. The following problems need to be addressed:

Child Symptoms

Depending on age level, child witnesses to domestic violence exhibit similar symptoms as those who have been directly abused (Wolak & Finkelhor, 1998).

- Toddlers and Preschool Children
  anxiety
  sadness
  somatic symptoms
  aggression and hyperactivity
  whiny and clinging behavior
  trouble sleeping
  regression in development (e.g., toilet training)
- School-Age Children
  anxiety
  depression
  low self-esteem
  aggression
  academic and social problems
  self-blame for the violence, but less often than preschoolers
- Adolescents
  drug and alcohol abuse
  delinquency
  running away

Preschoolers are more likely than older children to take responsibility for the violence. School age children have the coping resources of peer group interaction and greater cognitive/emotional maturity. Adolescents are least likely of all groups to assume blame for the marital violence

Boundary Issues and Disturbed Parent–Child Relationships

Johnston, whose typology of partner violence was discussed in a previous section, conducted one of the few studies that examined the effects of both male and female spouse abuse on parent–child relationships. Her research involved 160 separated or divorcing couples and their children. From extensive interviews and a battery of psychological tests, the following results were categorized according to type of marital violence (Johnston & Roseby, 1997):

Ongoing/Episodic Male Battering

Typical scenarios might include the following. Younger daughters are passive and fearful, cling to the mother, and react with regressed behavior. Fathers may lavish attention on these girls, sometimes in a seductive, sexualized manner, but at other times will ignore them. This causes these girls to have a dual image of father, as both loving and scary. Fathers seek affirmation of their self-esteem from these younger daughters, who "become watchful and oriented toward attempting to manage the father's equilibrium and anger" (Johnston & Rosedy, 1997, p. 31). Older, school-age girls are more likely to align with the mother and take it upon themselves to protect her by subtly influencing and managing the father. Some resent the mother for not standing up for herself.

Younger boys display oppositional and aggressive behavior toward the mother. At the same time, they worry about her safety. Older boys are afraid of their father, but are also attracted to the power he wields in the family. They are angry with him because of his marital and parental violence and his unavailability, but cannot express their anger overtly. Instead, these boys often turn on their mothers, behaving much like their fathers.

When the mother leaves the abusive father, the children often idealize him, repress memories of his violence, and blame the mother for his absence.

Female-Initiated Violence

Particularly with their sons, violent mothers alternate between nurturing and angry, abusive, rejecting behavior. A young daughter may assume a caretaker role with the mother, helping her unload some of her rage and is viewed by the father as "the good girl," in comparison with the bad, abusive wife. However, in spite of the father's idealization of her, the daughter typically grows up to be as temperamental and aggressive as her mother.

Boys in female-violent homes tend toward passive-aggressiveness and depression. Unless the father permits open displays of aggression, these boys suppress the rage they feel toward their mother. Younger boys are highly conflicted and unable to separate from the mother.

Male-Controlling Interactive Violence

Children in this situation exhibit a range of reactions, but aggression and passive-aggression are the primary behaviors. Because of the dual violence, children are left with no positive role model to help them successfully cope with stress. Children are conflicted, and their alliance shifts back and forth between the parents. Boys may develop an almost total lack of respect for authority figures, including their mother. "Fathers often have peer-like relationships with their sons, especially as they grow older. . . . Fathers are inclined to admire their son's toughness and acting-out, as the son replaces the father around the house" (Johnston & Rosedy, 1997, pp. 37–38).

Separation-Engendered and Post-divorce Trauma Violence

Parents typically align with the same-sex offspring in situations of violence precipitated by separation or divorce. Because of the unexpected nature of the violence, children sometimes show symptoms of PTSD, which may include fearfulness and nightmares. However, if the parent has relative strength and good parenting abilities, these children will be better able than those in other violent households to overcome their symptoms.

Family Education and Therapy

The goal of family interventions is to change the entire family unit, so that further abuse and violence will not continue and children will not transfer dysfunction from their family into their adult relationships. Change requires families to overcome denial and acknowledge the full extent of the abuse, learn alternative communication and conflict-resolution skills, and restructure and maintain healthy boundaries. Therapy that includes the entire family can effectively expose and break up/eliminate (1) unhealthy alliances/coalitions, (2) secret keeping, (3) denial, and (4) minimization. It can also supply accurate status reports, provide added safety by opening the family system to added scrutiny, and strengthen and support a healthy hierarchy.

Because of varying work and school schedules, a more practical alternative is to have the various family members seen separately, or in various combinations. A pioneer in the family-centered approach to the treatment of domestic violence is Family Violence Prevention Services (FVPS) in North Carolina. FVPS offers therapy groups for the male and the female partner, couples groups, and a group for children who have witnessed or experienced violence. The organization works closely with the courts to determine what services are appropriate and safe. Its director, David Maupin, writes:

> Most violence takes place in families that continue living together, and that violence affects all members of the family. We believe also that, in many instances, further violence can be prevented without breaking up the family. Most victims of relationship violence don't want to end the relationship, they just want the violence to stop. Further, we believe that all family members should have access to services in their community that will help them prevent the reoccurrence of violence. [2002, p. 1]

Working with Victims

After crisis intervention and the assessment phase, ongoing therapy begins. In working with victims of domestic violence, the therapist helps the family to honestly address the violence and all of its ramifications. The counselor

- Asks for detailed accounts of the family violence from all family members, gathering information on the worst and minutest details.
- Identifies the omissions, distortions, and/or distractions the child and family may exhibit and determines their emotional meaning for family members.
- Recognizes the intense impressions/perceptions of the domestic violence events.
- Corrects minimization or exaggeration of particular events.
- Discovers the fantasies of family members, particularly revenge fantasies.
- Assists the children and the entire unit to identify and cope with the emotions associated with the violence.
- Provides a sense of personal and family resolution that promotes a normal childhood and a nonviolent future (Lehmann & Rabenstein, 2002, p. 677).

Education Components

Cusik (2000) offers a good overview based on many years of working with victims. Because her research and experience focused on child witnesses of male-on-female violence, the section in her chart on gender roles is somewhat skewed. In families characterized by a dominant female perpetrator, for instance, children learn that women have all the power, not men. The information is otherwise quite useful, and may be imparted in a number of therapeutic modalities (e.g., parent education, couples or family therapy). A brief chart of her work can be seen in Table 8.5.

CHILD ABUSE AND CORPORAL PUNISHMENT

The two following sections, on types of child abuse and the deleterious effects of corporal punishment, are intended both for the clinician's edification, as well as the client's. These materials may be given as a handout, or be incorporated in the introductory section of a High Conflict Family Violence Parent Group.

CHILD ABUSE

Types of Child Abuse

Legally, child abuse falls into four categories: physical abuse, physical neglect, sexual abuse, and emotional maltreatment.

TABLE 8.5 Educating Families About Abuse

What Child Witnesses of Domestic Violence Learn	What Counselors Can Do
Violence is an effective way to solve conflicts 　poor impulse control 　aggression & violence 　passivity & desire to please 　the only response to anger is violence	Teach nonviolent conflict resolution 　anger management 　problem solving 　assertiveness 　stress-reduction (breathing, exercise)
Violence is a normal part of families 　no positive role models 　no personal boundaries 　no emotional security 　might means right	Teach about families 　different kinds of families and roles 　fairness & justice 　mutual respect 　provide appropriate role models for both 　　genders
Victims and children are helpless 　the abuser has all the power 　nothing will change 　no one can help	Teach about domestic violence 　what it is 　how children feel 　who can help 　safe people & places 　coping skills
Sexism 　men & women in stereotypical roles 　women are inferior to men 　men control their families	Teach tolerance 　gender roles 　stereotypes 　diversity
Victims cause the violence 　victims must change their behavior 　the abuser was justified	Teach self esteem 　personal responsibility 　failure is okay 　success comes from effort

Physical Abuse

According to California law (California Attorney General's Office, 1996, p. 1), "*child abuse* means a physical injury which is inflicted by other than accidental means on a child by another person" (Penal Code 11165.6).

The term *corporal punishment* refers to the use of physical force to discipline a child. Spanking and slapping are common forms of corporal punishment, but parents also hit with objects (e.g., belt, hair brush, paddle). Murray Straus, one of the pioneers in family violence research, defines corporal punishment as "the use of physical force with the intention of causing a child to experience pain, but not injury, for the purpose of correction or control of the child's behavior" (Straus & Donelly, 2001, p. 4). Most parents use corporal punishment in this way, without intending to cause the child physical or psychological injury.

It is not technically against the law to physically discipline a child, if it doesn't cause injuries. Unfortunately,*what begins as corporal punishment to correct misbehavior can easily turn into child abuse* when the child continues to act out, or the parent's anger escalates. Also, the psychological damage done to a child from spanking may not be noticeable for a long time.

Injuries due to physical abuse are typically found on the back of a child's body, from the neck to the knees, face, or several parts of the body. The *types of injuries* indicating child abuse include:

- Bruises
- Burns
- Bite marks
- Abrasions
- Lacerations
- Head injuries
- Internal injuries
- Fractures

Physical Neglect

According to California law, there are two categories of neglect: severe neglect and general neglect. Severe neglect means "the negligent failure of a parent to protect the child from severe malnutrition or a medically diagnosed non-organic failure to thrive" (California Attorney General's Office, 1996, p. 5). It also includes situations where the parent or caretaker willfully causes or permits the body or health of the child to be endangered. This includes the intentional failure to provide adequate food, clothing, shelter, or medical care.

In cases of *general neglect*, there has been no injury to the child, but the parent or caretaker has failed to provide the child enough food, shelter, clothing, medical care or supervision. Conditions indicating physical neglect include a child who lacks adequate medical care, is inadequately dressed for weather conditions, is dirty and has poor personal hygiene, appears malnourished, is poorly supervised, and lives in an unsafe or unsanitary environment. An untidy home does not necessarily mean that the home is unfit. It is the persistent and extreme presence of the above conditions that indicates neglect.

Sexual Abuse

This is defined as "acts of sexual assault or sexual exploitation of a minor." Sexual assault includes rape, incest, and "lewd and lascivious acts with a child under 14." Sexual exploitation includes "conduct or activities related to pornography depicting minors and promoting prostitution by minors" (California Attorney General's Office, 1996, p. 6).

Sexual abuse of children within the family, also known as incest, is the most secretive of all sexual abuse. Girls under the age of 11 are the most common victims, but boys are also victimized. Incest tends to recur and to escalate over the years. Children often blame themselves, wrongly thinking that they must have tempted or provoked the abuser.

Emotional Maltreatment

Emotional abuse includes the following parental behaviors:

- Verbal assaults such as belittling, screaming, threats, blaming, or sarcasm
- Unpredictable responses or inconsistent parenting
- Continual negative moods
- Constant family discord or "double-message" communication

Any type of emotional abuse may be reported to authorities, but "suspected cases of severe emotional abuse that constitute willful cruelty or unjustifiable punishment of a child must be reported by mandated reporters" (California Attorney General's Office, 1996, p. 14).

10 Myths About Corporal Punishment (from the book *Beating the Devil Out of Them*, by Murray Straus & Denise Donnelly, 2001)

Myth #1: Spanking works better.

Parents believe this myth partly because corporal punishment often takes less time and energy than other disciplinary measures, and has immediate results. But studies show that corporal punishment is *not* any more effective than talking, withdrawing privileges, and other non-physical approaches. In fact, some studies show that it is *less* effective (Crozier & Katz, 1979; Roberts & Powers, 1990; Webster & Stratton, 1990).

Parents may think that spanking is necessary because they find that when they stop, the child begins to misbehave again. But merely putting an end to the spanking is not enough. In fact, children who behave properly do so despite the corporal punishment they have suffered, not because of it.

> Parents who on their own accord do not spank also do many other things to manage their children's behavior. It is these other things, such as setting clear standards for what is expected, providing lots of love and affection, explaining things to the child, and recognizing and rewarding good behavior, that account for why children of non-spanking parents tend to be easy to manage and well-behaved. What about parents who do these things and also spank? Their children also tend to be well-behaved, but it is illogical to attribute that to

spanking since the same or better results are achieved without spanking, and also without adverse side effects. [pp. 150–151]

Another reason this myth persists is the phenomenon of "selective attention." The virtues of spanking are deeply ingrained in our culture. Strong beliefs tend to narrow a person's focus. For example, an employer who believes women are not assertive or intelligent enough to be office managers will overlook female applicants who may have those qualities. Likewise, parents don't remember the times that spanking is ineffective because this contradicts their belief that spanking works. Parents *will* remember when a warning, a time-out, or a loss of privilege failed to bring the child's behavior under control.

Myth #2: Spanking is needed as a last resort.

Spanking as a "last resort" is in some ways worse than as the first choice of discipline. By the time parents decide to use corporal punishment, they have already tried to reason with the child, have argued, used threats, and so forth, while the child typically has become more uncooperative and difficult. The parents' anger has now escalated to the point where they could easily lose control. And, in fact, research indicates that most episodes of physical abuse began as corporal punishment that got out of hand (Kadushin & Martin, 1981).

Myth #3: Spanking is harmless.

This myth persists because the harmful effects of spanking are not always obvious. Only a small proportion of children suffer serious effects, and often the effects are delayed. This is very much like the problems with smoking. That is to say, although most people who smoke do not die of smoking-related illness, it is equally true that people who smoke are at much greater risk than those who do not. The major problems with corporal punishment are as follows:

- As children get bigger and become better able to defend themselves, corporal punishment of any type becomes less effective. Parents then must either increase the severity of the punishment, which can lead to abuse, or be forced to give it up, which leaves them with less influence over their children.
- Children learn to behave more out of fear of being hit than because they think it is the right thing to do.
- The consequences of mild forms of corporal punishment, such as spanking, are not as severe as outright physical abuse. However, depression and delinquency later in life have been associated with corporal punishment in childhood.
- Children who are physically disciplined learn that it is okay to use physical aggression.

Myth #4: One or two times won't cause any damage.

A few instances of corporal punishment as a child slightly increase the likelihood of depression later in life, of physically abusing one's own children, and of engaging in violent or criminal behavior. Even if the likelihood is low, why take the risk at all?

Myth #5: Parents can't stop without training.

Most parents who use corporal punishment also use a variety of non-physical methods of controlling their children, such as time outs, withdrawing privileges, and so forth. Once they stop the spanking, they simply need to develop enough patience and determination to use these methods on a consistent basis. For other parents, parent training provides the support and additional tools necessary to make the transition.

Myth #6: If you don't spank, your children will be spoiled or run wild.

Children who are not spanked will likely become spoiled brats or "run wild" if the parents do not find alternative ways to control their behavior. However, for a number of reasons the children of non-spanking parents are more likely to be responsible and well-behaved.

- Because they pay more attention to their children's behavior, good and bad, non-spanking parents tend to reward good behavior and ignore negative behavior more often than parents who do spank.
- Without spanking as an option, they rely on such methods as child-proofing the home for younger children, and clear rules and consequences for older ones. The children, therefore, have fewer opportunities to get into mischief.
- They explain and reason more. Therefore, their children learn to think things through, understand the consequences of their actions, and learn to monitor their own behavior rather than depend on their parents' punishment.
- Because non-spanking parents more often reward good behavior, their interactions with their children are more positive. By not spanking, they also avoid the anger and resentment that come with this practice. A strong bond is therefore developed between parents and children. When such a bond exists, children identify with their parents, *want* to do as they are told, and develop a conscience.

Myth #7: Parents spank rarely or only for serious problems.

Parents who spank have a tendency to overly rely on this practice and to use it for many types of minor misbehaviors that could either be ignored, redirected, or otherwise handled differently. And they often use it without first warning the child. One national survey (Straus & Gelles, 1990) indicated that parents of toddlers spank an average of 15 times a year, and other surveys (e.g., Straus & Stewart, 1999) show higher rates.

Myth #8: By the time a child is a teenager, parents have stopped.

Parents who use corporal punishment continue to do so fairly regularly, into their children's early teen years. National surveys show that more than half of the parents of 13- and 14-year-old children hit their children, usually a slap rather than spanking. Even at age 17, one out of five parents continues to hit (Straus et al., 1980). By this age, of course, the child is bigger, and there is an increased danger that the slap may trigger a serious episode of violence, with either the child or the parent or both getting injured.

Myth #9: If parents don't spank, they will verbally abuse their children.

Studies actually indicate the opposite: Parents who use the least amount of corporal punishment also engage in the least amount of verbal aggression (Straus & Gelles, 1990).

Myth #10: It is unrealistic to expect parents to never spank.

It is no more unrealistic to expect parents never to hit their children than to expect spouses never to hit one another, or that no one should ever drive while intoxicated. Parents who don't have problems with their anger, who demonstrate a great deal of love for their children, and who routinely use a variety of non-physical alternatives to corporal punishment, may be forgiven somewhat for using a spanking or two. However, parents who have poor impulse control, don't handle stress well, and have poor overall parenting practices do not have that luxury.

High-Conflict/Family Violence Parent Group

Our center offers a 26–52-week group for parents who have been verbally and/or physically abusive toward their children. It is appropriate for self-referred clients and parents referred through Child and Family Services, but also meets the requirement of California PC 273.1 for parents convicted of physical child abuse. The program addresses parent-on-child violence, intimate partner violence, and sibling violence, and covers anger management, coping with stress, communication and conflict resolution skills, the family cycle of violence, maintaining appropriate family boundaries, stages of child development, disciplining with love, alternatives to punishment, and helping children overcome their own aggression.

Parents are given a workbook containing (1) introductory information, (2) log sheets to help them gauge their progress in overcoming abusive behaviors and using appropriate parenting skills, and (3) informational handouts/exercise sheets. Much of the material is identical to what is used in the 52-week batterers' group. A sample of the exercises specific to parenting can be found in Appendix E, pp. 261–283.

HIGH-CONFLICT FAMILY VIOLENCE PARENT GROUP CURRICULUM

1. Characteristics of healthy families
2. Anger management
3. Anger management
4. Anger management
5. Child abuse laws; physical child abuse facts; 10 myths about corporal punishment
6. Coping with stress
7. Coping with stress

27. Characteristics of healthy families
28. Anger management
29. Anger management
30. Anger management
31. Child abuse laws; 10 myths about corporal punishment; Parenting styles
32. Coping with stress; preparing for provocations

8. Goals of misbehavior; how children learn: modeling, reinforcement
9. Discipline; alternatives to punishment; behavior plans
10. Identifying distorted thinking
11. Challenging and replacing distorted thinking
12. Stages of child development: infancy to age 3
13. Stages of child development: age 3 through middle childhood
14. Stages of child development: preadolescence to young adulthood
15. Basic principles of communication; meta-communication
16. Active listening
17. Anger management review
18. Effects of parental and partner violence on children
19. Positive communication
20. Identifying feelings beneath anger
21. Identifying and expressing needs and wants; assertiveness
22. Assertiveness
23. Family violence cycle
24. Family conflict and conflict escalation
25. Resolving conflict
26. Responding to tantrums; helping children manage their own anger

33. Coping with stress
34. Goals of misbehavior; how children learn: modeling, reinforcement
35. Discipline; alternatives to punishment; behavior plans
36. Irrational beliefs
37. Irrational beliefs
38. Child development review
39. Child development review
40. Child development review
41. Basic principles of communication; meta-communication
42. Active listening; listening to criticism
43. Anger management review
44. Marital violence and child abuse
45. Positive communication
46. Developing empathy
47. Identifying and expressing needs and wants; assertiveness
48. Assertiveness
49. Overcoming resistance to change
50. Family conflict and conflict escalation
51. Resolving conflict
52. Coping with angry people; helping children manage their own anger; family meetings

Children's Groups

In addition to groups for men, women, and couples, the FVPS program in North Carolina, discussed earlier, offers a group for children who have witnessed spousal abuse, or who have been the victims of physical abuse at the hands of their parents. Led by experienced therapists and trained volunteers, the groups "provide a safe, accepting and fun environment where children can learn to express and to better understand their emotions" (Maupin, 2002, p. 2). Group facilitators teach children that feelings are valid, and encourage expression through story-telling and play activities. The children "experience appropriate adult responses to their behavior, and they learn to develop close, trusting relationships with adults" (p. 2).

The FVPS program has enjoyed a high rate of success. Perilla (2000) offers a similar program for Latino families, consisting of men's, women's, and children's groups that meet concurrently. A six-month outcome study indicated a wife abuse recidivism rate of less than 2%.

In their research, Johnston and Roseby (1997) found that school-age children of violent and divorcing families adopt very limited views of the world. These views allow children to make sense of the violence at home and to cope, by helping them lessen their anxiety. But developmentally, the children are alienated from the very peer group that might otherwise provide learning and support. Johnson and Roseby recommend a group format, for two reasons. First, school-age children can be distrustful of adults, and children from violent homes are particularly wary. Second, the group setting provides an alternative peer group where children feel accepted and can risk telling the truth about themselves and their families. Johnston and Roseby (1997) write:

> A central goal in the children's group work is to help them discover and revise the unconscious rules and expectations that govern their understanding of themselves, other people, and relationships. A second and equally important goal is to help the children access and tolerate a broader range of feelings as their scripted ideas begin to shift.
>
> Children ordinarily mature in their interpersonal understanding quite naturally, as they grapple with the demands of friendship. It is here that children must learn how to make sense of and balance their own needs, feelings, and point of view with someone else's. As children meet these challenges they learn about the codes of moral conduct, that is, how to conduct themselves as individuals who also belong to a community.
>
> Ironically, when children in high-conflict families defensively cling to their oversimplified and invariant scripts for understanding themselves and other people, the ordinary challenges of new relationships tend to deepen their constriction; it is the only response that feels safe. The group approach is designed to challenge this response in ways that the participants find safe, interesting, and pleasurable. [pp. 282–283]

Johnston's groups consist of 10 weekly meetings, open to both boys and girls. Groups for children 10–12 years old last for 2 hours each, and those for younger children (7–9) meet for an hour and a half. The groups are led by co-leaders, in order to help with any acting-out behavior during sessions. Many of these children repeat the group after they have completed it, whereas others go on to family or individual therapy. The group uses a variety of exercises, such as feeling-color charts, work with masks, human sculptures, and role plays. Participation in the group helps the children

- explore the language and complexity of feelings
- define and understand the self
- define, dramatize and revise family roles, relationships, and rules of moral conduct

Adolescent Anger Management Groups

Our center offers ongoing groups for adolescent boys and girls, ages 13 to 17, who live in high-conflict families and have exhibited verbal and physical aggression. A complete family assessment is conducted in which other family members, including the parents, are directed to participate in counseling as needed. Before any client is allowed to enter the group, we seek to obtain the parents' full cooperation, so that participation in the program is rigorously enforced with the use of consequences at home. A minimum 26-week commitment is required to allow clients to acclimate to the group culture, relinquish defensive posturing, and address issues in a serious manner.

The group is appropriate for teens with aggressive tendencies at school, at home, and in intimate relationships with the opposite sex. From our experience working with adolescents, we formulated a program that takes into account the unique needs of this population. In particular, adolescents will expend much energy fighting over excessive structure, and are uninterested in being lectured. They are also naturally disinclined to share feelings or reveal too much about their families. The group therefore incorporates the following features:

- primarily open-discussion format
- material adapted from the adult 52-week group program woven into the discussions naturally, when it seems relevant
- videotaping and role-play to demonstrate new skills and dramatize family and relationship conflicts, and to elicit more teen participation by making sessions interesting

Child–Parent Therapy

Recognizing that abused mothers perpetrate abuse on their offspring in various ways, Van Horn and her colleagues (1998) put together a successful program in San Francisco for female victims and their children. The program was designed to help mothers who have endured severe violence, 70% of whom met the criteria for Post Traumatic Stress Disorder. In working with these families, Van Horn observed that witnessing assaults on the mother disrupted the mother–child attachment because mother was no longer viewed as a dependable protector from father's abuse. Furthermore, the abused mothers had been abused as children, or witnessed abuse, and tended to pass on their relationship expectations (as dangerous and exploitative) to their children. For instance, the mother would attribute negative motives to the child, when none existed.

> Susan regularly referred to Tony (the child), in his presence, as "evil," "cruel," and a "devil." She also frequently expressed her fear of him. In one session, she said to the therapist, "There are times when I forget he is a five-year-old person. I forget he is my five-year-old boy. At those times, I believe that if I cannot keep him under control my life will be in danger." In one treatment session, Tony approached his mother, hugged her and rubbed her head. She stiffened and turned away from him, telling him not to be so rough. When the therapist wondered aloud if Tony was expressing affection for her, Susan said, "It's my body. I don't have to let anyone touch it if I don't want to." The therapist agreed that she didn't and then said that she could see how, in her fear, Susan might confuse Tony with men in her life who had badly hurt her. As the therapist spoke, Tony walked across the room and slowly and deliberately poured a glass of grape juice onto the white carpet, staring into his mother's face as he poured. In treatment, the therapist addressed the ways that Susan's fear compelled her to cast Tony in an aggressive light, and the ways in which Tony responded by becoming cruel and aggressive. [Van Horn et al., 1998, p. 7]

Van Horn's program consists of weekly sessions with the mother and child for a period of one year.

The major intervention in our treatment model involves using words and symbolic play to focus on the traumatic experiences and on the conflicted areas of the child–mother attachment, with the aim of helping the child and the mother articulate their emotional experiences, regulate affect, and promote a sense of partnership. . . . We use the therapeutic relationship to contain and explore the mother's anxiety and depression, and simultaneously give the child the opportunity, through play in which the mother and therapist are participant observers, to express her feelings in a containing environment. As the therapist interprets the child's experience in ways in which both the mother and child can hear, the mother begins to see her child in more objective and less threatening ways, releasing the child from the pressure of the mother's misattributions. The child's experience of being understood and accepted by her mother diminishes her need for externalizing behavior to express her feelings, diminishes her need to internalize those feelings, and enhances her capacity to empathize with others. We believe that this increased empathy diminishes the child's risk for reenacting violence in her relationship with her mother, and in other relationships. [p. 8]

Working with the Entire Family

Writing about treatment of Latino male batterers, Carrillo and Goubaud-Reyna (1998) conclude that

Contemporary services for family violence are fragmented in their focus. Services are available for "victims," "offenders," and children suffering from the effects of domestic violence. The end result appears to have essentially taken the "family" out of family violence. Within the current treatment programs, each individual family member is treated out of the context of the family system, many times at odds with each other. Each separate population has its own issues and advocates. The treatment itself retraumatizes the family, first, by catching family members in the vicious cycle of violence, and second, by developing fragmented treatment systems. [p. 54]

Family sessions involving all or most of the family members may not be appropriate in cases of severe, unilateral battering, when family members are afraid and feel unsafe, the perpetrator continues to be assaultive, and considerable pathology exists in either parent. Otherwise, it can be the most powerful, direct means for creating change. In working with Asian batterers, Lee (2000) advocates family sessions in which respected members of the family, including members of the extended family, confront the perpetrator about his violence. More recently, Mills (2003) has propounded the concept of the IAC, or Intimate Abuse Circle, which includes members of the larger community.

Family therapy affords the therapist an opportunity to observe firsthand the complexity of dysfunctional communication, interactions, alliances, and boundary problems. In addition, the presence of the children provides a corrective check on the parents' tendency to minimize their abuse. Depending on the family's functioning level, the format can be either semi-structured, with psychoeducational material presented at a specific point, or woven naturally into the session when indicated. An excerpt from a family session recently conducted at our center follows:

The Stuart family was asked to come in for a session, following two unsuccessful conjoint sessions with the parents. The mother, Lori, a petite, attractive redhead with long, flowing hair, had initiated couples counseling because of ongoing arguments with her husband, Ron, over money issues and their older son's school problems. The focus of the first conjoint meeting was on Ron's problems finding work after a three-month layoff from his accounting job. During the second conjoint session, as the therapist proceeded with her routine domestic violence assessment, it was revealed that Lori had a long history of violent outbursts directed at Ron and the children. She had once slapped the older son, Mike, in the face so hard it caused his nose to bleed. Four years previously, Lori had hurled an ashtray at Ron, striking him in the head and causing a large gash, which necessitated medical attention. In Lori's mind Ron was the aggressor because he sometimes yelled back, and recently bruised her arms when trying to restrain her from hitting him. "He's two-hundred pounds," Lori pointed out. "I'm barely a hundred. It's not the same." In session, Ron was content to talk about his lay-off and criticize Lori for not sticking to their budget. Ron dismissed his wife's violence as due to her Portuguese background. "Hot blooded, these women," he said. "You should meet her mother."

The therapist suggested that Ron and Lori bring their two children, Mike, age 14, and Corey, age 10, to the next session. The stated reason for the family meeting was to understand how the family coped with stress, but the therapist's more immediate goal was to help the couple overcome denial about Lori's violence. During the session, Ron and Lori presented as good-natured, well-meaning parents, who were trying to make ends meet. They expressed concern over Mike's plummeting grades at school. Corey sat between his parents quietly, preoccupied with a painting on the wall, sometimes laughing nervously at something his brother said. When asked questions about the family's well-being, he responded with brief, noncommittal responses, and would glance up at each of his parents for reassurance. Mike sat with a sullen expression between his dad and the therapist. When the issue of grades was raised, Mike launched into an extended critique of his history teacher, whom he accused of not caring about the students. Mom said her son was "goofing off." Dad agreed with Mom's assessment that Mike's grades needed to improve, but shared his son's opinion of the history teacher.

Tx: (therapist)	Mike, as your father was talking I noticed you kept looking up at him, but when your mom talked, you were looking at your brother, playing a kind of staring game. In fact, what I've observed is that for the whole first part of this session, about 40 minutes now, you haven't once looked at your mom. What's that all about?
Mike:	(looking down, mumbling) I dunno.
Tx:	Are you . . . upset with her?
Mike:	(sounding irritated) What do you mean?
Tx:	Well, are you maybe . . . angry with her for some reason?

Mike grimaces and shifts his body in his chair, looking highly uncomfortable. After a few moments, he notices that Corey is giggling nervously.

Mike:	(to Corey, snapping) What? What's your problem?
Corey:	Shut up!

After the brothers exchange a few insults, Mom tells Mike to "knock it off." The therapist reminds the family of the counseling rule that everyone speaks to each other with respect. The therapist turns her attention to Corey.

Tx:	When I was asking Mike if he was angry with Mom. Why did you find that funny?

Corey looks at each of his parents, as if wanting to see if it's okay to respond.

Mike:	Go on. What are you waiting for? We're in therapy. We're supposed to talk about stuff. (looks at therapist) Right?
Tx:	Yes. That's what we're here for.

Ron: C'mon, sport. Listen to the lady. She's a *professional.* She's trying to help us, help us be a happier family.

Mike: (laughs derisively) Oh, yeah. One big happy family. (Looks at Mom for the first time, eyeing her contemptuously) One big happy, screaming, yelling family.

Lori stares back at him for a moment, then looks away, appearing both angry and hurt. Everyone falls silent. Ron appears embarrassed, and Corey focuses his attention on the painting again. The therapist purposely allows the silence to continue, so the family may take in the moment and contemplate more fully what Mike has said.

Tx: (to the whole family) Well, now, maybe we're getting somewhere. (turns to Mike) Finally got some eye contact there, with your mom. . . . Is there something you want to tell us, about the way your mom acts when she's angry?

Following this exchange, Mike was able to talk about his mother's rants against Dad and those she directed at him. Once the violence was exposed, Corey also was able to open up. The issue of Mike's grades was abandoned, and the therapist steered the family into a discussion of Mom's violence and the family dynamics around it, including Corey's attempts to placate, and Mike's alliance with Dad. Ron, reluctantly, validated his sons' reports of abuse but continued to downplay the violence Lori perpetrated on him. In subsequent conjoint sessions, Ron finally relinquished the tough-guy façade and openly discussed the immense hurt he felt. Ron expressed humiliation at being called a "loser" in front of Mike. Only then did Lori begin to accept responsibility for her behavior. This led to a discussion of Ron's emotional dependence on Lori and her feelings of engulfment. From then on, the therapy continued in a couple format, with a focus on Lori and Ron's families of origin, particularly the sexual abuse she experienced as a child. Lori agreed to participate in individual therapy on her own.

III

Appendices

Appendix A

Assessment Forms

GENERAL PSYCHOSOCIAL ASSESSMENT

Man's name _____ Age _____ Occupation/School _____

Woman's name _____ Age _____ Occupation/School _____

Address _____ Phone: h (___) _____ w (___) _____

Referral source _____ Phone: (___) _____ Today's date _____

Client's/couple's household members

Name	Age	Relation	Location/phone/ other information

Children living outside of household/ex-spouse information

Name	Age	Relation	Location/phone/ other information

PRESENTING PROBLEMS:

MAN'S PREVIOUS COUNSELING:

MAN'S MOOD, PERSONALITY, MENTAL STATUS:

DSM-IV diagnosis
Motivation—will client benefit?

WOMAN'S PREVIOUS COUNSELING:

WOMAN'S MOOD, PERSONALITY, MENTAL STATUS:

DSM-IV diagnosis
Motivation—will client benefit?

MAN'S DEVELOPMENTAL HISTORY:

Family of origin today:

MAN'S ADULT HISTORY—school, work, major events

WOMAN'S DEVELOPMENTAL HISTORY:

Family of origin today:

WOMAN'S ADULT HISTORY—school, work, major events

Ex-spouse/co-parent

Name _____ Age _____ Occupation/School _____
Address _____ Phone: h (____) _____ w (____) _____
Referral source _____ Phone: (____) _____ Today's date _____

Household members/children living outside of household

Name	Age	Relation	Location	Notes

PRESENTING PROBLEMS:

DEVELOPMENTAL HISTORY:

Family of origin today:

ADULT HISTORY

MOOD, PERSONALITY, MENTAL STATUS

DSM-IV diagnosis
Motivation—will client benefit

FAMILY COURT INFORMATION

Docket #: _____

Judge _____   Court/Department #_____

Professionals currently involved in case:

Father's attorney _____   Mother's attorney _____

Mediator _____   Evaluator _____

Others working with father (e.g., therapists):

Others working with mother:

Approximate dates/outcomes of previous mediation and evaluation sessions, court appearances:

Upcoming dates:

Reports (evaluations, police, etc.):

Current custody arrangement:

Method of child transfer/restraining orders:

Father wants:

Mother wants:

CONFLICT TACTICS SCALE QUESTIONNAIRE

Name _____ Partner _____ Yrs. together ____ Date _____

No matter how well couples get along, there are times when they disagree, get annoyed with one another, want different things from each other, or just have spats or fights because they are in a bad mood, are tired, or are upset for some other reason. Couples also have many different ways of trying to settle their differences. I am going to read to you a list of things that might happen when you have differences. Please tell me how many times you did each of these things in the past year, and how many times your partner did them in the past year. Then state the total number of times each of you did these things during the entire relationship.

	PAST 12 MONTHS		TOTAL RELATIONSHIP (Total, *or* average/year)	
Behavior	me	partner	me	partner
1. Discussed an issue calmly				
2. Got information to back up your side of things				
3. Brought in, or tried to bring in, someone to help settle things				
4. Yelled at, insulted, or swore at partner				
5. Sulked or refused to talk about an issue				
6. Stomped out of the room or house or yard				
7. Cried (this item *not* scored)				
8. Did or said something to spite him/her				
9. Threatened to hit or throw something at him/her				
10. Threw or smashed or hit or kicked something				
11. Threw something at him/her				
12. Pushed, grabbed, or shoved him/her				
13. Slapped him/her				

14. Kicked, scratched, bit or hit
    him/her with a fist

15. Hit or tried to hit him/her
    with something

16. Beat him/her up

17. Choked him/her

18. Threatened him/her with a
    knife or gun

19. Used a knife or fired a gun

20. Other (e.g., burned)

21. SEXUAL COERCION (used
    force, threat of force)

NOTES (specifics about incidents, context, extent of injuries, provocations, etc.)

RELATIONSHIP BEHAVIORS

No matter how well couples get along, there are times when they disagree, get annoyed with the other person, want different things from each other, or just have spats or fights because they are in a bad mood, are tired, or for some other reason. Couples have many different ways of trying to settle their differences. This is a list of things that might happen when you have disagreements. Please circle how many times you did each of these in the past year, and how many times your partner did them in the past year. If you or your partner did not do one of these things in the past year, but it happened before that, circle "7."

How often did this happen?

1 = Once in the past year
2 = twice in the past year
3 = 3–5 times in the past year
4 = 6–10 times in the past year
5 = 11–20 times in the past year
6 = more than 20 times in the past year
7 = not in the past year, but it did happen before
0 = none

Example Negotiation Scale Items

1. I showed my partner I cared   1   2   3   4   5   6   7   0
    even though we disagreed.
59. I suggested a compromise to a   1   2   3   4   5   6   7   0
    disagreement.

Example Psychological Aggression Scale Items

35. I shouted or yelled at my partner.
49. I stomped out of the room or house or yard during a disagreement.

Example Physical Assault Scale Items

53. I slapped my partner.
27. I punched or hit my partner with something that could hurt.

Example Sexual Coercion Scale Items

51. I insisted on sex when my partner did not want to (but did not use physical force).
57. I used force (like hitting, holding down, or using a weapon) to make my partner have sex.

Example Injury Scale Items

11. I had a sprain, bruise, or small cut because of a fight with my partner.
41. I needed to see a doctor because of a fight with my partner, but I didn't.

RELATIONSHIP BEHAVIORS, PART 2

People have different reasons for acting physically aggressive toward their partners. For each possible reason listed below, circle a number from 1 to 3, to show how often this is *your* reason.

(1 = never or rarely   2 = sometimes   3 = often or always)

	Reason For My Physical Aggression	How Often		
1.	I thought it was the only way to get through to him/her	1	2	3
2.	I was getting back at him/her for something nasty he/she said or threatened to do to me	1	2	3
3.	I was getting back at him/her for some physical action he/she had used against me	1	2	3
4.	To stop him/her doing something	1	2	3
5.	To make him/her do what I wanted	1	2	3
6.	I thought he/she was about to use a physical action against me	1	2	3
7.	I was under the influence of alcohol or drugs at the time	1	2	3
8.	It is my character. That's the way I am	1	2	3
9.	No particular reason. I don't know	1	2	3
10.	Other:	1	2	3

Source: M. Carrado et al. (1996), "Aggression in British Heterosexual Relationships: A Descriptive Analysis." *Aggressive Behavior, 22,* pp. 401–415.

ORAL INTERVIEW

Current Relationship

A. Specific incidents of violence

Date   Location   What Happened

B. Initiation of aggression
When you have differences with your partner, what percentage of the time do you:
Start the yelling or swearing? ____%   Start the *physical* fighting? ____%

C. Self-defense
What percentage of the time is your physical aggression in self-defense, strictly to
protect yourself from his/her physical aggression? ____%

D. Extent of blaming/justification/contrition
When you and your partner have a fight, what percentage of the time is it his/her
fault? ____%
When you have been abusive toward your partner, what percentage of the time do
you feel sorry or bad afterwards? ____%

E. Alcohol and drug use
When you have been abusive toward your partner, what percentage of the time were
you under the influence of alcohol or drugs? ____% What about him/her? ____%

Childhood

How parents settled their disputes—Verbal, physical fighting?

How parents disciplined you—Corporal punishment? Severe? Psychological abuse?

Your aggression at home

Your aggression at school and elsewhere

Other abuse in family (e.g., siblings, elderly abuse)

What were you taught about anger and aggression?

Previous Adult Relationships

Years	Name	Nature of relationship (e.g., violence, police called, substance abuse, cause of break-up)

Other Violence/Criminal History

(Conflicts at work, with extended family, friends, in traffic; any arrests, for violent or non-violent offenses?)

Aggression-Related Medical Conditions

Brain injury _____ Stroke _____ Epileptic seizures _____ Other _____

Current Parenting

Please tell me about when your children do things that are wrong, disobey, or make you angry. What kinds of things do they do? Why do you think they act that way?

How do the children get along with one another? Do they ever have physical fights? Who initiates them, and who usually gets hurt?

Are any of your children ever aggressive with you, or the other parent? Verbal, or physical? Give me some examples.

How do you normally respond to your children when they misbehave? Are there times when you "lose it" or just don't respond very well? What happens then?

What about your partner?

Do you and your partner agree or disagree on how to handle your children when they do things that are wrong, disobey, or make you angry? Tell me about that. Who usually has the last say?

Lethality/Dangerousness Checklist (check when applicable):

(Characteristics of the perpetrator, unless otherwise indicated)

_____ Increase in severity/frequency of violence in previous year
_____ Owns a gun
_____ Victim has left after living together with perpetrator during past year
_____ Unemployed
_____ Previously used or threatened to use weapon against victim
_____ Threatens to kill victim
_____ Has avoided being arrested for domestic violence
_____ Victim has child that is not his/hers
_____ Forced sex on victim
_____ Has tried to choke
_____ Uses illegal drugs
_____ An alcoholic or problem drinker
_____ Highly controlling of victim's daily activities
_____ Violently and constantly jealous
_____ Assaults victim when victim is pregnant
_____ Perpetrator or victim has threatened or tried to commit suicide
_____ Harms victim's children
_____ Victim believes perpetrator is capable of killing him/her
_____ Engages in stalking behavior

Treatment Plan

Overall impressions of client(s)—e.g., affect, motivation, truthfulness, attitudes

Therapeutic goals and recommendations

ANGER STYLES QUESTIONS

1.	I try never to get angry.	YES	NO
2.	I get really nervous when others are angry.	YES	NO
3.	I feel I'm doing something bad when I get angry.	YES	NO
4.	I tell people I'll do what they want, but then I often forget.	YES	NO
5.	I say things like "Yeah, but . . . " and "I'll do it later."	YES	NO
6.	People tell me I must be angry but I'm not sure why.	YES	NO
7.	I get jealous a lot, even when there is no reason.	YES	NO
8.	I don't trust people very much.	YES	NO
9.	Sometimes it feels like people are out to get me.	YES	NO
10.	My anger comes on really fast.	YES	NO
11.	I act before I think when I get angry.	YES	NO
12.	My anger goes away very quickly after I explode.	YES	NO
13.	I get very angry when people criticize me.	YES	NO
14.	People say I am easily hurt and oversensitive.	YES	NO
15.	I get angry when I feel bad about myself.	YES	NO
16.	I get mad to get what I want.	YES	NO
17.	I try to scare others with my anger.	YES	NO
18.	I can pretend to be very mad when I'm really okay.	YES	NO
19.	Sometimes I get angry just for the excitement or action.	YES	NO
20.	I like the strong feelings that come with my anger.	YES	NO
21.	My anger takes over and I go out of control.	YES	NO
22.	I seem to get angry all the time.	YES	NO
23.	I just can't break the habit of getting angry a lot.	YES	NO
24.	I get mad without thinking—it just happens.	YES	NO
25.	I become very angry when I defend my beliefs and opinions.	YES	NO
26.	I become outraged about what others try to get away with.	YES	NO
27.	I always know I'm right in an argument.	YES	NO
28.	I hang onto my anger for a long time.	YES	NO
29.	I have a hard time forgiving people.	YES	NO
30.	I hate people for what they've done to me.	YES	NO

From *Letting Go of Anger* by Ronald T. and Patricia Potter-Efron, published by New Harbinger, Oakland, CA, 1996, pp. 4–6. Reprinted with permission of New Harbinger.

ASSESSMENT OF SELF AND PARTNER'S RELATIONSHIP FUNCTIONING*

Name ————————— Date ————

Rate your partner for each of the 7 areas of relationship functioning as either very poor, poor, fair, good, or excellent. Put a check mark in the middle of the text that best reflects your partner's functioning. You can also put a check mark on one of the two vertical lines between text (to indicate "poor" or "good"). Afterwards, go ahead and rate yourself, using an "x".

Area of Functioning	Very poor	Poor	Fair	Good	Excellent
Personal responsibility	Blames partner, expects her/him to change first. Minimizes own behavior, rarely admits being wrong.		Tends to blame, but willing at times to admit wrongs and change own behavior.		Accepts and expresses responsibility for behavior. Promptly admits wrongs.
Anger management	Short fuse. Temper tantrums. High level of verbal aggression; any kind of physical aggression.		Tries to express feelings properly, but often reacts before thinking. Some verbal, no physical agg.		Rarely lets partner push his/her buttons. Able to think through options, choose his/her actions.
Coping with stress	"Type A" personality. Driven, a perfectionist. Unable to unwind. No lifestyle balance.		Experiences moderate stress levels. Knows signs of stress, and sometimes makes lifestyle adjustments.		Experiences low levels of stress. Has lifestyle balance.
Communication	Poor listener. Interrupts. Doesn't express feelings. Highly critical, rarely gives praise.		Satisfactory listener. Some efforts to share feelings and understand other points of view.		Excellent listener. Communicates in a clear and respectful manner.

Conflict resolution	Ignores problems, allows arguments to spin out of control. Takes things personally. Always wants to win.	Somewhat able to keep conflicts from escalating. Tries to resolve issues. Sometimes willing to compromise.	Rarely lets conflicts escalate. Negotiates. Finds acceptable solutions, or is able to move on, without resentment.
Control	Insists on being in charge and making all the decisions. Keeps partner on "short leash." Possessive.	Can be flexible in making decisions. Grudgingly allows spouse right to independence.	Encourages partner's full participation in making decisions. Not threatened by his/her independence or success.
Isolation/social support	Suspicious of others. Won't ask for help. No friends or family support. No outside activities except job.	Requests help in crises. Gets some support. A few outside interests. Occasionally goes out w/partner.	Large network of supportive family and friends. Regular outside activities with and w/o partner.

*Adapted from *Spouse Abuse: A Treatment Program for Couples,* by P. Neidig & D. Friedman (1984).

CONTROLLING AND ABUSIVE TACTICS QUESTIONNAIRE (CAT)*

Read each statement and circle how often your partner/ex-partner has done each of the following behaviors *to you*, and how often you have done each of them *to your partner*.

My Name _____ Name of Partner or Ex-partner _____

1. My partner/ex has threatened to hurt me.
   Never   Rarely   Occasionally   Very Often

   I have done this to my partner/ex.
   Never   Rarely   Occasionally   Very Often

2. My partner/ex has tried to intimidate me with looks or gestures, or has done things to scare me.
   Never   Rarely   Occasionally   Very Often

   I have done this to my partner/ex.
   Never   Rarely   Occasionally   Very Often

3. My partner/ex has threatened to hurt someone I care about.
   Never   Rarely   Occasionally   Very Often

   I have done this.
   Never   Rarely   Occasionally   Very Often

4. My partner/ex had done cruel things to pets.
   Never   Rarely   Occasionally   Very Often

   I have done this.
   Never   Rarely   Occasionally   Very Often

5. My partner/ex has tried to control who I spend my time with, including my family and friends.
   Never   Rarely   Occasionally   Very Often

   I have done this to my partner/ex.
   Never   Rarely   Occasionally   Very Often

6. My partner/ex has kept me from doing things I want to do, and has tried to restrict my movements.
   Never   Rarely   Occasionally   Very Often

   I have done this to my partner/ex.
   Never   Rarely   Occasionally   Very Often

7. My partner/ex has kept me from leaving the house (for example, by standing in front of the door).
   Never   Rarely   Occasionally   Very Often

   I have done this to my partner/ex.
   Never   Rarely   Occasionally   Very Often

8. My partner/ex has withheld the car keys, or disabled my vehicle.
   Never   Rarely   Occasionally   Very Often

   I have done this to my partner/ex.
   Never   Rarely   Occasionally   Very Often

9. My partner/ex has accused me of flirting with other people.
   Never   Rarely   Occasionally   Very Often

   I have done this to my partner/ex.
   Never   Rarely   Occasionally   Very Often

10. My partner/ex has accused me of being unfaithful, and has checked up on me.
    Never   Rarely   Occasionally   Very Often

    I have done this to my partner/ex.
    Never   Rarely   Occasionally   Very Often

11. My partner/ex has interrogated me about where I have been.
    Never   Rarely   Occasionally   Very Often

    I have done this to my partner/ex.
    Never   Rarely   Occasionally   Very Often

12. My partner/ex has controlled the money, and excluded me from having a say in financial decisions.
    Never   Rarely   Occasionally   Very Often

    I have done this to my partner/ex.
    Never   Rarely   Occasionally   Very Often

13. My partner/ex has spent our money excessively/has put us into debt.
    Never   Rarely   Occasionally   Very Often

    I have done this.
    Never   Rarely   Occasionally   Very Often

14. My partner/ex has refused to work or otherwise contribute financially to our household.
    Never   Rarely   Occasionally   Very Often

    I have done this.
    Never   Rarely   Occasionally   Very Often

15. My partner/ex has threatened to get me fired.
    Never   Rarely   Occasionally   Very Often

    I have done this to my partner/ex.
    Never   Rarely   Occasionally   Very Often

16. My partner/ex has lied about child expenses to get more child support.
    Never   Rarely   Occasionally   Very Often

    I have done this to my partner/ex.
    Never   Rarely   Occasionally   Very Often

17. My partner/ex has told me that I am physically or sexually unattractive, or that no one else would ever want me.
    Never   Rarely   Occasionally   Very Often

    I have done this to my partner/ex.
    Never   Rarely   Occasionally   Very Often

18. My partner/ex has flirted with others, or threatened to have affairs.
    Never   Rarely   Occasionally   Very Often

    I have done this.
    Never   Rarely   Occasionally   Very Often

19. My partner/ex has said hurtful things (for example, calling me "ugly," "fat," "whore," or "loser").
    Never   Rarely   Occasionally   Very Often

    I have done this to my partner/ex.
    Never   Rarely   Occasionally   Very Often

20. My partner/ex has humiliated me in front of others.
    Never   Rarely   Occasionally   Very Often

    I have done this to my partner/ex.
    Never   Rarely   Occasionally   Very Often

21. My partner/ex has pressured me do things that are degrading or against my values.
    Never   Rarely   Occasionally   Very Often

    I have done this to my partner/ex.
    Never   Rarely   Occasionally   Very Often

22. My partner/ex has ridiculed me, or treated me like I was stupid.
    Never   Rarely   Occasionally   Very Often

    I have done this to my partner/ex.
    Never   Rarely   Occasionally   Very Often

23. My partner/ex has told me I am incompetent, or that no one will want to hire me again.
    Never   Rarely   Occasionally   Very Often

    I have done this to my partner/ex.
    Never   Rarely   Occasionally   Very Often

24. My partner/ex has told me I'll never be able to manage things on my own.
    Never   Rarely   Occasionally   Very Often

    I have done this to my partner/ex.
    Never   Rarely   Occasionally   Very Often

25. My partner/ex has told me that what I want, feel or care about is unimportant.
    Never   Rarely   Occasionally   Very Often

    I have done this to my partner/ex.
    Never   Rarely   Occasionally   Very Often

26. My partner/ex has made fun of my sexual performance.
    Never   Rarely   Occasionally   Very Often

    I have done this to my partner/ex.
    Never   Rarely   Occasionally   Very Often

27. My partner/ex has spread false rumors about me to others, or done other things to wreck my relationships.
    Never   Rarely   Occasionally   Very Often

    I have done this to my partner/ex.
    Never   Rarely   Occasionally   Very Often

28. My partner/ex has tried to convince other people that I am crazy.
    Never   Rarely   Occasionally   Very Often

    I have done this.
    Never   Rarely   Occasionally   Very Often

29. My partner/ex has routinely blamed me for all our problems.
    Never   Rarely   Occasionally   Very Often

    I have done this to my partner/ex.
    Never   Rarely   Occasionally   Very Often

30. My partner/ex has ordered me around, expecting me to "hop to it."
    Never   Rarely   Occasionally   Very Often

    I have done this to my partner/ex.
    Never   Rarely   Occasionally   Very Often

31. My partner/ex has repeatedly nagged me, and has refused to take "no" for an answer.
    Never   Rarely   Occasionally   Very Often

    I have done this to my partner/ex.
    Never   Rarely   Occasionally   Very Often

32. My partner/ex has followed me around, criticizing my every move.
    Never   Rarely   Occasionally   Very Often

    I have done this to my partner/ex.
    Never   Rarely   Occasionally   Very Often

33. My partner/ex has insisted on talking late at night, keeping me awake.
    Never   Rarely   Occasionally   Very Often

    I have done this to my partner/ex.
    Never   Rarely   Occasionally   Very Often

34. My partner/ex has called/come to my place of employment, to harass me.
    Never   Rarely   Occasionally   Very Often

    I have done this to my partner/ex.
    Never   Rarely   Occasionally   Very Often

35. My partner/ex has followed me around (stalked me).
Never   Rarely   Occasionally   Very Often

I have done this to my partner/ex.
Never   Rarely   Occasionally   Very Often

36. My partner/ex has called or paged me constantly, against my wishes, or has left numerous unwanted messages on my voice mail.
Never   Rarely   Occasionally   Very Often

I have done this to my partner/ex.
Never   Rarely   Occasionally   Very Often

37. My partner/ex has threatened to commit suicide.
Never   Rarely   Occasionally   Very Often

I have done this.
Never   Rarely   Occasionally   Very Often

38. My partner/ex has deliberately ignored me, or withheld affection and sex to punish me.
Never   Rarely   Occasionally   Very Often

I have done this to my partner/ex.
Never   Rarely   Occasionally   Very Often

39. My partner/ex has locked me out of the bedroom or house when he/she was angry.
Never   Rarely   Occasionally   Very Often

I have done this to my partner/ex.
Never   Rarely   Occasionally   Very Often

40. My partner/ex has refused to cooperate with me.
Never   Rarely   Occasionally   Very Often

I have done this.
Never   Rarely   Occasionally   Very Often

41. My partner has been passive-aggressive—e.g, "forgot" to give me important information.
Never   Rarely   Occasionally   Very Often

I have done this.
Never   Rarely   Occasionally   Very Often

42. My partner/ex has told the children negative things about me, or used them as spies.
Never   Rarely   Occasionally   Very Often

I have done this.
Never   Rarely   Occasionally   Very Often

43. My partner/ex has excluded me from child-rearing, or has joined with the children against me.
    Never   Rarely   Occasionally   Very Often

    I have done this to my partner/ex.
    Never   Rarely   Occasionally   Very Often

44. My partner/ex has threatened to take the children, or kept them from me against an agreement/court order.
    Never   Rarely   Occasionally   Very Often

    I have done this to my partner/ex.
    Never   Rarely   Occasionally   Very Often

45. My partner/ex has refused to let the children see their grandparents.
    Never   Rarely   Occasionally   Very Often

    I have done this.
    Never   Rarely   Occasionally   Very Often

46. My partner/ex has filed false domestic violence or child abuse charges against me.
    Never   Rarely   Occasionally   Very Often

    I have done this to my partner/ex.
    Never   Rarely   Occasionally   Very Often

47. My partner/ex has threatened to have me deported, or to report me to welfare.
    Never   Rarely   Occasionally   Very Often

    I have done this to my partner/ex.
    Never   Rarely   Occasionally   Very Often

48. My partner/ex has pressured me to engage in sexual practices I am uncomfortable with.
    Never   Rarely   Occasionally   Very Often

    I have done this to my partner/ex.
    Never   Rarely   Occasionally   Very Often

49. My partner/ex has pressured me to have sex when I didn't want to.
    Never   Rarely   Occasionally   Very Often

    I have done this to my partner/ex.
    Never   Rarely   Occasionally   Very Often

50. My partner/ex has physically forced me to have sex (raped me).
    Never   Rarely   Occasionally   Very Often

    I have done this to my partner/ex.
    Never   Rarely   Occasionally   Very Often

*This questionnaire may be copied without permission.

MARITAL HAPPINESS & COMMUNICATION

A.   Below is a list of areas that are important to having a satisfying relationship. Please circle the number corresponding to how satisfied you are for each specific area.

	Very Satisfied	Mostly Satisfied	Satisfied	Somewhat Unsatisfied	Very Unsatisfied
1. The way we interact on a daily basis	5	4	3	2	1
2. Level of affection shown	5	4	3	2	1
3. Our sex life	5	4	3	2	1
4. Our overall communication	5	4	3	2	1
5. The trust we have in one another	5	4	3	2	1
6. How we handle conflict	5	4	3	2	1
7. Dividing household chores	5	4	3	2	1
8. Cooperation in raising children	5	4	3	2	1
9. Our money management	5	4	3	2	1
10. Amount of free time spent together	5	4	3	2	1
11. Quality of free time spent together	5	4	3	2	1
12. Amount of individual free time	5	4	3	2	1
13. Our ability to cope in a crisis	5	4	3	2	1

B. Now please indicate how much each statement below accurately describes your communication.

	Nearly Always	Often	Sometimes	Rarely	Almost Never
1. My partner listens attentively when I speak	5	4	3	2	1
2. I listen attentively when my partner speaks	5	4	3	2	1
3. My partner understands what I say	5	4	3	2	1
4. I understand what my partner says	5	4	3	2	1
5. My partner speaks to me with respect	5	4	3	2	1
6. I speak to my partner with respect	5	4	3	2	1
7. My partner compliments/encourages me	5	4	3	2	1
8. I compliment/encourage my partner	5	4	3	2	1

EXPERIENCES IN CLOSE RELATIONSHIPS—REVISED

The statements below concern how you feel in emotionally intimate relationships. We are interested in how you *generally* experience relationships, not just in what is happening in a current relationship. Respond to each statement by marking a circle to indicate how much you agree or disagree with the statement.

I often wish that my partner's feelings for me were as strong as my feelings for him or her.

Strongly
Disagree   O   O   O   O   O   O   O   Strongly
Agree

I prefer not to be too close to romantic partners.

Strongly
Disagree   O   O   O   O   O   O   O   Strongly
Agree

I tell my partner just about everything.

Strongly
Disagree   O   O   O   O   O   O   O   Strongly
Agree

I feel comfortable sharing my private thoughts and feelings with my partner.

Strongly
Disagree   O   O   O   O   O   O   O   Strongly
Agree

It's not difficult for me to get close to my partner.

Strongly
Disagree   O   O   O   O   O   O   O   Strongly
Agree

When my partner is out of sight, I worry that he or she might become interested in someone else.

Strongly
Disagree   O   O   O   O   O   O   O   Strongly
Agree

It makes me mad that I don't get the affection and support I need from my partner.

Strongly
Disagree   O   O   O   O   O   O   O   Strongly
Agree

I worry that I won't measure up to other people.

Strongly
Disagree   O   O   O   O   O   O   O   Strongly
Agree

I often worry that my partner doesn't really love me.

Strongly
Disagree   O   O   O   O   O   O   O   Strongly
Agree

I feel comfortable depending on romantic partners.

Strongly
Disagree   O   O   O   O   O   O   O   Strongly
Agree

My romantic partner makes me doubt myself.

Strongly
Disagree   ○   ○   ○   ○   ○   ○   ○   Strongly
Agree

I prefer not to show a partner how I feel deep down.

Strongly
Disagree   ○   ○   ○   ○   ○   ○   ○   Strongly
Agree

My partner really understands me and my needs.

Strongly
Disagree   ○   ○   ○   ○   ○   ○   ○   Strongly
Agree

I am nervous when partners get too close to me.

Strongly
D isagree   ○   ○   ○   ○   ○   ○   ○   Strongly
Agree

I find it difficult to allow myself to depend on romantic partners.

Strongly
Disagree   ○   ○   ○   ○   ○   ○   ○   Strongly
Agree

I do not often worry about being abandoned.

Strongly
Disagree   ○   ○   ○   ○   ○   ○   ○   Strongl y
Agree

It helps to turn to my romantic partner in times of need.

Strongly
Disagree   ○   ○   ○   ○   ○   ○   ○   Strongly
Agree

I talk things over with my partner.

Strongly
Disagree   ○   ○   ○   ○   ○   ○   ○   Strongly
Agree

My partner only seems to notice me when I'm angry.

Strongly
Disagree   ○   ○   ○   ○   ○   ○   ○   Strongly
Agree

I find that my partner(s) don't want to get as close as I would like.

Strongly
Disagree   ○   ○   ○   ○   ○   ○   ○   Strongly
Agree

I usually discuss my problems and concerns with my partner.

Strongly
Disagree   ○   ○   ○   ○   ○   ○   ○   Strongly
Agree

I don't feel comfortable opening up to romantic partners.

Strongly
Disagree   ○   ○   ○   ○   ○   ○   ○   Strongly
Agree

I find it easy to depend on romantic partners.

Strongly
Disagree ○ ○ ○ ○ ○ ○ ○ Strongly
Agree

I rarely worry about my partner leaving me.

Strongly
Disagree ○ ○ ○ ○ ○ ○ ○ Strongly
Agree

I am very comfortable being close to romantic partners.

Strongly
Disagree ○ ○ ○ ○ ○ ○ ○ Strongly
Agree

It's easy for me to be affectionate with my partner.

Strongly
Disagree ○ ○ ○ ○ ○ ○ ○ Strongly
Agree

I worry a lot about my relationships.

Strongly
Disagree ○ ○ ○ ○ ○ ○ ○ Strongly
Agree

I'm afraid that once a romantic partner gets to know me, he or she won't like who I really am.

Strongly
Disagree ○ ○ ○ ○ ○ ○ ○ Strongly
Agree

I get uncomfortable when a romantic partner wants to be very close.

Strongly
Disagree ○ ○ ○ ○ ○ ○ ○ Strongly
Agree

I often worry that my partner will not want to stay with me.

Strongly
Disagree ○ ○ ○ ○ ○ ○ ○ Strongly
Agree

My desire to be very close sometimes scares people away.

Strongly
Disagree ○ ○ ○ ○ ○ ○ ○ Strongly
Agree

I'm afraid that I will lose my partner's love.

Strongly
Disagree ○ ○ ○ ○ ○ ○ ○ Strongly
Agree

I find it relatively easy to get close to my partner.

Strongly
Disagree ○ ○ ○ ○ ○ ○ ○ Strongly
Agree

I worry that romantic partners won't care about me as much as I care about them.

Strongly
Disagree ○ ○ ○ ○ ○ ○ ○ Strongly
Agree

When I show my feelings for romantic partners, I'm afraid they will not feel the same about me.

Strongly   Strongly
Disagree   ○   ○   ○   ○   ○   ○   ○   Agree

Sometimes romantic partners change their feelings about me for no apparent reason.

Strongly   Strongly
Disagree   ○   ○   ○   ○   ○   ○   ○   Agree

The above Experiences in Close Relationships—Revised (ECR-R) Questionnaire, by Fraley, Brennan, and Waller, can also be taken online. Go to www.YourPersonality.net. Follow the instructions and a profile of your attachment style will be provided for you.

Reprinted with permission of R. Chris Farley, Department of Psychology (MC285), University of Illinois, Chicago, IL.

OBSESSIVE RELATIONAL INTRUSION/STALKING CHECKLIST

Indicate whether your ex-partner has engaged in the following behaviors by circling "yes" or "no":

(1)	Spies on you	Y	N
(2)	Follows you	Y	N
(3)	Sends you notes	Y	N
(4)	Makes unwanted phone calls	Y	N
(5)	Leaves messages on your telephone	Y	N
(6)	Secretly records your conversations	Y	N
(7)	Sends gifts*	Y	N
(8)	Sends offensive photos	Y	N
(9)	Waits for you in car	Y	N
(10)	Leaves notes on your windshield	Y	N
(11)	Leaves notes at your home	Y	N
(12)	Stays outside your home, or drives by	Y	N
(13)	Stays outside your work, or drives by	Y	N
(14)	Waits around when you are talking with someone	Y	N
(15)	Shows up where you are	Y	N
(16)	Visits you at work	Y	N
(17)	Calls you at work	Y	N
(18)	Leaves items for you to find	Y	N
(19)	Communicates verbally against your will	Y	N
(20)	Damages your property	Y	N
(21)	Does unrequested favors*	Y	N
(22)	Contacts your family	Y	N
(23)	Asks others about you	Y	N
(24)	Knocks on your window	Y	N
(25)	Asks you out as friends*	Y	N
(26)	Asks you out on a date*	Y	N
(27)	Threatens to release harmful information about you	Y	N
(28)	Takes up an activity to be closer to you	Y	N
(29)	Manipulates you into dating	Y	N
(30)	Scares you	Y	N
(31)	Secretly takes your belongings	Y	N
(32)	Gives you unusual parcels	Y	N
(33)	Attempts to, or verbally abuses you	Y	N
(34)	Harasses you	Y	N
(35)	Breaks into your house or car	Y	N
(36)	Visits your home	Y	N
(37)	Threatens or attempts to hurt you	Y	N
(38)	Is physically violent to you	Y	N
(39)	Threatens emotional harm	Y	N
(40)	Threatens or attempts to harm someone you know	Y	N
(41)	Threatens to, or harms your pet	Y	N
(42)	Forces you to have sexual contact	Y	N
(43)	Takes photos of you	Y	N

(44)	Kidnaps you	Y	N
(45)	Uses profanity about you	Y	N
(46)	Argues with you in public places	Y	N
(47)	Spreads false rumors about you	Y	N
(48)	Claims to still be in relationship	Y	N
(49)	Violates restraining orders	Y	N
(50)	Will not take hints he/she is not welcome	Y	N
(51)	Tries to keep you away from the opposite sex	Y	N
(52)	Harms your new partner or his/her property	Y	N
(53)	Threatens to harm him/herself	Y	N
(54)	Tells others stories about you	Y	N
(55)	Constantly apologizes for past wrongs	Y	N
(56)	Exaggerates claims of affection for you	Y	N
(57)	Describes acts of sex to you	Y	N

*Indicates normal courtship behavior in most cases

The above checklist has been adapted from K. Davis & I. Frieze (2000), "Research on Stalking: What do We Know and Where Do We Go?" *Violence and Victims*, Vol. 15, No. 4. The checklist incorporates measures from the National Violence Against Women Survey, Cupach and Spitzberg's Obsessional Relational Intrusion Scale, Sinclair and Friezes's Courtship Persistence Inventory, Palarea and Langhinrichsen-Rohling's Pursuit Behavior Inventory, and measures by Coleman and Davis, et al. Reprinted with permission.

DANGER ASSESSMENT*
Jacquelyn C. Campbell, Ph.D, R.N., Copyright ©2003

Several risk factors have been associated with increased risk of homicides (murders) of women and men in violent relationships. We cannot predict what will happen in your case, but we would like you to be aware of the danger of homicide in situations of abuse and for you to see how many of the risk factors apply to your situation. Mark Yes or No for each of the following. ("He" refers to your husband, partner, ex-husband, ex-partner, or whoever is currently physically hurting you.)

_____ 1. Has the physical violence increased in severity or frequency over the past year?

_____ 2. Does he own a gun?

_____ 3. Have you left him after living together during the past year?

_____ 4. Is he unemployed?

_____ 5. Has he ever used a weapon against you or threatened you with a lethal weapon? (If yes, was the weapon a gun? _____)

_____ 6. Does he threaten to kill you?

_____ 7. Has he avoided being arrested for domestic violence?

_____ 8. Do you have a child that is not his?

_____ 9. Has he ever forced you into sex when you did not wish to do so?

_____ 10. Does he ever try to choke you?

_____ 11. Does he use drugs? By drugs I mean uppers or amphetamines, speed, angel dust, cocaine, crack, street drugs, heroin, or mixtures.

_____ 12. Is he an alcoholic or problem drinker?

_____ 13. Does he control most or all of your daily activities? For instance, does he tell you whom you can be friends with, how much money you can take with you shopping or when you can take the car? (If he tries, but you do not let him, check here _____)

_____ 14. Is he violently and constantly jealous of you? (For instance, does he say, "If I can't have you, no one can."?)

_____ 15. Have you ever been beaten by him while you were pregnant? (If never pregnant by him, check here _____)

_____ 16. Have you ever threatened or tried to commit suicide?

_____ 17. Has he ever threatened or tried to commit suicide?

_____ 18. Does he threaten to harm your children?

_____ 19. Do you believe he is capable of killing you?

_____ 20. Does he follow or spy on you, leave threatening notes or messages on your answering machine, destroy your property, or call you when you don't want him to?

*Reproduced with permission of Jacquelyn C. Campbell, Johns Hopkins University, School of Nursing, Baltimore, MD.

FAMILY BEHAVIORS

Children often do things that are wrong, disobey, or make their parents angry. We would like to know what you have done when your child did something wrong or made you upset or angry. This is a list of things that parents sometimes do and that you may have done in the past year. For each one, please indicate whether you have done it once in the past year, twice in the past year, 3–5 times, 6–10 times, 11–20 times, or more than 20 times in the past year. If you have not done it in the past year but have done it before that, then circle "7" as your answer. Please focus on only one child when giving your answers.

How often did this happen?

1 = Once in the past year
2 = Twice in the past year
3 = 3–5 times in the past year
4 = 6–10 times in the past year
5 = 11–20 times in the past year
6 = More than 20 times in the past year
7 = Not in the past year, but it did happen before
0 = None

Example Non-Violent Discipline Scale Item

2. You put your child in "time out"   1   2   3   4   5   6   7   0
   (or sent the child to his/her room)

Example Psychological Aggression Scale Items

6. You shouted, yelled, or screamed at your child

Example Minor Assault (Corporal Punishment) Scale Items

8. You spanked your child on the bottom with your bare hand

Example Severe Assault (Physical Maltreatment) Scale Items

20. You threw or knocked your child down

Example Very Severe Assault (Severe Physical Maltreatment) Scale Items

11. You beat your child up, (hit him or her over and over as hard as you could)

COLLATERAL INTERVIEW WITH CHILD

Note: Children should be interviewed when the standard interview process, outside documentation and collateral contact information fail to resolve the parents' conflicting accusations. Children should first be reassured that they have done nothing wrong, and that they are being asked merely to provide some information that will help the counselor resolve some problems that their parents are having.

Sometimes parents disagree. What happens when your parents don't get along, with each other or with the stepparents?

Do your parents or stepparents ever yell, or use bad words? Can you give me an example—something that happened recently (not too long ago)?

Does one parent/stepparent yell or swear more than the other(s), or do they do it about the same?

Does either of your parents, or stepparents, ever throw things, or grab or push or hit the other one? Tell me about something that happened recently (not too long ago).

Does one parent/stepparent throw things, or grab or push or hit more than the other(s), or do they do it about the same?

What's the worst fight your parents ever had? Tell me about that. Have there been times when one of your parents got really hurt because of something the other parent or stepparent, did?

Sometimes, parents get angry with their kids. What happens when your parents/stepparents get angry with you (are mad)? What about with your brothers and sisters?

If they say bad things, what kinds of things do they tell you?

Do your parents/stepparents ever spank you, or your brothers and sisters (hit you on the rear with an open hand)? When does that happen? Who usually gives you the spankings?

Besides spankings, do either of your parents or your stepparents hit you in other ways? Tell me about that.

Have there been times when you got hurt because of something one of your parents/ stepparents did to you? What was the worst thing that happened?

Are there other things your parents/stepparents do that you don't like, or that make you afraid?

SUBSTANCE ABUSE QUESTIONNAIRE

Substances Currently Used   Pattern of Use (how often, amount, circumstances)

Current symptoms—physical, psychological

Past Substance Abuse History

From _____ to _____   Substances Used   Pattern of Use

Previous mental health and substance abuse treatment

Arrest record/DUIs

Substance abuse in family of origin

Periods of abstinence—good or bad, reasons for relapse

Tolerance factor—increase over time?

Control factor

AGGRESSIVE BEHAVIOR/SUBSTANCE ABUSE LOG

On the chart below, indicate the name of the substance used (including alcohol), each time you had an aggressive episode (verbal or physical), and check the stage of using you were in at the time.*

day/ date of aggr.	drug used	immediate use	intoxication	immediate withdrawal	next-day withdrawal	procurement

*This chart has been adapted from R. Potter-Efron & P. Potter-Efron (1991), *Anger, Alcoholism and Addiction.*

Appendix B

Victim Safety Plan

PRECAUTIONS

1. Make sure you understand your partner's use of violence. Recognize situations when he/she is becoming increasingly agitated, and be aware of how the violence escalates over time. It is crucial to quickly determine when your partner is becoming dangerous, and when you are at risk for being harmed.
2. Prearrange a safe place to stay—with a trusted friend or family member. While your partner is out, remove any weapons that may be in the house. If you don't feel comfortable removing weapons, call the police and ask them to assist you. Then make your escape to the safe place and stay there. If you have children, bring them with you.
3. Train the eldest and most responsible child to be aware of your partner's cycle of violence, and how to call the police in an emergency. Also see to it that the same safe place, or an alternative, is available for your children. Make sure they understand the importance of secrecy. Very young children can inadvertently reveal private information.
4. Inform anyone about your situation whom your partner might contact. Ask the people who are providing the safe place not to disclose your location. Alert your employer about the situation and ask that he/she not speak to your partner without your permission.
5. Inform children not to disclose your safe place to anyone.

What to Do During a Violent Incident

1. Escape from the abuse at the earliest opportunity.
2. Take a survival kit with you. A survival kit includes items you will need after leaving. These should be kept in an easily accessible location, such as the trunk of your car, or somewhere close at hand. You may have more than one kit in several locations. Your kit should include the following

Money: If you don't have time to bring a checkbook and credit card with you, it is important to put aside enough cash to pay for lodging and food for a few days. You will need cash even if you have a credit card, because your partner could cancel your credit card. Cash may be necessary if you do not have a cell phone and need to use a pay phone.

Clothing: The kit should include a small, portable bag with enough clothes for you and your children, including warm clothes in case of cold weather.

Keys: You should have an extra set of keys to your vehicles, your house, or anything else you will need access to (e.g., place of business).

Important phone numbers:

- Police (911)
- Local shelter
- County victim/witness programs
- County social services
- County probation
- Legal assistance
- Your therapist, and the phone number of your partner's therapist
- Any friends or family members who can help you

Vital Documents: Your kit should contain necessary documents. If you are unable to secure the originals in advance, then have copies available, or a plan on how to retrieve the originals when you need them. Important documents to have include:

- Driver's license (for both you and your partner, or copies)
- Bank account numbers and paperwork
- Social security numbers for you, your partner, and your children
- Birth certificates for you, your partner, and your children
- Recent pay stubs for you and your partner
- Mortgage papers and other documents for jointly owned properties
- Marriage license
- Various insurance policies

3. After securing your physical safety, if time allows, secure valuables, such as jewelry, and anything else that may be of importance to you.

Appendix C

Client Workbook Introduction, Group Guidelines, and Exercises

Introduction

You have completed the assessment phase of the anger and conflict management/ domestic violence treatment program. The next phase consists of regular group meetings for a period of 26 to 52 weeks. Laws in each state vary (California law requires anyone convicted of spousal abuse to complete 52 weeks). During this period you will learn how to manage interpersonal relationships better, with an emphasis on conflict resolution, anger management, and the elimination of violent, controlling, and abusive behaviors. How well this program works for you, and how well your relationship improves, will depend largely on three factors: *effort, consistency, and setting priorities.* You will be asked to change behaviors that have been established over a lifetime, behaviors deeply ingrained in your personality. They won't go away overnight. But you'll make steady progress if you attend each meeting, participate in the program, and apply what you learn. Progress may be slow, but it will last.

The *number one priority* is taking responsibility for your behavior, including verbal and emotional abuse, controlling behaviors, and physical assaults upon others. Controlling your behavior starts by managing your anger. When you are in a conflict with another person, *you must first control your anger* to have any chance of resolving the problem. Resolving conflict depends on clear, respectful communication, which is impossible when one person is very angry.

Make an effort to resolve those problems that you can. Don't worry about resolving all conflicts right away, especially the difficult ones, until you have learned healthy communication and conflict resolution skills. *By managing your anger, you'll gain confidence and feel more in control.* Increased confidence will promote even more changes, generate goodwill, and reestablish trust with your partner. For now, concentrate on two things: *awareness and acceptance.* You can't control what you aren't aware of, so don't ignore or stuff your anger. Before you know it, the conflict has escalated, and the damage has been done. Begin by identifying your anger at lower levels, before it becomes too intense and escalates into emotional or physical abuse. You can do this by taking your *anger temperature*, rating anger intensity on a scale of 1 to 10.

10 9 8	High anger (rage)	You have lost the ability to think rationally, and have lost control of your anger. Example: During the argument, you find out that your partner had an affair (or you suspect an affair, even though it may never have happened). You start throwing things (or punch a hole in the wall), verbally threaten your partner and maybe physically assault him/her.
7 6 5	Medium anger	Your anger has begun to affect your thinking. You are focused more on your own needs, doing a poor job of listening to the other person, and find it difficult to express yourself clearly and calmly. Example: The two of you argue, raising voices. You accuse one another of being selfish and insensitive.
4 3 2	Low anger (frustration or irritation)	Something or someone is bothering you, but your thinking and communication skills have not yet been seriously affected. Example: Your spouse is late coming home from work and hasn't called.
1	No anger	

Frustration is anger at a lower level. Don't discount it. After a hectic day at work, a sarcastic remark may be all that it takes for your anger to jump from a 4 to a 6, or even higher. Acknowledging that you are frustrated can help you anticipate what will likely provoke you in order to better respond to the situation. Practice *identifying* your anger by randomly taking your anger temperature during the day—at work, in traffic, at home, even when you seem to be feeling fine.

Like all emotions, anger serves several important functions. Anger lets us know that others may be mistreating or taking advantage of us. Without at least mild anger we would not stand up for ourselves. Properly expressed, anger can communicate to others our limits and boundaries. Think of anger as a smoke alarm. When a smoke alarm goes off it is loud and obnoxious and never tells us if there is a fire, how large the fire might be, or how to put the fire out. The alarm is only a warning.

Accepting anger as a normal human emotion is equally important. Fear of the intense energy behind anger tends to cause many individuals to either ignore and stuff it, or to let it out in an uncontrolled, aggressive manner, hoping to relieve themselves of the tension. People associate anger with aggression, and fear they will react aggressively if they let themselves acknowledge their anger. But refusing to acknowledge anger is to ignore reality. Stuffing keeps individuals from addressing situations they are angry about, and may lead to stress-related physical problems, such as ulcers or hypertension. And letting it out aggressively, while sometimes providing tension relief, creates more problems and, ultimately, more tension. Although you'll learn how to lessen the frequency and intensity of your anger, you will experience anger long after you complete our program. There will always be occasions when no matter what you do, your anger will remain. Don't panic. Anger is uncomfortable and unpleasant, but you will never explode as a result of feeling this emotion. If you do absolutely nothing, the anger will eventually go away.

Accepting and controlling anger is more difficult when the other person is mean, unreasonable, or unfair. However, we have little or no control over other people, whereas we have a lot more control over ourselves, especially our behavior. The following box illustrates this point, with one's potential level of control arranged from most to least:

MOST	your behavior
	your thoughts, feelings, wants, etc.
	other people's behavior
LEAST	other people's thoughts, feelings, wants, etc.

Until you learn how to alter your thinking and defuse your anger at those who may provoke you, concentrate on altering your behavior. This includes keeping your lips pressed together to avoid saying something you will regret later, offering an apology when you are responsible for the conflict, or taking a *time out* by walking away from the situation.

Take a time out whenever your anger temperature is at 5 or above, or you sense that the argument is getting out of control. If you're becoming increasingly tense, unable to really listen to the other person, then remove yourself from the situation. Let the other person know where you are going and for how long. Don't blame or take "parting shots" as you leave. Go to another room, to the bathroom, walk around the block, or go see a friend. Do not go to a bar or use mind-altering substances. If your temperature is in the "rage" range of the anger scale, avoid driving. Leave your location and walk. Walk for at least a half hour, until your anger level has dropped. *If you have been physically aggressive in the past, don't return until you are sure your anger is under control.* Stay with a relative or friend or go to a hotel. Stay the night, a week, or as long as you need.

Taking a time out is *not* giving in. It is taking control over a volatile situation the best way you can, by altering your behavior. Remember: your priority is to gain greater control over your anger and to refrain from reacting aggressively. The better you do this, the more quickly and comfortably you'll be able to discuss and resolve the most controversial and volatile issues.

If you follow the program to the best of your ability, good things will happen. Change will be slow at first, and hard-earned, but it will be real—the kind of change that lasts a lifetime. You will sometimes resist this change. Right now, your aggressive/ dysfunctional behaviors feel normal or right to you, but this is only because they are so deeply ingrained, and are literally part of your brain physiology. Although you cannot completely unlearn old, dysfunctional behaviors, you can, by practicing new and more appropriate behaviors, build alternative neural connections in your brain. As these alternative connections replace the old ones, the new behaviors you have been practicing will begin to feel more normal.

USING THE WORKBOOK

Completing the workbook as requested will help you gain greater awareness and control of your behavior. It is divided into three sections. The first part includes guidelines for group participation, a copy of the batterer program agreement, a sample progress/termination report, and definitions of dirty fighting and controlling/emotionally abusive behaviors. Read this section carefully, and then go on to the second section, containing the log sheets. Each page in the log section represents a month. Keeping track of these behaviors will make it easier for you to overcome and replace them with more appropriate, healthier, more effective behaviors. It is recommended that you fill out the log on a weekly basis. The third section contains all of the worksheets and handouts used during the program. *Bring your workbook to group each week.* You will refer to your progress log during the check-in portion of the meeting. In addition, you will need the workbook to complete the readings and assignments that will be assigned.

DEFINITIONS OF DIRTY FIGHTING* AND CONTROLLING BEHAVIORS

Dirty Fighting

The underlying motive when using these behaviors is to win the argument at all costs. The purpose is to make the other person feel too confused, overwhelmed, guilty, or worn out to effectively make his/her case, so that in your mind you have "won."

1. Timing—Insisting on talking when your partner is tired or busy (e.g., late at night)
2. Brown-bagging—Bombarding the other person with all the complaints you have been wanting to talk about, all at once, including many from the distant past
3. Overgeneralizing—(e.g., "You're always late." "I can never count on you.")
4. Cross-complaints—Instead of answering the question or taking responsibility for your actions, you complain about something your partner did.
5. Blaming
6. Pulling rank—You use your authority to get your way, instead of presenting facts (e.g., "I'm the mother, that's why!" or "I'm the man of the house")
7. Not listening/Talking over the other person
8. Listing injustices—You name all of the bad things your partner has done to you, with an emphasis on how you have been wronged, and how it isn't "fair"
9. Mind-reading—You tell the other person what he/she thinks, feels, or wants
10. Fortune-telling—(e.g., "You'll never change.")
11. Being sarcastic
12. Rejecting compromise
13. Playing martyr—Intentionally mentioning things with the intent of causing another person to feel guilty, or beholden. (e.g., "I'm nothing but a slave in this house.")
14. Giving advice—The other person doesn't want advice, but you give it anyway.

---

*This list has been adapted from *Spouse Abuse: A Treatment Program for Couples*, by Neidig & Friedman (1984).

15. Terminal language—You imply/state that if you don't get your way, you'll leave your partner.
16. Lecturing

Emotionally Abusive and Controlling Behaviors

The intent behind these behaviors is not only to win the argument, but to dominate and/or to emotionally hurt the other.

1. Threats and intimidation—Verbally threaten to hurt partner, or intimidate with gestures (e.g., staring). Harm pets. Threaten to harm someone partner cares about.
2. Isolation and jealousy—Attempt to control who partner spends time with. Restrict partner's movements, keep him/her from leaving (e.g., by standing in front of the door). Withhold car keys, disable the vehicle. Accuse partner

of being unfaithful or of flirting with others. Check up on partner, interrogate about where he/she has been.

3. Economic abuse—Control the money, exclude partner from financial decisions. Or spend money excessively, refuse to work or contribute financially. Threaten to have partner fired. Lie about expenses to get more child support.

4. Diminishment of self-esteem—Call partner unattractive, call him/her names (e.g., "bitch," "loser"), make fun of partner's sexual performance. Threaten to have an affair. Humiliate partner in front of others, pressure him/her to do things against his/her values. Ridicule, treat partner like he/she is stupid, or say he/she is incompetent and helpless. Tell partner that what he/she wants or cares about is unimportant. Spread false rumors about partner, or try to convince others that partner is crazy. Blame partner for problems in relationship.

5. General control—Order partner around, expect him/her to "hop to it." Nag, refuse to take "no" for an answer. Follow partner around, criticizing every move. Insist on talking late at night, keeping partner awake.

6. Obsessive relational intrusion—Call or go to partner's place of employment to harass him/her. Follow partner around. Page constantly, or leave numerous unwanted messages on partner's voice mail.

7. Passive-aggressiveness and withdrawal—Threaten to harm yourself to get attention. Deliberately ignore partner, or withhold affection or sex as punishment. Lock partner out of bedroom when angry. Refuse to cooperate. Act in a passive-aggressive manner (e.g., "forgetting" to pay a bill or to convey some important information).

8. Using children—Tell the children negative things about partner, or use them as spies. Exclude partner from child-rearing, or join with children against him/her. Threaten to take the children or keep them from partner. Refuse to allow the children to see their grandparents on the partner's side.

9. Legal system abuse—File false or exaggerated domestic violence charges or false child abuse charges. Threaten to have partner deported, or reported to welfare.

10. Sexual coercion—Pressure partner to have sex when he/she doesn't want to, or to engage in unwanted sexual practices. Physically force sex (rape).

CLIENT PROGRESS LOG

Month _____ Year _____ Complete on a weekly basis:

A. At the end of each week, enter the number of times you engaged in the behaviors listed below; then enter the total at the end of the month.

name(s)	name(s)
Week #: 1 2 3 4 Total	Week #: 1 2 3 4 Total

days contact

conflicts

Discuss w/o aggression

Aggression
Yell, shout
Swear at, put down
Threaten to hurt
Throw, hit things
Grab, push
Slap
Punch, kick
Bite/choke/pull hair
Other

Dirty Fighting
1. Timing
2. Brown bagging
3. Overgeneralizing
4. Cross-complaints
5. Blaming
6. Pulling rank
7. Not listening

8. Listing injustices
9. Mind-reading
10. Fortune-telling
11. Being sarcastic
12. Rejecting compromise
13. Playing the martyr
14. Giving advice
15. Using terminal language
16. Lecturing

Abusive/control tactics
Threats and intimidation
Isolation and jealousy
Economic abuse
Diminish self-esteem
General control
Obsessive relational
   intrusion
Passive-aggressiveness/
   withdrawal
Using children
Legal system abuse
Sexual coercion

B. What I need to work on:

C. Record times when you got aggressive/angry in the past month. Include situations outside home.

Date   Situation

Anger temp. (1–10)   Other emotions

Thoughts

What I did wrong/right

Date   Situation

Anger temp. (1–10)   Other emotions

Thoughts

What I did wrong/right

Date   Situation

Anger temp. (1–10)   Other emotions

Thoughts

What I did wrong/right

Date   Situation

Anger temp. (1–10)   Other emotions

Thoughts

What I did wrong/right

D. Think of the situations in which you were angry and acted aggressively or engaged in dirty fighting/controlling behaviors. Keeping in mind that one function of anger is to alert you to the possibility that some of your needs are being threatened, answer the following questions:

1. What need(s) seemed to be threatened—BASIC (food, water, etc.), SELF-ESTEEM/PRIDE, or LOVE/BELONGING?

2. If my needs weren't actually threatened, what were my unrealistic expectations?

3. How could I have responded to my anger differently, to better take care of myself?

GROUP GUIDELINES FOR CLIENTS*

1. Come to every session, unless you are sick or on vacation, and attend each session on time. The effectiveness of the program depends on your consistent attendance.
2. Come to each meeting alert, free of chemical influence, and ready to participate.
3. Listen attentively to the group leader and to your fellow participants.
4. Share, as much as possible, about how you are doing.
5. Speak with respect, both to the other group members and when referring to people outside the meeting. Referring to your partner, or others, in demeaning terms (e.g., "bitch," "asshole") is unnecessary and destructive. Using demeaning language only reinforces old, dysfunctional behavior, and will hinder your progress.
6. Some limited griping about your partner and others in your life is permissible, but you are encouraged to focus on *your* behavior, and what *you* can do to make things better.
7. When someone brings up a problem, avoid advice-giving unless specifically requested to do so. Instead, share any experiences you had with the problem in question.
8. Show positive support of your fellow group members. This means being empathetic and concerned when they are having a hard time, and praising them when they are making positive changes in their lives. Refrain, however, from supporting abusive, illegal, or antisocial behavior. The group works best when each person holds him/herself and everyone else accountable for their actions.
9. Everyone is allowed to share, for purposes of identification, the circumstances under which they were referred to the group. If you are court ordered, you may briefly inform the group of major new developments in your case, such as having a restraining order lifted or instituted. However, extended complaints about "the system" are not allowed. This includes how unfair the judge was, your attorney fees, why your partner wasn't arrested, and so on. You are in the group to learn how to overcome anger and violence and improve your relationships. Legal complaints should be discussed with an attorney. If you are unhappy with public policy or laws regarding domestic violence, write to your local congressperson or state representative.
10. Honor the confidentiality of other members. If you want to tell someone outside the group about your group experiences, focus on the curriculum, the facilitator, and your own participation. Do not, under any circumstances, disclose anyone's name or identity.
11. Complete your progress log and all in-class and homework assignments as requested. This will help you get more out of the program, and will accelerate your progress.

---

*A sample batterer treatment program agreement for court-ordered clients can be found in appendix D, pp. 258–260.

CLIENT WORKBOOK EXERCISES

Complete Set for 52-Week Program

MEETINGS #3 & 29: ANGER—GOOD AND BAD

#3: Misuses of Anger

A.   Anger can be a negative or a positive emotion, depending on what you do with it. Because it is such a strong emotion, it can easily be misused. For each of the misuses listed below, please give one or two recent examples from your own life.

1.   Intimidate:

2.   Control:

3.   Punish:

4.   Protect self from hurt:

5.   Feel morally superior:

6.   Maintain a connection with partner:

7.   Get a rush, or "high":

B.   Now go back to each misuse of anger, and ask yourself:

1.   Did my aggression work in the short run? Do people comply out of respect—or fear?

2.   Did my aggression work in the long run? Did my aggression have negative consequences, such as hurt feelings and resentments in the other person, or guilt and shame in myself?

MEETINGS #6 & 32: STRESS BASICS

#6: Identifying Stress

A. *Symptoms of Stress:* Please circle the symptoms you have experienced in the past 6 months. Which of these are signs of depression? Anxiety? Anger?

Physical
rapid heart rate
tight neck, back or chest
headaches
difficulty breathing
sweaty palms
diarrhea, frequent urination
nausea, vomiting
constant fatigue
tendency to get sick

Behavioral
poor appetite
sleep problems
increase in smoking, drinking
poor concentration
restlessness
crying spells
decreased involvement with other people
declining performance at work or school

Psychological
depression, inability to experience joy
feelings of worthlessness
jealousy, suspiciousness
anxiousness
lack of initiative
tendency to blame others
negative attitude
self-critical
forgetfulness
lack of concentration, poor attention to details
preoccupation with the past
boredom
decreased creativity
decreased sexual interest
anger outbursts, or constant irritability

B. *External Sources of Stress*—LCU = Life Change Units, or degree of adjustment required by each event. Please circle the ones you have experienced in the past 6 months, and then separate those into two categories: those you have little control over and those you do have control over. If you are not already trying to resolve those you can, make a commitment to do so.

Event	LCU	Event	LCU
Family		Major change in recreation	19
Death of a spouse	100	Major change in church activities	19
Divorce	73	Major change in sleeping habits	16
Marital separation	65	Major change in eating habits	15
Death of a close family member	63	Vacation	13
Marriage	50	Christmas	12
Marital reconciliation	45	Minor violations of the law	11
Major change in health of family	44	*Work*	
Pregnancy	40	Being fired from work	47
Addition of new family member	39	Retirement from work	45
Major change in arguments		Major business adjustment	39
with spouse	35	Changing to different line of work	36
Son or daughter leaving home	29	Major change in work	
In-law troubles	29	responsibilities	29
Wife starting or ending work	26	Trouble with the boss	23
Major change in family		Major change in working	
get-togethers	16	conditions	20
Personal		*Financial*	
Detention in jail	63	Major change in financial state	38
Major personal injury or illness	53	Mortgage or loan over $10,000*	31
Sexual difficulties	39	Mortgage foreclosure	30
Death of a close friend	37	Mortgage or loan less than	
Outstanding personal achievement	28	$10,000*	17
Start or end of formal schooling	26		
Major change in living conditions	25		
Major revision of personal habits	24		
Changing to a new school	20		
Change in residence	20		

*Dollar amounts considerably higher today, due to inflation.

Source: T. H. Holmes & R. H. Rahe (1967). "The Social Readjustment Rating Scale." *Journal of Personal and Social Psychology, 21,* pp. 296–301.

MEETINGS #7, 8, 33 & 34: MANAGING STRESS

#7: Grounding Meditation

A.   Procedure:

Close your eyes and sit still and quietly in your chair. There is nothing more that you have to do, other than to be aware of the experience.

(Participants sit quietly for a period of 3–5 minutes. The group leader then asks participants to open their eyes again.)

B.   Questions for discussion:

1.   How did you experience this meditation? What were you aware of externally? Sounds, temperature in the room, feeling of your body against the chair or couch?

2.   What were you aware of internally? Current thoughts, memories, speculation about the future? Feelings . . . bored, excited, annoyed, happy?

3.   If we were to do this exercise again later this weekend, in a different location (e.g., shopping mall, your house), do you think you would have the same thoughts, feelings and an awareness of the same external environment?

C.   The goal: improve capacity for self-observation and detachment

There is no right or wrong way to do this meditation. The purpose of the exercise is to help you get grounded, so that you can develop a capacity for self-observation and detachment, essential qualities for managing anger and coping with stress.

Remember: Thoughts and feelings, even sensations of the outside environment, are always changing, sometimes from second to second. The part of you that is aware of thoughts, feelings and sensations, which psychologists call the *self* or *observing ego*, changes very little and very gradually over time. When you say, "I" feel good, bad, tired, the "I" is the self or observing ego. The "I" is the core of who you are, and it is basically whole, pure and good.

D.   Homework:

Next time you feel overwhelmed by stress or life events, when you are confused, unsure, about to blow up with anger, etc., REMEMBER THAT THIS TEMPORARY EXPERIENCE DOES NOT DEFINE YOU! DON'T LET FLEETING EMOTIONS AND THOUGHTS CAUSE YOU TO ACT AGAINST YOUR OWN BEST INTEREST!

MEETINGS #7, 8, 33 & 34: MANAGING STRESS

#8: Progressive Relaxation (long version)

Introduction

The following relaxation exercise, developed by Edmond Jacobsen in the 1920s, has been the most widely used relaxation technique over several decades. It is based on the premise that our body responds to anxiety and anger-provoking thoughts and events with muscle tension. The physical tension then increases our subjective experience of anxiety and anger. But deep muscle relaxation lessens physical tension and is incompatible with anxiety and anger.

The Exercise

You can do this exercise either lying down or sitting. The chair should be comfortable, and tall enough to support your head. During the following procedure, you will be identifying areas of the body where tension tends to be located. At each location, you will be asked to tense, then relax, the particular muscle or muscle group. This may seem odd at first; however, it is necessary to locate tensions outside of conscious awareness. Once you have identified the muscle groups, and have practiced the exercise several times, you may be able to skip directly to the relaxation part. The entire exercise takes about 15–20 minutes.

Clench your left fist for about five seconds. As you do so, pay attention to the tension. You will also experience tension in your hand and forearm. Now relax your left hand for about 15–20 seconds, as loose as possible. Notice how different this feels, compared to when it was tense. Repeat the procedure with your right fist, then both fists at once.

Turn your attention to your elbows. Bend them, tensing your biceps, as hard as possible without hurting yourself. Afterwards, straighten out your arms. As you do so compare the relaxation with the tension you experienced previously. You may want to repeat this procedure, and all the subsequent ones, a second time. In each procedure, the tension phase should last about 5 seconds, and the relaxation phase about 20 seconds.

Frown. Notice the tension throughout your forehead. After five seconds, let your brow become smooth again. Now wrinkle your forehead, hold the tension, and relax. Smooth out your forehead and your scalp. Now close your eyes and squint, tighter and tighter. Can you feel the tension? After five seconds, relax, letting your eyes stay peacefully closed. Then clench you jaw. Clench it tightly, without hurting your teeth. Relax your jaw, allowing your lips to be parted somewhat. There should be a noticeable contrast between this feeling and the prior experience of tension. Shape your lips into the form of an "O," so that your lips are tight, and maintain this position for five seconds. Now relax your lips. Push your tongue against the roof of your mouth. Hold it, even if it hurts a bit, then relax.

The next step is to tilt your head back as far as it can. Roll it to the left. As you do so, pay attention to change in tension, from one part of your neck to the other. Roll your head to the right. Afterwards, let it relax. Relax, and really appreciate that difference. Now look down, and press your chin against your chest. As you hold this position for five seconds, feel the tension in the back of your neck and in your throat. Lift your head back to its normal position and relax. Let go of all the tension, allowing the relaxation to deepen. After 20 seconds, hunch your head tightly down between your shoulders, in an exaggerated shrug. Hold it, then relax. Can you feel that tension disappear? Repeat the procedure if you need to.

Draw a deep breath, letting your lungs fill with air. As you hold your breath, you should notice the tension in your chest. Hold your breath for 15–20 seconds, then exhale. Relax, allowing your chest to become loose. Breathe easily and freely. Repeat this procedure a few times. Each time you exhale, imagine all your tension and stress flowing out from your body. Now tighten your stomach. Focus on the tension as you do so. Hold it for 20 seconds, then relax. Let the relaxation deepen. Arch your back, without straining. Pay attention to the tension in your lower back, while you keep the rest of your body as relaxed as possible.

Now tighten your buttocks. Press your heels down on the floor, and feel the tension in your thighs. Relax your feet. Wait 20 seconds, then tighten your calves by curling your toes downward. Notice the tension as your toes dig into the soles of your feet, or into the carpet. Relax. Afterwards, point your toes upwards and feel the tension in your shins. Relax your toes.

Your entire lower body should be relaxed and at rest—toes, feet, ankles, calves, shins, thighs, knees and buttocks. Allow the relaxation to spread upwards to the rest of your body, starting with your lower stomach, lower back and chest. Let all the tension out, every last trace of it. Notice the looseness in your shoulders, arms and hands. Feel the relaxation deepening in your neck and in your jaw, and throughout all your facial muscles.

Suggestions

- Your initial success may be limited. Practice the exercise a couple of times a day for several days, and you'll soon experience the full benefits.
- Be careful when tensing your back and neck. Overdoing this may lead to muscle damage, or even spinal damage. And biting down too hard may damage your teeth.
- Once you have remembered the steps (listening to an audiotape of the procedure is helpful), you can do the procedure from memory. Do it every day if you can, or at least several times a week.
- This exercise should be practiced regularly, to help you manage general stress. But you can also use it whenever you are experiencing acute stress, or a situation in which you are experiencing a lot of anger. When you have mastered this procedure, you'll find it easier to relax on the spot. For instance, when you give yourself a 5-minute time out at home, or during your break at work, you can quickly scan your body for tension and will your body to relax.

Source: M. Davis et al. (1988), *The Relaxation & Stress Reduction Workbook* (3rd edition, pp. 22–23).

MEETINGS #10, 35 & 36: OVERCOMING IRRATIONAL THOUGHTS AND BELIEFS

#10: Self-Coaching

A. Events don't cause emotions—your thoughts about events, your attitudes, cause those emotions. Having more control over your emotions requires that you be able to identify and challenge your negative, distorted thinking, and replace it with clear, reality-based thinking.

Negative, distorted thinking	Emotional consequence	Reality-based thinking
Mind-reading		
"she's trying to mess with me"	anger	"how do I know?"
"he doesn't really love me"	depression	"I can't read minds"
		"better check it out first"
Labeling		
"jerk," "bitch," "lazy," etc.	anger	"everyone has a good side"
		"better focus on his/her behavior—what is it I don't like?"
Futurizing		
"she/he is never going to change"	anger, anxiety, depression	"I don't have a crystal ball"
"I'll never get another job"	anxiety, depression	"better focus on right now"
Magnification		
"this is horrible, terrible"	anxiety, depression, anger	"how horrible is this, compared to losing someone I love, or if I were badly injured?"
"the weekend's ruined"		
"my life's a joke"		
Absolutes		
(rigid, unrealistic expectations)		"she can do what she wants, but I don't have to like it"
"she/he can't talk to me like that"	anger	"I don't have to accept this. I can choose to change this."
"this has to change"	anxiety, anger	

B. Useful self-talk: "First things first," "Feelings are not facts," "This, too will pass," "My thoughts cause my feelings," "Take action and the feeling will follow."

C. Rules for Rational Thinking*
    1. It doesn't do anything to me. (Your thoughts, not events, cause your feelings and reactions. No one "makes" you angry or violent.)

---

*Source: D. Goodman (1974), *Emotional Well-Being Through Rational Behavior Training.*

2. Everything is exactly as it should be. (That is, everything may not be the way you would like it to be, but all events occur for a reason, and are the consequence of prior events. To expect things to be different is irrational, because it ignores causality. Focus on controlling your behavior *now*.)

3. All humans are fallible (imperfect) creatures

4. It takes two to have a conflict

5. The original cause is lost in antiquity. (Avoid needless arguments with your partner trying to determine with certainty who caused the problem. In relationships, causes are complex and circular, not linear. Blaming solves nothing. Instead, decide whether or not you approve of your partner's behavior and act to take care of your best interests.)

6. We feel the way we think

MEETINGS #11 & 37: IDENTIFYING VULNERABLE FEELINGS

#11: Identifying Feeling in Oneself

Situation	Feeling(s)
Your daughter says that she'll be working at K-Mart after graduation, instead of going to college, as you had hoped.	
While dining in a 4-star restaurant, your partner tells you, in a voice loud enough so that the people at the next table can overhear, that you are "slurping your soup like a pig."	
Your 13-year-old son finally comes home at 1:30 a.m., two hours past his curfew.	
Although you are next in line for a promotion, the boss gives the job to his son-in-law.	
Your partner says he/she wants his/her "own space," and hasn't returned your phone calls in three weeks.	
Your partner is glad to be with you one day, but irritable and distant the next, and won't talk about it. Then he/she announces he/she has an appointment with a therapist.	
Once again, you miss a concert when your boss announces that he wants you to finish a project. Your boss keeps repeating how much he *needs* you, but you're on salary, without overtime pay.	
At a party, you and your partner are talking politics with friends. You chime in with your opinion, but your partner cuts you off so another person can speak.	
While you are fixing dinner, your children are fighting at the table. The phone rings, and there is a knock at the door.	
For the third time this week, your ex calls you wanting to know what you did with your son's raincoat. You have already explained that it was stolen at school.	
Your partner is hurt because you yelled at him/her, even though you had promised not to do that again.	

Vulnerable Feelings: afraid, ashamed, betrayed, confused, disappointed, disrespected, embarrassed, guilty, harassed, helpless, hurt, ignored, inadequate, jealous, lonely, overwhelmed, sad, taken advantage of, unimportant, used, worried.

MEETINGS #12 & 38: ANGER MANAGEMENT FLOW CHART

Experience anger arousal

↓

Acknowledge anger

↓

Determine anger level

Anger level: 1–4	*Anger level: 5–7*	*Anger level: 8–10*
No anger, or mild frustration or irritation, but able to think clearly, to express yourself appropriately, and to listen. Feeling in control.	Moderate anger affecting your ability to think clearly, to express yourself appropriately, and to listen attentively. Feeling like you might possibly lose control.	High anger/rage. Thinking is confused, dominated by negative, aggressive thoughts. Completely unable to properly express yourself. Not wanting to listen, but instead wanting to vent or do harm. Feeling very out of control.
Action: go on to next step.	Action: reduce anger through "self coaching," breathing, relaxing body (e.g., sitting down, leaning back, loosening hands), or take a short, creative time out (get drink of water, change rooms, etc.).	Action: immediately take a full time out by leaving the house or situation completely, and not returning for at least an hour.

↓

Ask yourself: "What else might I be feeling?" (e.g., hurt, overwhelmed, disrespected, embarrassed, etc.)

↓

Ask yourself: "Is this person intentionally trying to harm me, or violate my rights?" (to determine if anger is justified)

↓

If the answer is "no," ask yourself: "What am I telling myself about this situation?" (to identify distorted "self-talk")	If the answer is "yes," ask yourself:"Is my anger helping me in this situation?" (to determine if anger is helpful or useless)

↓

If answer is "yes," continue to direct anger in a productive way.

If answer is "no," try a different approach, or let go of the anger.

MEETINGS #13 & 39: SOCIALIZATION OF VIOLENCE

#13: Relationship Power, Gender Roles and Aggression

A. Relationship Power

Researchers at the Family Violence Laboratory examined the relationship between marital power, conflict and violence.* Power was measured according to who had the final say in decisions regarding: buying a car, having children, what residence to live in, what job either partner should accept, whether a partner should go to work or quit work, and how much money to spend each week on food. The table below shows how power and conflict are related:

Marital Power Type	Number	Level of Marital Conflict %		
		Low	Medium	High
Male dominant	200	25.0	36.0	39.0
Female dominant	160	23.8	43.1	33.1
Divided power	1146	20.5	45.7	33.8
Equalitarian	616	32.5	47.1	20.5

The survey also found:

*   The lowest conflict existed among equalitarian couples, and the highest in male-dominant relationships.
*   Few male-dominated households had a consensus about that arrangement, but those that did had significantly less conflict.
*   Twenty-six percent of the high-conflict couples were physically violent.
*   When conflict is high, rates of violence increase substantially, with the greatest increase in female-dominated households, the second highest in the male-dominated relationships.
*   The authors conclude: When conflict occurs in an asymmetrical power structure (the male-dominant and female-dominant types) there is a much greater risk of violence than when the conflict occurs among the equalitarian couples. Equalitarian relationships appear to tolerate more conflict before violence erupts than other power structures do. Consensus reduces conflict, and when conflict does arise it is associated with a much higher risk of violence in asymmetrical structures than when similar conflict occurs in equalitarian families.

B. Gender Roles

Individuals who dominate decision-making at home often do so because of gender roles they have adopted. Please answer the following questions about the decision-making process in your home.

---

*Source: D. Coleman & M. Straus. (1990). "Marital Power, Conflict and Violence in a Nationally Representative Sample of American Couples." In: M. Straus & R. Gelles (eds.), *Physical Violence in American Families.*

Would you characterize your relationship as equalitarian, male-dominant, fe-male-dominant, or divided power? Who makes the important decisions in your home?

(MEN) Do you see yourself as the "man of the house"? Do you refuse to do household chores because it's "women's work"? Do you expect sex or having your dinner prepared each night because it is your *right* as a man?

(WOMEN) Do you think of the home as your domain, or that being a woman or mother gives you certain privileges? When you ask your husband to help with household tasks, do you supervise him, and re-do those tasks so they are done properly?

Where did you pick up these attitudes?

Does your partner go along with you? Willingly, or unwillingly? Describe some of the conflicts you have had as a result.

Do you use your attitudes/beliefs to justify abusive behavior toward your partner?

MEETINGS #14 & 40: CONTROLLING AND ABUSIVE TACTICS

#14: Consequences of Abuse

A.   Take a look at the list of abusive/controlling behaviors in part A of your log sheet, also represented in the "Intimate Partner Relationship Abuse and Control Wheel," depicted in the introduction to your workbook. Which of these have you engaged in the most since you have joined the program? Which ones were you using prior to having joined the program?

   Behaviors I have used recently   Behaviors I have used in the past

   _____   _____
   _____   _____
   _____   _____
   _____   _____
   _____   _____
   _____   _____

B.   Pick three of these behaviors. Then imagine how your partner felt when you acted that way, Using the list below (from session #11).

   afraid   disrespected   helpless   jealous   taken advan-
   ashamed   embarrassed   hurt   lonely   tage of
   betrayed   guilty   ignored   overwhelmed   unimportant
   confused   harassed   inadequate   sad   used
   disappointed   worried

             My behavior   Partner probably felt

   _____   _____
   _____   _____
   _____   _____

C.   Which of these behaviors have been done to you? Think about either current or past intimate partner relationships, as well as your family of origin. List the behaviors, who did them to you, and how you felt as a result:

   Abusive/controlling   Who did it to me   How I felt at the time
   behavior

   _____   _____   _____
   _____   _____   _____
   _____   _____   _____
   _____   _____   _____
   _____   _____   _____

   Were the abusive and controlling behaviors that were done to you the same as, or different from, those that you engaged in yourself?

D.   What usually happens after you engage in these behaviors? Please check off the consequences to the relationship from the list below:

1.   The argument stops, and we all feel better.
2.   My partner backs down, but everyone feels terrible, and there is tension in the home long afterwards.
3.   The problem gets resolved.
4.   My partner retaliates with emotionally abusive/controlling behavior of his/her own, and then we stop fighting.
5.   My partner retaliates with emotionally abusive/controlling behavior of his/her own, and the conflict escalates even more.

MEETING #15: WHAT MAKES A GOOD RELATIONSHIP?

A.   The following is a list of conditions necessary for a healthy, happy relationship, that each partner must be committed to. How well are *you* doing in these areas?

	doing a great job	doing a fair job	doing a bad job
1. WILLING TO TAKE RESPONSIBILITY FOR MY OWN HAPPINESS: Taking care of myself when I need to, instead of expecting my partner to make me feel better.			
2. RESPECTING MY PARTNER'S IDENTITY: Allowing my partner to be who he/she is, including his/her faults, without exerting criticism or control.			
3. RESPECTING MY PARTNER'S INDEPENDENCE: Allowing my partner to make his/her own decisions and trusting that he/she knows what is best for him/her.			
4. MAINTAINING GOOD COMMUNICATION: Being a good listener, being respectful, and generally maintaining an open, two-way flow of communication.			
5. ROLE FLEXIBILITY: Changing roles when necessary, such as helping out with tasks I don't normally do.			
6. WILLING TO NEGOTIATE: Seeking compromises, rather than always trying to win an argument. Committed to solutions that satisfy everyone. Being part of a team.			
7. STRIVING FOR RELATIONSHIP INTIMACY: Striving for an emotional, intellectual, spiritual and sexual connection to my partner. Willing to do the hard work of making this happen.			

B.   What are some of the ways you can better meet these conditions?

MEETING #16: CONFLICT: MAINTAINING THE RIGHT ATTITUDE

People don't like having conflicts with their partners. Conflicts bring up negative feelings, take up a lot of emotional energy, and can lead to unhealthy and destructive behaviors. The chart below* describes two attitudes that people can have about conflict. The first is closed, the other open. Those with a closed attitude fear conflict and want to avoid it at all costs. Those with an open attitude don't like conflict either, but are willing to work it out in order to better their relationship and to emotionally connect with their partner. *As you go over this chart, determine which attitude you normally have, and how it affects your own relationship.*

CLOSED ATTITUDE ——— CONFLICT ——— OPEN ATTITUDE

INTENT: Avoid open, honest, two-way discussion

STATED REASONS:

Issues not important enough

No time

Angry with partner

Have dealt with this before

UNDERLYING REASONS:

Fear of getting emotionally hurt

Fear of "rocking the boat," and of not getting something you want, or else losing something you already have

Fear of losing partner's love

Fear of uncovering unpleasant emotions and revisiting unhappy events from the past

Fear of taking responsibility

BEHAVIORS:

Compliance: Pretend to agree, stuff anger, put your needs and wants aside

Control: Attempt to squash discussion through aggressive and/or controlling behaviors, and by insisting on your solution to the problem

Indifference: Withdraw

INTENT: Improve emotional connection w/partner

WILLING TO:

Take responsibility for one's feelings, behaviors and their consequences

Be affected by the other person

Experience the emotional pain of learning the truth about yourself or your partner

OPEN TO EXPLORING AND CONFRONTING:

Fears

Embarrassing/shaming/painful issues

Childhood

Internal defenses

Core beliefs and values

CONSEQUENCES:

Learn more about oneself

Learn more about partner

Feeling in love, joyful, connected to partner

Relationship growth

Personal growth and personal freedom

Resolution to conflicts

DYNAMICS:

Control–Control, Control–Compliance

Indifference–Indifference

CONSEQUENCES:

Power struggles, lack of positive connection and sex, deadness, feeling unloved and unloving

---

*Adapted from: J. Paul & M. Paul (1983), *Do I Have To Give Up Me To Be Loved By You?*

MEETINGS #17 & 42: EFFECTIVE PARENTING

Research indicates that effective parenting generally results in children who are responsible, therefore competent with high self-esteem. Children who have high self-esteem do not need to act out. You, the parent, have less of a reason to get angry with them. (For more information on the table below, and research on parenting, see: *Social Development: Psychological Growth and the Parent–Child Relationship* by Eleanor Maccoby, 1980.)

Productive Pattern	*Destructive Pattern*
1. High parental acceptance/warmth	1. Low parental acceptance/warmth (rejection)
2. Moderate to highly restrictive	2. Unyielding restrictiveness or extreme permissiveness
3. Insistence on mature behavior	3. Little insistence on mature behavior
4. High responsiveness	4. Inconsistent responsiveness
5. High positive involvement	5. High negative involvement

Additional suggestions for effective parenting:

1. Give choices, rather than commands. Say: "First you _____, then you may _____." Or: "You have a choice. You can _____ (what you expect), and then _____ (the positive consequence that follows); or you can _____ (the misbehavior about to be committed), and then _____" (the negative consequence that follows).
2. Say "do _____," rather than "don't do." When kids are told they are doing it wrong, they often sulk or rebel.
3. Always follow through with consequences. Kids cannot become competent and responsible unless they experience a connection between their actions and the consequences.
4. Never defend your actions when enforcing your rules—that will only lead to unnecessary arguing. Offer to hear your kid's opinions and feelings later, *after* the rule has been enforced.
5. Present a united front with your spouse. Whatever differences you have individually about parenting should never be discussed in front of the kids.

MEETINGS #18 & 43: GENDER ROLES

#18: Childhood Socialization

A. Sociobiologists argue that both *ultimate* causes (long-term, evolutionary explanations as to *why* certain behaviors develop) and *proximate* causes (short-term, social explanations as to *how* certain behaviors develop) influence human behavior.

A visit to the local toy store ought to make anyone skeptical about the imminent advent of unisex socialization. Despite women's greater access to economic, political, legal and economic resources, and the existence of laws such as Title IX, little boys still favor action toys and little girls still prefer dolls. Reasons may have to do with nature as much as nurture. Nevertheless, gender differences contribute to relationship conflict, which in turn increases the likelihood of partner violence.

The gender differences listed below come from two sources: W. Farrell, (1988), *Why Men Are The Way They Are*, and D. Tannen, (1990), *You Just Don't Understand.*

Boys:

Generally play in large, hierarchically structured groups, and arrive at decisions based on status in the group

Engage in competitive games in which there are clear winners and losers

Aggression is permissible and even encouraged under certain conditions; are given greater latitude than girls when it comes to physical fighting

Vulnerable feelings are better left unexamined and unexpressed; and expect adults to minimize their physical injuries

Girls:

Tend to play in smaller groups or in pairs, and make decisions based on consensus

Play games that involve taking turns and cooperation, such as jump rope or hopscotch

Suppress outward aggression, but engage in gossip, ostracizing foes, and other indirect forms of aggression

Vulnerable feelings ought to be expressed, and expect adults to respond quickly and empathetically to their physical injuries

Note: These are only a few general differences, and the degree of ultimate and proximate influences on gender specific behavior is unknown.

B. Questions for Discussion:

Think back to your childhood, from kindergarten through high school. Imagine yourself at play. Answer the following questions:

1. What were the most important things you learned about being a boy, or a girl?

2.   At the time, what did you consider the ideal boy? The ideal girl?

3.   What did you like about being a boy/girl? What did you dislike?

4.   Do you intend to raise your own children the same way? If "no," please
      indicate why not, and what you plan to do differently

MEETINGS #19 & 44: BASIC COMMUNICATION PRINCIPLES

#19: Messages Sent and Received

A.   Below is a conversation between a man and his wife.* It has been broken into four parts to illustrate communication principle number one, *the message sent is not always the message received.* By following the number sequence, you will see how each person's failure to metacommunicate allows the interaction to quickly deteriorate.

The situation: Jim comes home from work. When he opens the door, he is greeted by his wife, Amanda, who is wearing a new leather jacket.

Jim—his thoughts	Jim—what he says	Amanda—her thoughts	Amanda—what she says
(1) *What a nice looking jacket. Makes her look sexy. I don't remember seeing it before. Wonder if it's new.*	(2) "Is that a new jacket?"		
		(3) *Oh, no, here comes the interrogation, treating me like a child.*	(4) "I got it on sale! Want to see the tags?"
(5) *I drive that beat-up old Chevy so we can save money, and this is how she treats me.*	(6) "No need to be sarcastic. Where'd you get it, anyway?"		
		(7) *I'm not going to put up with this.*	(8) "I'm an adult! You don't need to know where I got it!"

---

*Adapted from P. Neidig & D. Friedman, (1984), *Spouse Abuse: A Treatment Program for Couples.*

(9) *If she thinks I'm going to stick with the budget now, she must be crazy.*	(10) "Well, I'm an adult, too. Guess you don't need to know about the Beemer I'm going to buy."		
		(11) *What a jerk.*	(12) "I don't care what you do."

B.   Questions:

1.   How did "mind-reading" contribute to the misunderstandings?
2.   What could Jim have said to keep the situation from escalating? What about Amanda?

MEETING #20: PRACTICE QUIZ FOR ACTIVE LISTENING

A.   When someone is talking to you about something important, you should:
   1.   Look away if you're bored
   2.   Stare at the person without blinking
   3.   Maintain appropriate eye contact

B.   You should say nothing while the other person is speaking, even if he/she speaks for a long time.
   1.   Yes, this is a good thing to do
   2.   No, this will make the person uncomfortable. Better to nod, or ask a question, or occasionally make encouraging comments, like, "Go on."

   What are some of the other helpful comments you can offer to help move the conversation along and let the other person know you are really listening?

   What would be some good ways to use questions?

C.   Paraphrase in one or two short sentences the following *for content and feelings*:

   "I want to talk about the money situation. Yesterday, I went over the account, and it doesn't look good. There's only two hundred dollars in the checking account, and we've got the Visa bill due next week. That's about a hundred dollars right there. Plus, I haven't done the shopping yet. That's going to be seventy-five dollars, at least. And I haven't even mentioned the utilities. I know you have a check coming in Friday, but between the mortgage and car payments, I figure we'll be down to nothing. We don't have much in savings, either. What are we going to do?"

   Paraphrase:

   "McGuire's been hassling me all week about those reports I sent him. This morning, he phones me up, right in the middle of a project, wanting to go over the June account. I told him that I worked on it for a month, did all I could, but that Stanley's got me on a new assignment. Got to do what the boss says. But McGuire won't take no for an answer. He kept hounding me all morning. I finally had to take an early lunch, just to get away for a while. Didn't come back until almost five. I guess McGuire's going to make a big deal out of that, too."

   Paraphrase:

MEETINGS #21 & 46: POSITIVE COMMUNICATION AND BEHAVIOR

*#21: The Emotional Bank Account**

A.   Inspecting Your Account

Think of your relationship like an emotional bank account, in which your behaviors are either **deposits** (positive communication and actions) or **withdrawals** (negative communication or actions). In the left column below, write down the withdrawals, or negative things you said and did in the past month. This might include yelling, putdowns, criticisms, blaming, dirty fighting, ignoring your partner, coming home drunk, etc. In the right column, write down the deposits, or positive things you said or did. This might include thanking your partner for something, praising or congratulating your partner, offering to help out with chores, giving your partner a back rub, letting your partner play an extra round of golf or game of cards with the guys (or the gals).

Withdrawals	Deposits

B.   Questions for Discussion

1.   Are your deposits less than your withdrawals? If your deposits are only somewhat greater, that may not be enough to bring your account into balance. A man, for instance, cannot call his girlfriend or wife a bitch and expect her to forgive him after he buys her flowers and does the dishes.

2.   What are some of the ways you can increase the deposits? Think of things you said or did in the past that were successful and try to do more of these.

---

*For more information on the emotional bank account concept, see: J. Gottman (1999), *The Marriage Clinic.*

MEETINGS #23 & 48: ASSERTIVENESS

#23: Assertiveness vs. Aggressiveness

Situation #1

All week, Bob's ten-year-old son, Jimmy, has failed to clean up his room. Bob is irritated with Jimmy because Bob doesn't want to pick up after him. This kind of behavior has happened before. Bob is also angry with Jimmy for slacking off on his homework. The night before, Bob specifically asked Jimmy to have his room cleaned before Bob got home from work. Bob arrives home to find that the room has not been cleaned. Jimmy's clothes are all over the floor and his bed is unmade.

Aggressive response: Bob stands over Jimmy, pointing his finger at him, speaking loudly: "What's the matter with you? Don't you listen to anything I tell you? Look at your room. It's a pigsty. Now clean up this mess right now, or you're grounded. Do you hear me? I'm tired of this, Jimmy. Your room's a mess and you haven't done your homework. I'm fed up."

Assertive response: Bob speaks in a normal tone of voice: "Jimmy, last night I asked you to have your room cleaned up by the time I came home from work. I see that your clothes are still on the floor, and that you haven't made your bed yet. I'm really irritated about this. I like a clean house, and I should not have to clean up after you. Please make your bed, and put your clothes away where they belong, in the dresser and the closet, by the time we eat dinner in fifteen minutes."

Situation #2

As Alice speaks on the phone with her close friend, Fay, Alice's husband, Steve, interrupts her. While Alice listens to Fay express sadness over her mother's terminal illness, Steve repeatedly asks Alice where the TV guide is. He continues asking, even after Alice tells him she doesn't know, and after she asks that he not interrupt. Alice feels embarrassed and angry. She wants to be supportive of her friend and not have her friend hear an argument. Steve has interrupted many times before, and Alice is angry with Steve about a lot of other things, too. Due to Steve's voluntarily accepting overtime, he hasn't been available most nights, and has refused to go to marriage counseling.

Aggressive response: Alice yells: "Jerk! Why can't you keep your big mouth shut while I'm on the phone? This has been going on for years, and you're still doing it. I guess TV is more important. Look, Steve, I don't expect you to care about Fay, but I *do* expect you to care about me. I've had it. Unless we get into some counseling and you get your act together, that's it for us. It's over."

Assertive response: The next day Alice says calmly: "Last night, while I was speaking with Fay, you asked me three times where the TV guide was, even after I told you I didn't know. Your interruptions made it hard for me to pay attention to what Fay was telling me about her dying mother, and I was embarrassed and angry. When I'm on the phone, please wait until I get off before asking me questions."

MEETING #24: COMMUNICATION SKILLS REVIEW OUTLINE

Basic Principles

The message sent is not the message received. In the role of listener, strive to be attentive. As a speaker, strive to be clear and concise.

We constantly communicate with those we live with. Even silence conveys attitude, mood, etc.

There are verbal and nonverbal messages, and the nonverbal are more believable. Make sure that the verbal and nonverbal match.

Meta-communicating: Commenting on how the communication is going to get it back on track: for example, saying you need a time out, or asking for clarification, etc.

Listening Skills

1. Be ready and willing
2. Face the other person and maintain eye contact
3. Don't interrupt
4. Make helpful comments ("Go ahead." "I see.") and gestures (appropriate facial expressions, a nod)
5. Ask questions
6. Paraphrase what the other has said. Use your own words, don't just parrot. When listening to criticism, remember to disagree only *after* you have listened to the entire message, and have acknowledged what is true.

Positive Expression

1. Demonstrate affection (hugs, back rubs, offer to make dinner). Frequent small gestures are better than infrequent large ones.
2. Praise and compliments.

   • Avoid *qualifying* hooks that undermine the message ("That was a great dinner, *but* why didn't you remember to press my shirt?")
   • Specific praise is more meaningful than general praise.

3. Encouragement and support

   • Be a good listener
   • Avoid giving advice until asked
   • Mention *specifically* the other person's areas of strength

Assertiveness Skills

1. State what is bothering you. Talk only about the behavior. Don't attack the person.
2. State how the behavior affects you. This includes expressing your feelings.
3. Request, don't demand, a change in behavior. Start a request with, "I would like it if . . . " or "Please, could you . . . "

MEETINGS #25 & 51: CONFLICT RESOLUTION SKILLS

A.   Three Levels of Conflict*:

Relationship level (threats to move out, divorce or have an affair)

Personality level (name calling, dirty fighting)

Issue level (you stick to the issue and talk respectfully)

B.   Basic Principles

1.   "Change first"—Do your part, and don't wait for your partner to make things better.
2.   Discuss only one problem at a time.
3.   Use a win–win approach.
4.   Use healthy communication skills—active listening, speaking with respect.
5.   Identify the underlying issue. What's *really* going on? (For example, an argument over what movie to see is really an issue over who makes decisions in the family.)
6.   Avoid controlling or dirty fighting techniques.
7.   Find something to agree about. Be willing to compromise, and allow the other person to have some influence over you.
8.   Arrive at decisions together, even if you end up using your partner's solution.

C.   Problem Solving (for the most difficult conflicts)†

1.   S—State the problem. Remember to define it in such a way that both parties can accept the definition.
2.   O—Outline previous solutions to the problem. There is no need to reinvent the wheel.
3.   L—List new alternatives. Use a brainstorming process in which you list all ideas without judgment, no matter how extreme, silly, or unworkable they may seem.
4.   V—Visualize the consequences of implementing each solution.
5.   E—Execute the best solution(s).

Remember: You have nothing to lose and everything to gain by trying these steps. Even if you don't find an ideal solution, the above process allows you and your partner to experience working as a team, and these steps will help establish trust as you experience some measure of success in solving the problem.

---

*Source: P. Neidig & D. Friedman, (1984), *Spouse Abuse: A Treatment Program for Couples*.
†Source: H. Weisinger (1985), *The Anger Workout Book*.

MEETINGS #3 & 29: ANGER—GOOD AND BAD

#29: Making Anger Work for You

A.   All emotions are valid and necessary. Anger is a powerful emotion that can have positive or devastating consequences. Properly expressed, anger is very useful. Expressing anger constructively is necessary in order to communicate our limits (boundaries), and as a means of holding others accountable for their actions. Keep in mind that *anger will be useful only when we control how it is expressed.* The chart below presents the positive functions of anger. Please match the situations from the first column with one or more of the positive anger functions listed in the second.

Situation/Behavior	Positive Anger Function
Your boss insists that you work overtime again, and his insistence triggers your anger "smoke alarm." You realize he has taken advantage of you.	Energizer Motivator
Your girlfriend makes demeaning jokes at your expense. You have been wanting to talk to her about it, but have worried that she will be upset with you. Eventually, you decide to assertively confront her.	Provides you with information about a situation so you can better deal with it
Unemployed for three months, you are feeling depressed, and drinking more. One day, as you watch another rerun of *People's Court*, you begin to feel angry. You think, "I'm sick of lying around all day. I need to start looking for a job."	Allows you to communicate the seriousness of your concern Communicates limits and boundary violations
You discover your son playing with matches in his room. In a firm, quiet, voice, you tell him that you are very angry about what he has done, how he has put the family's safety in jeopardy.	

B.   Think of situations in which other people have used anger in a constructive way (e.g., the protestors in the civil rights movement of the '60s):

C.   Now think of situations in your own life when you appropriately expressed your anger:

MEETING #30: VIOLENCE—WHEN IS IT JUSTIFIED?

A. Read each vignette below. Determine if the violence is justified by circling either *yes*, *no*, or *somewhat*, for each behavior and its alternative.

   1a. After suffering several hours of Sara's nonstop verbal abuse and threats to divorce him and take custody of the kids, Bill chokes Sarah.

   Yes   No   Somewhat

   1b. Bill lightly pushes Sarah aside, without physically injuring her.

   Yes   No   Somewhat

   2a. Alphonso twists his wife's hair and slams her up against a wall after finding that they'll have to declare bankruptcy for the $5,000 in credit card debts she incurred from shopping sprees.

   Yes   No   Somewhat

   2b. Alphonso grabs her by the arms and shakes her slightly.

   Yes   No   Somewhat

   3a. When Henrietta catches Joe viewing pornography on the Internet, she punches him in the face, causing his nose to bleed.

   Yes   No   Somewhat

   3b. Henrietta slaps Joe.

   Yes   No   Somewhat

   4a. When Brandon learns that Margie has again been driving under the influence with their kids in the car, he shoves her down a flight of stairs and calls her a "worthless drunk." She suffers a concussion.

   Yes   No   Somewhat

   4b. Brandon throws the car keys at Margie, resulting in minor scratches.

   Yes   No   Somewhat

   5a. After catching John in bed with David, Ted beats John with his fists.

   Yes   No   Somewhat

   5b. Ted slaps John once and leaves.

   Yes   No   Somewhat

   6a. When Jack again interrogates Rhonda on her whereabouts, and refuses to give her grocery money, Rhonda threatens Jack with a knife.

   Yes   No   Somewhat

   6b. Rhonda kicks Jack in the shin.

   Yes   No   Somewhat

7a. Margaret has been harassed daily by her jealous, controlling boyfriend. One night, as they watch television, he calls her a "tramp." When he stands up to get a sandwich, Margaret grabs a vase and cracks it over his head.

               Yes   No   Somewhat

7b. Margaret pushes him.

               Yes   No   Somewhat

     Score 0 points for each *no*, 1 for each *somewhat*, and 2 for each *yes* (score sheet at end of section).

     Total _____

B.   The correct score for the violence questionnaire is, 0. As the bumper sticker reads, "THERE IS NO EXCUSE FOR DOMESTIC VIOLENCE."

C.   Definitions, under California law:

     1. "Domestic Violence" is abuse committed against an adult or a fully emancipated minor who is a spouse, former spouse, cohabitant, former cohabitant, a person with whom the suspect has had a child or is having or has had a dating or engagement relationship. Same sex relationships are included.
     2. PC 13700 defines "abuse" as "intentionally or recklessly causing, or attempting to cause bodily injury, or placing another person in fear of injury to self or another."

D.   Some legal provisions:

     1. Under PC243(e), a person can be charged with a misdemeanor for perpetrating domestic violence, even if there is no visible injury.
     2. Under PC273.5, a person can be charged with a felony for perpetrating domestic violence involving a "traumatic condition," usually visible.
     3. A 52-week batterer intervention program is mandated for individuals convicted of PC243(e), PC273.5, or for 273.6 (violation of a protective order).

MEETINGS #6 & 32: STRESS BASICS

#32: Preparing for Provocations

Learning ways to manage your anger during the heat of a situation is crucial. If you have practiced such skills as taking time outs and disputing your irrational self-talk, you will be better able to handle the unexpected situations that test your ability to control yourself. And of course, using these skills is an important first step in your quest to effectively communicate, resolve conflicts, and improve your personal relationships. However, many potentially volatile situations can be predicted (e.g., a visit to in-laws you resent). When possible, you should be proactive and plan ahead. Think of recurring high-conflict situations and, using the information from parts A and B, prepare a plan to more productively deal with them.

Provocation	Anger Temperature	My Plan
1.		
2.		
3.		

A. To generate an effective plan, use the problem-solving steps. (You may do this by yourself, without your partner.)

  S   State the problem.
  O   Outline previous solutions.
  L   List alternative solutions.
  V   Visualize the consequences of each possible solution.
  E   Execute the best solution(s).

B. Useful tools you might want to incorporate in your plan:

  1. Take your anger temperature (scale of 1–10).
  2. Take a time out, or a creative time out (go to another room, count to 50, etc.).
  3. Do a meditation or relaxation exercise.

4. Self-coach (challenging beliefs and distorted, irrational self-talk).
5. Use the anger flow chart.
6. Be a good listener.
7. Be assertive, rather than aggressive.
8. Engage in positive communication—be supportive, encouraging and attentive.
9. Remain at the issue level and strive toward a win–win approach.

MEETINGS #7, 8, 33, & 34: MANAGING STRESS*

A.   *Meeting #33: Breath Counting Meditation (takes about 10–15 minutes)*

1.   Find a quiet place and sit comfortably. Scan your body for tension and try to relax. Make sure you feel somewhat centered and grounded. Either close your eyes, or pick a spot on the floor a few feet in front of you and gaze at it.

2.   Notice your breathing. Breathing in through your nose, take a deep breath, hold for a moment and release. Inhale, exhale, and pause, breathing in an easy, natural manner. Be aware of your breathing. As you exhale, say to yourself, "one." Continue to repeat "one" each time you exhale.

3.   If thoughts or outside noises distract you, bring your focus back to the sound and sensation of your breathing, to your lungs as they fill and collapse like a balloon with each breath. Continue to breathe in and out, saying "one" each time you exhale.

B.   *Meeting #34: Progressive Relaxation (short version)*

Curl both of your fists and tighten your forearms and biceps, as though you were a body-builder. Then relax . . . Wrinkle your forehead. As you do this, press your head back as far as possible and roll it clockwise in a complete circle, and then reverse the circle. Now, wrinkle your face muscles like a walnut: frowning, eyes squinted, lips pursed, tongue pressed on the roof of your mouth, and shoulders hunched. Then relax . . . Arch your back as you take a deep breath. Hold the breath. Relax. Take a deep breath, pressing out the stomach. Hold. Relax . . . Pull your feet and toes back toward you, tightening your shins. Hold. Relax. Curl your toes, as you tighten your calves, thighs and buttocks. Relax.

C.   *Meeting #34: Visualization Exercise*

Close your eyes . . . Imagine leaving the area where you live . . . Leaving all the daily hassles behind . . . Imagine going across a valley, moving closer and closer to a mountain . . . Now imagine reaching the mountain . . . and begin to climb a winding path. Look around. Notice the lush plants and trees, the smell in the air, and the light breeze over your face. Up ahead you will see a place on the path to stop and rest . . . Take some time as you rest here to examine the tension, stress and anger in your life . . . The tension, stress and anger have shapes and colors . . . Look at them carefully . . . Then put each one in the can on the side of the path and place the lid securely on the can . . . Continue walking without effort until you reach the top . . . Look out over the valley . . . What do you see? Nearby is an inviting, peaceful place you are drawn to . . . a place just for you. What do you see, right now, right here, in your special place? Take a slow, deep breath and take in the smells as you listen to the sounds of nature around you. Feel how relaxed, how calm and safe you feel. You are now feeling completely relaxed . . . Experience being totally relaxed . . . Sit or lie down and pause for five minutes to enjoy your special place. When you are ready to return, remember this is your own special place, and you can return here anytime you want.

---

*The above exercises were adapted from: M. Davis et al. (1988), *The Relaxation & Stress Reduction Workbook*, 3rd edition.

MEETINGS #10, 35, & 36: OVERCOMING IRRATIONAL THOUGHTS AND BELIEFS

*#35: Identifying Irrational Beliefs**

A. Beliefs are a major cause of problems and unhappiness. In each section, decide if you agree or disagree with each statement listed below the belief. The more strongly you agree with each statement, the more anchored you are to the belief. These beliefs are irrational because they include distorted self-talk. For each, determine whether the distortion is one of *magnification* (exaggerating things) or *absolutes* (rigid thinking). Then rewrite each belief, taking out the distortions. Does the new way of thinking seem more rational?

1. It is an absolute necessity that I have love and approval from peers, family and friends.

    I want everyone to like me and approve of me.
    I worry about what others think of me.
    I don't like to express disagreement, or go against what others think.

    Type of Distortion:
    Rational Belief:

2. I must be entirely competent in all that I undertake.

    If there's something I can't do well, I avoid it.
    I need to be successful in everything I do, and can't stand to fail at anything.
    It bothers me when others are better at some things than I am.

    Type of Distortion:
    Rational Belief:

3. Some people are evil and wicked, and should be punished.

    People who do wrong deserve what they get and ought to be blamed.
    Too many bad people avoid the punishment they deserve.
    Fear of punishment helps people be good.

    Type of Distortion:
    Rational Belief:

4. It is horrible when people and things are not the way I would like them to be.

    Things should be different from the way they are.
    I can't stand being frustrated.
    I often become upset over the mistakes of others.

    Type of Distortion:
    Rational Belief:

---

*Sources: A. Ellis (1975), *A New Guide to Rational Living*, and M. Davis et al. (1988), *The Relaxation & Stress Reduction Workbook*, 3rd edition.

5. Human misery is caused by external events.

   People react to events that trigger their emotions.
   The more problems a person has, the less happy he will be.
   People are upset by situations, not by the view they take of them.

   Type of Distortion:
   Rational Belief:

6. It is easier to avoid than to face the difficulties and responsibilities of life.

   I tend to put off important decisions.
   I avoid facing my problems.
   Life is too short to spend it doing unpleasant tasks.

   Type of Distortion:
   Rational Belief:

7. The past determines the present.

   A zebra cannot change his stripes—people basically never change.
   It's impossible to overcome the past.
   We are slaves to our personal histories.

   Type of Distortion:
   Rational Belief:

MEETINGS #10, 35, & 36: OVERCOMING IRRATIONAL THOUGHTS AND BELIEFS

#36: More Irrational Beliefs

Here are other irrational beliefs. For each one, try to determine why it is irrational. Then, as with the previous list, rewrite each to represent reality. (For more information on these beliefs, see: M. Davis et al. (1988). *The Relaxation & Stress Reduction Workbook*, 3rd edition.)

1. I have no control over what I experience or feel.
    Why this belief is irrational:

    A more rational view is:

2. People are fragile and must never be hurt.
    Why this belief is irrational:

    A more rational view is:

3. If I don't go out of my way to please others, they will abandon or reject me.
    Why this belief is irrational:

    A more rational view is:

4. When people disapprove of me, it means I am wrong or bad.
    Why this belief is irrational:

    A more rational view is:

5. Being alone is horrible.
    Why this belief is irrational:

    A more rational view is:

6. There is perfect love and a perfect relationship.
    Why this belief is irrational:

    A more rational view is:

7. I shouldn't have to feel pain—I am entitled to a good life.
    Why this belief is irrational:

    A more rational view is:

8. My worth as a person depends on how much I achieve and produce.
    Why this belief is irrational:

    A more rational view is:

9. Anger is always bad and destructive.
    Why this belief is irrational:

    A more rational view is:

MEETINGS #11 & 37: IDENTIFYING VULNERABLE FEELINGS

#37: Identifying Feelings in Others (Developing Empathy)

Situation	What he/she might be feeling

You and your mate are excitedly making vacation plans. You suggest a trip to Hawaii, which will cost twice as much as the budget you both agreed on. Your partner is about to say something, then shakes his head silently.

Earlier, your partner was told that there might be layoffs at work. He has been cranky all day. You try to talk about the kids, and he angrily storms out of the room.

In front of the other guests at a party, you tell your boyfriend he's had too much to drink. He whirls around, spilling his drink on the carpet.

Last night, your partner had said something mean to you. You said how hurtful that comment was, but she didn't offer an apology. Now it's breakfast, and your partner, normally quiet this time of day, cheerfully asks you about your day and offers to get you a refill of coffee.

Your partner has wanted to tell you about her day. But you put her off for two hours to watch a movie. Later, you hear the door slam and the car start.

Your partner comes home in a bad mood, and goes into a 45-minute rant about how "impossible" the boss is, and complains to you that she is a week behind with a project. She says, "I can never please the bastard."

In family court, your husband's visitation time with his oldest child was cut back. Since then, your husband doesn't want to go out as much as before, and has been going to bed earlier than usual.

Your partner has just turned 40. He announces his intention to go back to college and study architecture. You say that you don't think he is cut out for that kind of work, and besides, it would be too expensive. He refuses to talk to you for two days.

Vulnerable Feelings: afraid, ashamed, betrayed, confused, disappointed, disrespected, embarrassed, guilty, harassed, helpless, hurt, ignored, inadequate, jealous, lonely, overwhelmed, sad, taken advantage of, used, unimportant, worried.

MEETINGS #13 & #39: SOCIALIZATION OF VIOLENCE

#39: Adult Problems from Childhood of Origin

A.   Abuse in childhood of origin

Taking responsibility for your *current* behavior is crucial in learning to overcome problems with anger and aggression. It is ultimately self-defeating to wallow in the past or to use it as a way to avoid changing the present. However, it is equally crucial that you have a thorough *understanding* of your aggression, and how you got that way. An awareness of the past will remind you of how you *don't* want to act, so that you don't pass on to your children the dysfunction you may have experienced growing up. Such an awareness is also necessary in order to work through the feelings of resentment, guilt, and shame that prevent you from healing. Answer the following questions as honestly as you can. Share with the group what you are willing to share. You may want to discuss the rest with a trusted confidant or therapist.

1.   How did your parents/stepparents settle their differences? Did they yell or swear at one another or throw things? Ever fight physically? Give some examples. Try to remember the worst fight. What happened? How did you feel about it at the time?

2.   Did your parents/stepparents ever spank you? What about other forms of physical punishment, such as hitting you with a belt or some other object? What was the worst episode? How did you feel about it at the time? What about now?

3.   Overall, how good a job did your parents do of caring for you? Were they there for you when you needed them? Did they provide for your needs—food, shelter, love, a sense of safety? Or did you resent them in any way, and if so, why?

4.   Did your parents ever swear at you, call you names, or put you down in front of other people? Give some examples. How did you feel?

5.   Were there any other times when they did something that made you feel bad, like there was something terribly wrong with you?

B.   Problems associated with having witnessed parental violence, according to the NFVS:*

Problem	Had Witnessed Violence by			
	Neither	Father	Mother	Both
Depression index (above 80th percentile)	20.0	31.0	33.6	32.9
Perceived stress index (range = 0–12)	3.1	3.7	3.9	3.8
Times drunk past year: men	2.82	7.52	3.37	3.66
Times drunk past year: women	1.02	2.24	1.61	1.62
Times high on drugs past year: men	3.18	9.0	15.45	4.48
Times high on drugs past year: women	1.76	5.0	9.87	1.96
Verbal aggression past yr: husband—wife	9.6	13.2	16.3	15.3
Verbal aggression past yr: wife—husband	9.9	14.6	16.4	15.4
Any violence past yr: husband to wife	10.5	18.3	23.0	22.2
Any violence past yr: wife to husband	11.4	21.7	21.4	22.7
Severe violence past yr: husband to wife	3.1	4.0	8.4	7.4
Severe violence past yr: wife to husband	*	*	*	*

*Source: M. Straus et al. (1990), *Physical Violence in American Families.*

C.   Abusive adult behavior from having been insecurely attached, rejected, shamed
     or physically abused by a parent; and from having witnessed marital violence*:

Socialization Experience	Psychological Consequences	Behavioral Consequences
I—Rejection, shaming	inflated self-esteem; problems with affect regulation; anger and rage; tendency to blame	frequent rage outbursts emotional abuse
II—Insecure attachment	jealousy and attachment anger	dominance/isolation behavior
III—Physical abuse victim	decreased empathy for victim	physical abuse
Witnessed physical abuse	unconscious images of violence, and lack of healthy conflict-resolution strategies	
I + II—Rejection, shaming, insecure attachment	anger focused on intimate partner relationship	intimate rage
I + II + III—Rejection and shaming; insecure attachment; victim of physical abuse, and witnessed physical abuse	ego integrity dependent on relationship	physical and emotional abuse, dominance/isolation behavior and stalking

*Source: D. Dutton (1998), *The Abusive Personality.*

MEETING #41: DEFENSES AGAINST ACCOUNTABILITY WORKSHEET

Minimization

You agree that you did something wrong, but insist that it is not as horrible as the victim claims. You believe the victim is overly sensitive. Minimizing thoughts or statements come in four types: those that include the word *only* or *just*, those that compare the behavior to something worse, those that suggest the behavior was simply an accident, and those that suggest the victim is not affected by the behavior.

Examples:

"I didn't mean for her to fall on the coffee table."   "I could have punched her out."

"What's the big deal about a slap? He's 6' 2."   "I only yelled at him."

Using your log, or from your memory, think of a few examples of how you used minimization to avoid taking responsibility for aggressive/abusive behavior.

Denial

When using denial, you cannot take responsibility and change your behavior because, as you see it, there is no problem to work on. The victim is getting the message that it's all in his/her mind, and is left feeling confused, helpless and angry.

Examples:

"I never touched you."   "I have no idea why they arrested me."

My personal examples:

Blame

You blame your actions on such factors as stress or alcohol use. But the most destructive defense is blaming the victim. In this case, the aggressor is not merely avoiding responsibility, but actually re-victimizing the victim. "You" statements are generally intended to blame.

Examples:

"You shouldn't have yelled at me."   "You pushed my buttons."

My personal examples:

MEETINGS #18 & 43: GENDER ROLES

#43: Impact on Adulthood

A. Boys and girls are not differentially socialized by accident.

For boys, being raised to be competitive and aggressive, minimize pain and vulnerable emotions, and maintain hierarchical organizations in play groups prepares them for the *world of work.*

For girls, being raised to be cooperative, consensus-seeking and nurturing, and to express pain and vulnerable emotions prepares them for the *world of home and family.*

Men often feel they are at a disadvantage in intimate relationships when it comes to negotiating wants and needs and resolving conflict. *Women appear to have the advantage in intimate communication because they simply have more practice.*

Differences in male and female socialization have other consequences as well, in terms of values, expectations, and motives. *These differences are potential sources of conflict, and, sometimes, violence.*

Deborah Tannen points out that although men and women both value *autonomy and intimacy,* men place a higher value on the former, and women place a higher value on the latter.

Men's need for autonomy and their desire to be seen as competent sometimes cause them to interpret sincere advice as nagging.

Women tend to engage in rapport *talk,* which often includes a more diffuse expression of feelings. *Men tend to engage in* report *talk,* which contains a greater proportion of facts. "Rapport" talk is often interpreted by men as indirect and manipulative, whereas "report" talk is often regarded by women as arrogant, boring, and/or insensitive.

For men, reading the morning newspaper is an opportunity to obtain facts and relates to autonomy and competence. Women can view this as a sign of rejection.

Men don't express a lot of feelings partly because they don't consider them important, and because such expression isn't natural for them. Men regard the task of identifying and expressing feelings as foreign and arduous work, which they are not very good at and would prefer to avoid after a long day at their job. But women interpret the avoidance as evidence that their partner doesn't care.

Men interpret their partners' complaints as invitations to solve a problem. They see help-giving, such as fixing things, as a way of connecting to their partners.

Women expect men to offer sympathy and emotional support, and often regard problem-solving efforts as presumptuous and controlling.

One way that women try to connect and offer support is through *complaint matching*—responding to a complaint their partner may have about something with one of their own. This is often interpreted by men as dismissing and belittling.

However, men will engage in complaint matching with other men for the same reason. They support other men by denying the problem, or refraining from offering advice. This is done out of respect for other men's autonomy.

Because of their hierarchical orientation, men tend to avoid asking for help. Help-seeking implies they are incompetent or inferior.

Women prefer *face-to-face* intimacy. Men bond to other men in what Tannen calls *shoulder to shoulder* intimacy.

Women expect their partners to look directly at them when they are talking, to show respect and support. But men tend to position themselves at an angle when engaged in conversation. With other men, they are concerned about coming off as too threatening, and with women they are concerned about being perceived as flirtatious.

When women interrupt in conversation, it is often a way to maintain rapport with the other. Men view this as annoying and disrespectful.

Because of their consensus orientation and lower tolerance for direct conflict, women soften commands to suggestions, and imply rather than state their intentions directly. Men often interpret this as manipulative.

According to Tannen, the same consensus orientation causes women to play the role of peacemaker more often than men. Because men have been socialized to be competitive and work within hierarchies, they regard conflict as a normal state of affairs.

Warren Farrell argues that because men are socialized to obtain sex, and because securing sex partners brings status and approval, *men often regard women as sex objects*, which women resent.

Traditionally, women have been socialized to pursue relationships, with the ultimate goal of securing a family. Although many women now work outside the home, Farrell reminds us that society grants women the option of being homemakers, whereas men who don't have regular jobs are regarded with scorn. It therefore pays for women to find a mate who can support them should they elect not to work. Thus, *women regard men as success objects*.

Sources: D. Tannen (1990), *You Just Don't Understand.*
W. Farrell (1988), *Why Men Are the Way They Are.*

B.   Questions for Discussion:

Couples' conflicts may be due to personality differences, communication styles, incompatible needs, stress, and sometimes from the differing values that come from being reared as a male or as a female. Read each scenario, and answer each question to determine how gender roles affect relationships.

1.   Wilma comes home in tears, and starts to tell Fred about her stressful day at work. Fred loves Wilma and is very concerned. As he listens, Fred is looking slightly away as he analyzes her problem and tries to think of a solution. After about a minute or two, he has come up with a sensible

plan of action and eagerly makes his suggestion. To his dismay, Wilma storms out of the room, accusing him of "not listening and not being supportive." Fred feels confused, hurt and unappreciated.

- What male value might have influenced the way Fred tried to help? What female value(s) might explain how Wilma reacted?
- Were Fred's actions misunderstood? What could they have done differently so that Wilma felt more supported and Fred felt more appreciated?

2.   Tina finally gets off the phone with her friend, Suzanne, after chit-chatting for an hour and a half about various topics, such as a new eyeliner she has purchased and the sale on children's underwear at Macy's. Her husband, Tony, is steaming. He accuses her of, "being inconsiderate and wasting time talking about crap." He then calls his friend, Joe, and they have a thirty-second conversation in which they arrange to play golf. Afterwards, Tina tells Tony that he's abusive, then cancels their dinner date.

- What male and female values explain Tony's frustration, and Tina's anger?
- Who is engaging in *report* talk? *Rapport* talk?

3.   Think of examples from your own life. When have you had a conflict with your partner because of differences in gender values, such as intimacy vs. independence?

MEETINGS #19 & 44: BASIC COMMUNICATION PRINCIPLES

#44: Practicing Meta-Communicating

When you have a conversation and there is any problem with the communication, someone needs to acknowledge that there is a problem (meta-communicate). In each scenario below, the communication has taken a bad turn. What could each person have said to get it back on track?

1. Jimmy is angry with his wife, Lisa, for canceling dinner plans at the last moment. His voice is rising. Lisa feels irritated and attacked, and has begun to stop paying attention, staring off in another direction.

    What Jimmy could meta-communicate:

    What Lisa could meta-communicate:

2. Lucy's boyfriend, Robb, has been watching football all afternoon, and Lucy feels ignored. She sits across from him on the couch, arms folded, looking sullen. Robb's not sure what she might be thinking.

    What Lucy could meta-communicate:

    What Robb could meta-communicate:

3. Ted is trying to explain to his wife, Karen, about some reorganization plans at his job. He has gone into great detail, trying to make himself clear, but Karen has a blank look on her face. Ted is feeling unheard and angry.

    What Ted could meta-communicate:

    What Karen could meta-communicate:

    Think of misunderstandings you and your partner may have had recently. Where did they go wrong? How could you have meta-communicated so that you resolved communication problems before the conflict escalated?

MEETINGS #21 & 46: POSITIVE COMMUNICATION AND BEHAVIOR

#46: Giving Encouragement and Support

DO'S	DON'TS
1. *Listen.* Remember that active listening is composed of several skills: eye contact; making comments such as, *uh-huh*, or, *go on*; asking questions; paraphrasing and summarizing what the other person said. Especially listen for *feelings*—e.g., say: "You sound depressed."	1. *Don't interrupt.* Don't argue or bring up other issues. Active listening comments should be brief and infrequent.
2. *Express Concern.* Tell the other person that you are concerned, worried about him or her, etc. Use "I" statements. For example, "I'm worried about your health."	2. *Don't criticize.* Even if other people seem to be doing something wrong or not in their best interests, refrain from telling them. They'll only feel hurt and attacked.
3. *Remind Others of Their Strengths.* You can make others feel better by reminding them of instances when they successfully handled a similar problem. Make sure that you give *specific* examples.	3. *Don't minimize.* People are entitled to their feelings. Comments such as, "There's no reason to be upset," may be *intended* to be reassuring, but instead they invalidate the other person's feelings.
4. *Offer to Help.* Let others know that you are there for them, to assist them in whatever way you can.	4. *Don't give advice.* Most of the time, when people have problems, they already know how to solve them. They just need you to listen, to be a sounding board. Giving advice may come off as patronizing, as though you know better.

MEETINGS #23 & 48: ASSERTIVENESS

#48: Responding to "Blocking Maneuvers*

A. ' Delivering your message in a clear, direct and respectful manner increases the likelihood that you will be heard, but there are no guarantees. Keep in mind that when you are assertive, you are telling others that they are doing something wrong. When people are confronted, they are often defensive. Don't be surprised if those at the receiving end try to avoid hearing you—if they can avoid hearing the message, then they don't have to take responsibility for their behavior! Below is a list of *blocking maneuvers*, ways that people deflect your message. Imagine that you have just made your assertive request and the other person tries to block it. What is your gut reaction?

Request: "Billy, your screaming hurts my ears. Please stop screaming."
Response: "Aw, you're funny, Dad. What a joker!"
Blocking maneuver: HUMOR
Your gut reaction:

Request: "Please take those tennis shoes off your bed, and put away your Barbies."
Response #1: "Check out *your* room, Mom. It's gross!"
Blocking maneuver: TURNING THE TABLES
Your gut reaction:

Response #2: "Why do I have to do this?"
Blocking maneuver: ASKING "WHY?"
Your gut reaction:

Response #3: "Whatever. Sure, later."
Blocking maneuver: PUTTING YOU OFF
Your gut reaction:

Request: "When you do that, it's hard for me to think. Please don't interrupt."
Response #1: "I didn't interrupt."
Blocking maneuver: DENIAL
Your gut reaction:

Response #2: "Back off. Can't you see how stressed I am?"
Blocking maneuver: BLAME/GUILT
Your gut reaction:

---

*Some of the material in this section has been adapted from H. Weisinger (1985), *Dr. Weisinger's Anger Workout Book.*

Response #3: "Don't control me! I'll really give you something to think about!"
Blocking maneuver: THREATS
Your gut reaction:

Response #4: "There go your mother issues again. I'm not your mother."
Blocking maneuver: PSYCHOLOGIZING
Your gut reaction:

B.   Go over the list, and for each item think about what would happen if you went
     with your gut reaction. Would it increase or decrease your odds of getting the
     other person to hear you? To comply?

C.   *Delivering your message in an assertive manner gives you the best possible chance of
     being heard, and possibly gaining compliance.* Anger and threats only serve to put
     the spotlight on you, and allow the other person to escape responsibility. Once
     you overreact, the other person doesn't have to listen. Instead of giving up,
     giving in, or getting angry, stick with your assertive message by trying one of
     the following countermaneuvers instead.

D.   *CounterManeuvers:*

     1.   THE BROKEN RECORD—Repeat your assertive request, calmly and
          firmly.

     2.   AGREEING—Helpful with "turning the tables." The other person has
          correctly pointed out that you do the same thing. You agree, but then go
          right back and repeat what you just said (broken record).

          Example:
          (He/She): "Me, late? What about you? You're *always* late!"
          (You): "Good point. I'm late sometimes. But I'd still like you to . . . "
          (broken record).

     3.   DEFUSING—Use with threats. Playing the broken record with someone
          who is angry can be dangerous. Instead, acknowledge, without blaming
          the other person, that the situation is volatile, and back off.

          Examples:
          "This might not be a good time to talk."
          "This situation seems to be getting out of hand."

          If you try these countermaneuvers but the other person persists in blocking
          your assertive message, then stop. You can use the "broken record" a few
          times, and then it becomes unproductive. At this point, your only recourse
          is to bow out gracefully.

4.   OFFERING THE OLIVE BRANCH—Refuse to get sucked into an argument, or to act in an immature, abusive or irresponsible manner. *Show that you really mean to be assertive, and not aggressive, and that you really want to work things out.*

Examples:
"Please think about what I said. We can talk about it later."
"I really want to work this out. I hope you do, too."

MEETINGS #26 & 52: IMPACT OF FAMILY VIOLENCE ON CHILDREN

#52: My Role in Family Violence Worksheet

Domestic violence, also known as intimate partner violence, typically is preceded and accompanied by yelling, swearing, and emotionally abusive and controlling behaviors. Also, parents who abuse one another often abuse the children. This is because abuse of any kind increases stress levels, making high-conflict situations even more volatile, and because of the behavioral principle of observational learning, the odds are increased that others will copy abusive behavior. Keep in mind that when you fight with your spouse, your children are usually aware. When you assume they are asleep, they are often awake. When you act like everything is OK, they sense the tension in the home, and read the fear and anger in your face and body language. Later, if you divorce your spouse, you and your children are at risk for bringing these patterns of dysfunction into the next relationships and the next family unit.

As a parent, you are responsible for the well-being of your family. IT IS CRUCIAL THAT YOU REFRAIN FROM BEING ABUSIVE AND NOT ALLOW OTHERS TO BE ABUSIVE, EITHER. OTHERWISE, YOU MAINTAIN A DYSFUNCTIONAL, STRESSFUL, AND DANGEROUS ATMOSPHERE FOR THE PEOPLE IN YOUR HOME.

Please answer the questions below, circling either *yes* or *no*. If you answer in the affirmative, what are you prepared to do to change that behavior or situation?

1. I have been physically abusive towards my spouse.   Y   N

2. I have been verbally abusive, emotionally abusive, or control-   Y   N
   ling with my spouse.

3. I have yelled at, put down, demeaned, shamed, ignored, or   Y   N
   hit my children.

4. I allow my spouse to yell at, put down, demean, shame, ignore,   Y   N
   or hit my children.

5. I allow my spouse to abuse me.   Y   N

6. I allow my children to abuse each other or me.   Y   N

Appendix D

Resources and Program Agreements for Court-Ordered Clients

SOURCES FOR CONTROLLING AND ABUSIVE TACTICS QUESTIONNAIRE (CAT)

Name of Questionnaire and Source	Subscales
1. Power and Control "Wheel" E. Pence & M. Paymar (1993), *Education Groups for Men Who Batter: The Duluth Model.*	Coercion/threats; intimidation; isolation; emotional abuse; minimizing, denying and blaming children; using children; male privilege; economic abuse
2. Psychological Maltreatment Inventory (PMI) M. Kasian & S. Painter (1992), "Frequency and Severity of Psychological Abuse in a Dating Population." *Journal of Interpersonal Violence, 7*(3).	Isolation and emotional control; diminishment of self-esteem; jealousy; verbal abuse; withdrawal
3. Psychological Maltreatment of Women Inventory (PMWI) R. Tolman (1989), "The Development of a Measure of Psychological Maltreatment of Women by Their Male Partners." *Violence and Victims, 4*(3).	(see PMI)
4. Controlling Behaviors Scale (CBS) N. Graham-Kevan & J. Archer (2002), "Does Controlling Behavior Predict Physical Aggression and Violence to Partners?" Unpublished manuscript, available at Ngraham-kevan@uclan.ac.uk	Economic abuse; coercion and threats; intimidation; emotional abuse; isolation

5. Female Aggression Wheel
    M. Koonin et al. (2003), *Treatment of Women Arrested for Domestic Violence: Women Ending Abusive/Violent Episodes Respectfully.* (Available from The Family Violence & Sexual Assault Institute, San Diego, (858) 623-2777, x357.)

    Physical violence; threats; verbal abuse; financial abuse; fear; psychological abuse; family

6. Waltz-Rushe-Gottman Emotional Abuse Questionnaire
    J. Gottman (1999), *The Marriage Clinic.*

    Social isolation; degradation; sexual coercion; property damage

7. Danger Assessment
    J. Campbell (1986), "Nursing Assessment for Risk of Homicide with Battered Women." *Advances in Nursing Science, 8*(4).

    Physical violence; threats; drug/alcohol use; jealousy and isolation; criminal behavior

---

Other Sources:

P. Cook (1997), *Abused Men: The Hidden Side of Domestic Violence.*

P. Pearson (1997), *When She Was Bad: Women and the Myth of Innocence.*

A. Shupe et al. (1987), *Violent Men, Violent Couples.*

W. Stacey et al. (1994), *The Violent Couple.*

L. Walker (1979), *The Battered Woman.*

SAMPLE RESOURCE LIST (FOR MARIN COUNTY, CALIFORNIA)

General info. line: HELPLINK—(415) 772-4357 (800) 273 6222

NOTE: The following are resource lists used at John Hamel & Associates to help us better serve our clients. Family violence practitioners are advised to compose their own list, including information appropriate to each of the five categories, for the geographical area in which they work.

FAMILY VIOLENCE COUNSELING

John Hamel & Associates	Greenbrae	(415) 472-3275	Individual, group and family counseling. 52-week certified batterer intervention programs for men and for women. 52-week high conflict family violence groups.

Building Better Families	San Rafael	(415) 601-7497	Individual, group and family counseling. 52-week certified batterer intervention programs for men and for women.

SHELTERS

Marin Abused Women's Services	San Rafael	(415) 924-6616	Shelter, counseling and support groups for women and child victims of family violence
Homeward Bound	San Rafael & Novato	(415) 457-2114	Shelter, transitional housing for men and women
Shelter Bed Hotline		(800) 774-3583	Referrals to temporary shelter

LEGAL ASSISTANCE

Family Law Center	San Rafael	(415) 492-9230	Low-fee legal help for divorce, child custody problems
Legal Aid of the North Bay		(415) 492-0230	Assistance with restraining orders
Victims of Crime		(800) 842-8467	Counseling referrals, legal assistance
Lawyer Ref. Service	San Rafael	(415) 453-5505	Low-cost consultations, help for family law problems
District Attorney Office, Victim Witness/ Assistance Unit	San Rafael	(415) 499-6450	Provides assistance in pursuing a legal case against a batterer, and securing victim aid

CHILD CARE

Marin Child Care Council	San Rafael	(415) 472-1092 x5774	Referrals to child care in Marin County

CHILD SEXUAL ABUSE

Family Service Agency	San Rafael	(415) 499-8490	Treatment programs for child sexual abuse; also, program for pregnant teens
Marin Family Therapy Center	Novato	(415) 892-0764	Child sexual abuse programs

DRUG AND ALCOHOL TREATMENT

Center Point	San Rafael	(415) 454-7777	Outpatient and residential drug and alcohol programs for adults and adolescents

Marin Treatment Center	San Rafael	(415) 457-3755	Treatment for opiate addiction, and methadone maintenance
Alcoholics Anonymous	Larkspur	(415) 499-0400	Self-help for alcohol problems
Narcotics Anonymous	San Rafael	(415) 456-1292	Self-help for drug problems

OTHER RESOURCES

National Domestic Violence Hotline
(800) 799-7233
www.NDVH.org
A general information line for victims of domestic violence—e.g., shelters, counseling

National Resource Center on Domestic Violence
(800) 537-2238
www.NRCDV.org
Provides statistical information about domestic violence, with emphasis on battered women

Domestic Abuse Helpline for Men
(888) 743-5754
Resources for male victims and female perpetrators throughout the U.S.

Stop Abuse for Everyone (SAFE)
www.safe4all.org
Information and resources for all victims of domestic violence, with an emphasis on men, and gay and lesbian populations

Family Violence Treatment and Education Association (FAVTEA)
www.FAVTEA.com
A consortium of family violence treatment providers in the greater San Francisco Bay Area, and throughout the U.S., who take a gender-inclusive, systemic approach to domestic violence treatment

Child Help U.S.A.
(800) 4 A CHILD
(800) 422-4453
Crisis counseling for parents or children; also provide resources and information

Prevent Child Abuse America
www.preventchildabuse.org
Family violence information and resources; chapters located in 39 states

Elder Abuse Hotline
(202) 898-2586
Resources for elder and dependent victims of violence and mistreatment

Batterer Treatment Program Agreement for Court-Mandated Clients

A. I am required to attend a weekly, same-sex group, each lasting 2 hours and not to exceed 15 people, for 52 consecutive sessions, and a final individual session afterwards. The primary goal of the program is to stop domestic violence. As an offender, I am the responsible party, and understand that domestic violence is a crime. While in the program, *I agree to*:

1. Attend each session as scheduled and pay my fees as required (see below).
2. Respect the confidentiality of each group member, so as to encourage more honest participation and build trust. I agree to not disclose any information regarding other participants obtained through participating in the program.
3. Never attend sessions under the influence of alcohol or drugs.
4. Listen attentively; show an interest in the material discussed, and what the other participants are saying; make an effort to talk about my issues (e.g., relationship problems, anger management, stresses), while avoiding frivolous topics; give support and constructive feedback to the other group members; share experiences, but avoid giving unwanted advice.

B. I understand that I will be held accountable for the use of violence, or threats of violence. *To successfully complete the program*, I must demonstrate that

1. I have been violence free for a minimum of 6 months.
2. I have cooperated and participated as required in the program.
3. I practice and demonstrate an understanding of anger management and conflict resolution skills.
4. I have not blamed, degraded, or committed acts which dehumanize the victims of my behavior or put at risk their safety—including, but not limited to, molesting, harassment, stalking, striking, attacking, threatening, sexually assaulting, or battering them.
5. I have not made threats to harm anyone in any manner.
6. I have complied with any requirements to receive alcohol or drug counseling, if necessary.

C. *Attendance Requirements*

1. I agree to *miss no more than 3 sessions*. If I miss a fourth session, the group leader will notify the court in writing that my attendance has become a problem. Although the group leader is under no obligation to immediately drop me from the program, the court may order him/her to do so.
2. The *maximum number* of sessions I am allowed to miss is 6—excused or unexcused. After that, I will automatically be dropped from the program.
3. I am required to call the group leader any time I miss a session—on the same day. Failure to call will result in an unexcused absence. I am allowed an absolute *maximum of 2 unexcused absences* for the duration of the program. After that, I will be terminated.
4. Late attendance policies:
    a. I am allowed to be late 6 times, and then will be dropped from the program.

    b.   No one will be allowed into group, under any circumstances, after 20 minutes.

    c.   After each 2 sessions I am late, I will be required to complete 1 additional session.

5.   If terminated for poor attendance, I may be allowed to *re-enter* the program, without losing credit for previous sessions. At a minimum, I must:

    a.   Demonstrate, with documentation, that I have a legitimate reason for my absence, and have made a reasonable effort to correct the problem.

    b.   Have otherwise been an appropriate participant in group.

    c.   Pay the $75.00 re-enrollment fee.

6.   A *leave of absence* may be granted in some cases—e.g., being put on a different shift at work, having to temporarily drop out because of financial problems, extended vacations. Sessions missed during a leave of absence will *not* count against my attendance. *Requests for a leave of absence must be put in writing in advance* (available from group leader).

D.   *Policy Regarding Fees*

1.   Group fees are *due on the first week* of the month. I am required to pay the entire amount (for 4 weeks) at that time. *No partial payments will be accepted.*

2.   If the group meets for a fifth week that particular month, that week is *free.*

3.   A *late fee surcharge* will be added to my regular fee if I don't pay on time:

    a.   Additional 10% the second week.

    b.   Additional 30% the third week.

    c.   Additional 50% the fourth week.

4.   Payments will not be allowed beyond this point. If I have not paid the fees in their entirety by the fourth week, I will automatically be put on a *mandated 1 month leave of absence.*

5.   I am not required to pay for any sessions while I am on an official leave of absence. Otherwise, I agree to pay for the *entire* month, *every* month.

E.   *Release of Information*

I grant John Hamel & Associates permission to exchange information with the following individuals and organizations regarding my participation in this program. I understand that a report regarding my progress in the program will be sent to the courts and/or probation every 3 months.

Name/Organization	Address	Phone	Fax

I understand that I may be removed from the program, and that the courts and/or probation will be notified, if it is determined that I have not been benefiting from the program, or have been disruptive to the program.

NAME _____ SIGNATURE _____ DATE _____

Appendix E

Client Exercises for High Conflict Family Violence Parent Group

EFFECTIVE PARENTING

Research indicates that effective parenting generally results in children who are responsible, therefore competent with high self-esteem. Children who have high self-esteem do not need to act out. You, the parent, have less of a reason to get angry with them. (For more information on the table below, and research on parenting, see: *Social Development: Psychological Growth and the Parent–Child Relationship* by Eleanor Maccoby, 1980.)

Productive Pattern	*Destructive Pattern*
1. High parental acceptance/warmth Never criticize the child, only the behavior Demonstrate affection with hugs, etc.	1. Low parental acceptance/warmth (Rejection)
2. Moderate to high restrictiveness Clear rules, firm limits Parent willing to listen and be flexible, but always in charge	2. Unyielding restrictiveness or extreme permissiveness
3. Insistence on mature behavior Child given age-appropriate responsibilities Parental expectations are high, but realistic	3. Little insistence on mature behavior
4. High responsiveness Parent promptly attends to the child's physical, emotional, and other needs	4. Inconsistent responsiveness
5. High positive involvement Show interest by asking questions and doing activities together Spend some one-on-one time with each child in the family	5. High negative involvement

Additional suggestions for effective parenting:

1. Give choices, rather than commands. Say: "First you _____, then you may _____." Or: "You have a choice. You can _____ (what you expect), and then _____ (the positive consequence that follows); or you can _____ (the misbehavior about to be committed), and then _____ (the negative consequence that follows)."

2. Say "do _____," rather than "don't do _____." When kids are told they are doing it wrong, they often sulk or rebel.

3. Always follow through with consequences. Kids cannot become competent and responsible unless they experience a connection between their actions and the consequences.

4. Never defend your actions when enforcing your rules—that will only lead to unnecessary arguing. Offer to hear your kid's opinions and feelings later, *after* the rule has been enforced.

5. Present a united front with your spouse. Whatever differences you have individually about parenting should never be discussed in front of the kids.

MEETINGS #1 & 27: CHARACTERISTICS OF HEALTHY FAMILIES

#1: Healthy Family Checklist

Below are the conditions required for a healthy, happy family. How good a job are *you* doing?

	great	fair	bad

1. MAINTAIN CLEAR BOUNDARIES BETWEEN CHILDREN AND PARENTS—I have the responsibility to raise my children and, therefore, have authority over them. I can be their friend, but I am a parent first, and do not use them to get my emotional needs met. I take care of my needs, and my spouse and I have a relationship apart from the children. We do not side with any child or encourage "alliances." My children are individuals, even if they remind me of people I'm angry with, and I don't take my frustrations out on them.

2. USE AN AUTHORITATIVE STYLE OF PARENTING—My style of parenting is neither permissive nor authoritarian, and my rules are reasonable. My spouse and I act like "benevolent dictators" with our children. We are willing to hear them out, but reserve the right to have the final say. Our decisions are made out of love, and to meet the best interests of the family.

3. COMMUNICATION IS RESPECTFUL—With my spouse and children, communication is always respectful. I am an attentive listener, and talk in a non-aggressive manner, careful to avoid put-downs and comments that shame my children. I am secure enough to allow my children to express strong feelings and opinions.

4. DISCUSSION AND NEGOTIATION PREFERRED—My partner and I never try to impose our will on each other, but are open to hearing each other's points of view. When appropriate, I engage in discussion and negotiation with my children, allowing them to contribute to the problem-solving process. I am open to changing the rules if necessary.

5. AUTONOMY ENCOURAGED—I give my children as much responsibility as they can handle. Although I am responsible for their welfare, and seek to keep them safe, I avoid overprotecting or over-controlling them. I teach them in such as way that they *internalize* my rules and lessons, and they behave because they think it is the right thing to do, rather than out of fear.

6. MARITAL RELATIONSHIP HEALTHY AND SE-
CURE—I actively nurture my relationship with my partner. We help each other, are flexible in our roles, and
show mutual respect. We set aside time to talk, but we
also go out on dates and have fun together, so that our
home is not simply a "child rearing business."

MEETING #8: GOALS OF MISBEHAVIOR*

1. The four basic goals and the unhelpful and helpful ways parents can respond:

Child's Goal	Behavior	Unhelpful Parental Response	Helpful Parental Response
Attention	Clowning around, engaging in minor mischief, unique dress, forgetting, neglecting chores	Become annoyed, remind, nag	Refuse to give attention on demand; ignore inappropriate bids for attention; wait for the child to do something right and give proper attention
Power	Aggressive, disobedient, defiant, hostile, resistant, stubborn	Feel angry and provoked; either fight power with power or else give in	Withdraw from conflict and enforce consequences for misbehavior; help child use power constructively by asking him/her to help work things out
Revenge	Rude, hurtful, destructive, violent, glaring	Feel deeply hurt, retaliate	Try to empathize with the child; build a trusting relationship through understanding/acceptance
Prove child's inadequacy	Avoid trying, quit easily; school truancy, escape through alcohol, drugs	Feel hopeless, discouraged; agree with child that nothing can be done; give up	Avoid criticism or pity; arrange for child to have successful experiences and praise positive efforts

2. Other goals of misbehavior, common with adolescents: excitement, peer acceptance, superiority
3. Questions for discussion:

    *   Based on the list above, why do you think *your* child misbehaves?
    *   What are some of the negative and positive ways you tend to respond?

---

*Adapted from D. Dinkmeyer & M. McKay (1983), *The Parent's Guide: Step teen.*

MEETINGS #9 & 35: BEHAVIOR PLANS

A.   Behavior Plan #1

    Name _____   Week Ending _____

DESIRED BEHAVIOR   PRIVILEGE OR REWARD

B. Behavior Plan #2 (Point Chart)

Name _____ Week Ending _____

BEHAVIOR—and points possible for each (Assign each behavior 1–5 points)	M	Tu	W	Th	F	Sa	Su	Tot

Total points earned:

Rewards:

Total points possible:

_____ to _____ points:

_____ to _____ points:

_____ to _____ points:

MEETINGS #12, 13, 14, 38, 39, & 40: STAGES OF CHILD DEVELOPMENT*

Meetings #12 & 38: Infancy to Age 3

Read the information below. Which problems have you had, and how have you dealt with them?

BIRTH–8 MONTHS: INFANTS

CHILD CHARACTERISTICS/NEEDS/ TYPICAL PROBLEMS	WHAT PARENTS SHOULD BE DOING
1. *Dependence*—Babies are completely dependent on their caregivers, and need to feel absolutely secure.	1. Be highly responsive to your baby's needs. It is nearly impossible to "spoil" an infant. The more secure an infant feels, and the more he trusts you, the easier it will be for him to separate later on.
2. *Differences*—Infants differ in temperament, activity level, reaction to stimulation, sensitivity to the environment, how loud and often they cry, and how well they sleep. No two babies develop at exactly the same rate in any of these areas. By the second or third month, babies' personalities begin to emerge in terms of what they like to look at, how much stimulation they need, and how they wish to be held.	2. Expect your child to develop at her own pace, and respond accordingly. Consult with your pediatrician if the baby's development is highly unusual.
3. *Sucking*—Infancy is also known as the "oral-sensory" stage, due to baby's need to suck. This need is stronger in some infants than others. Babies, however, will put anything into their mouths.	3. An infant's need to suck should not be denied. Keep dangerous objects out of reach. Pacifiers can be used in addition to the breast or bottle. If the infant has begun to use his own hand, a pacifier won't be needed. You can use a pacifier between feedings, but limit its use to times when the baby is being highly fussy, so he doesn't become too dependent on it. Pacifiers are not a substitute for cuddling and holding.
4. *Crying*—Crying may signal physical distress (e.g., hunger, stomach cramps, needing to change position) or a desire	4. Tend to the baby's needs. To comfort, hold and rock, sing, or play a music tape. You may need to burp her, because

*Much of the material in the following sections on child development has been adapted from *Parent Power!*, by John Rosemond (Published by Andrews & McMeel, 1990) for comforting. Because they don't achieve "object permanence" until around 8 months, babies think that if you are out of sight, you disappear. But babies may cry just because they can.

5. *Feeding*—Newborns need to be fed every 3–5 hours, but 3 a.m. feedings may stop by the second or third month. Can take breast or bottle. Bottle-fed babies get more diseases, are more overweight, and have more control over the feeding process. Solid foods accepted sometime after the fourth month, but breast feeders will often resist them. At six months, they will want to feed themselves, using their fingers.

6. *Sleeping*—Each baby will prefer a particular sleeping position. Often cry themselves to sleep. Typically begin sleeping through the night in the second or third month, but will sometimes wake up for short periods in middle of night. Will give up late night feeding by fourth month. Need several naps each day, until around the eighth month, when only one nap may be needed. By then, they are more mobile, and will protest their bedtime.

babies swallow air as they cry. If you have to leave the room, call to her—your voice is reassuring. Let her cry for a while if you've already tended to her needs. Infants like to be snugly wrapped and to be held upright, to look over your shoulder. An infant carrier comforts the baby while freeing your hands.

5. Feed your baby when he's hungry. Don't force feed, and never use bottles as pacifiers. Introduce new foods one at a time, at the beginning of a meal. Don't let the baby take a bottle to bed—causes tooth decay and bottle dependence. Breast-fed babies will often reject bottles from mom, but accept them from others.

6. Go along with the preferred sleeping position. Establish a consistent bedtime (e.g., 8:00 p.m.) once the baby has given up the late night feeding. Let baby cry himself to sleep, and ignore short periods of crying during night, but respond to prolonged crying. Don't force the baby to stay up past bedtime in an attempt to make him tired—he will only become agitated. Be firm with bedtime. Don't walk on tiptoes—babies can tolerate a good deal of noise when asleep.

---

8 MONTHS–18 MONTHS: TODDLERS

CHILD CHARACTERISTICS/NEEDS/ TYPICAL PROBLEMS	WHAT PARENTS SHOULD BE DOING

---

1. *Need to explore*—Toddlers experience rapid growth in motor, communication, and cognitive skills, and can begin doing many things on their own (begin to crawl around 9 mos). Curious, driven to master their environment by exploring, manipulating objects.

2. *Stranger and separation anxiety*—Exploring is exciting but scary. Toddlers

1. Provide a safe environment, that also encourages exploration. Playpens OK for very short periods, but toddlers need to roam so they can have more control. Child-proof house (e.g., locks for doors and drawers, gates; remove breakable and small objects, etc.).

2. Let the child determine the pace of exploration. Be patient. Be available,

realize they are separate persons, develop an identity. Object permanence lets them distinguish between mom and strangers, causing anxiety. Repeatedly return to mom/primary caregiver for security, even as they actively seek independence. Fear of strangers—will even reject toys from them. May reject dad and other familiar relatives.

and let him cling if he needs to. Don't force him on others.

3. *Biting*—Babies use their mouths to explore their environment and to get pleasure. Biting is natural, and can help relieve the pain of teething. In their second year, toddlers bite when frustrated.

3. If she bites you, don't take it personally and don't punish. Say "No!" firmly, and put child in a time out. Afterwards, you can hold her, but don't talk about the biting incident.

4. *Weaning*—Most pediatricians believe that weaning, from the breast or the bottle, should occur after the child is 12 months old. Some toddlers will want a bottle when upset or sleepy.

4. The more you deny the bottle, the more he will want it. Let the child have a bottle when he asks, but insist that he use a cup during meals.

5. *Playing with b.m.'s*—Very normal. Satisfies their need to explore. May also hold their b.m.'s.

5. Supervise the child, but don't overreact if she makes a mess. Calmly clean up.

6. *Bedtime problems*—Toddlers often will resist going to sleep and scream in protest.

6. Start 30 minutes before bedtime with a bath or by reading a story. Tuck him in and leave the room. If the screaming continues, go back every 5 minutes or so to reassure him. Tuck him in, kiss him (but don't pick him up) and leave right away.

---

18 MONTHS–36 MONTHS: THE "TERRIBLE TWOS"

CHILD CHARACTERISTICS/NEEDS/ TYPICAL PROBLEMS	WHAT PARENTS SHOULD BE DOING
1. *Experimenting*—At this age, children realize that they can cause things to happen. Are constantly on the go, getting into things. Want to be independent.	1. Allow as much exploring and experimenting as possible, while providing for his safety. Have toys available that are age appropriate but challenging.
2. *Frustration*—Physical development lags behind cognitive skills, causing frustration (e.g., can't put a puzzle piece into place). Also frustrated because they can't express thoughts and feelings into words (only know about 10 words at 18 mos). Often reject help.	2. Assist child when frustrated, but back off when she refuses help. Let her figure things out herself, or encourage her to do something else.

3. *Rebellion*—Won't respond when you talk to them. Throw loud, violent tantrums. Won't cooperate. Say "no!" a lot.

3. Enforce limits in a firm but gentle way. Don't try to explain. Show him what needs to be done, step-by-step. Remove him from trouble, redirect him to other activities, or put him in his room. Reinforcement should be immediate (e.g., "pick up that toy and then we go swimming"). Don't react in anger—this increases his anxiety and convinces him that he is more powerful than you! Remember that rebelling is good: it helps children establish an identity, understand cause-and-effect, and figure out what they can and cannot do.

4. *Social aggression*—Even more difficult with other children than with adults. Very possessive of their toys, and territorial. Hit, push, pull hair, bite, etc. No patience, want everything "right now." Self-centered, not able to empathize with the feelings of others, incapable of remorse, and don't know right from wrong. Don't know how to make friends.

4. Supervise play. Best to pair your child with playmates who have a similar temperament. If one child takes another's toy, gently take it and give it back, then separate the children until they calm down. Don't try to reason with her. Model for her the right way to play. With severe aggression, such as biting, sternly say "no!" before removing her from the situation.

5. *Separation anxiety*—New independence is scary. Will often cling, follow parent from room to room. Have a favorite toy or "security blanket." Can be ritualistic about arranging toys or going to bed.

5. Allow him to cling and to follow you. Hold him if he wants that. He'll let go when he feels ready. If clinging is excessive, redirect him to a fun activity that you can join in at first but walk away from later. Go along with his ritualistic activities.

6. *Sibling rivalry*—Their self-centeredness won't let them tolerate rivals for parent's attention. Show aggression to babies, or act up. Sometimes will regress— e.g., want to wear a diaper again or nurse.

6. Give her plenty of love and attention. Reward appropriate attempts to get attention. Set aside time just for her. Continue to have reasonable expectations, but make her feel special by telling her that she's a "big girl" and is more capable than her baby brother.

7. *Bedtime problems*—Children will insist on staying up past their bedtime, may scream to get their way.

7. As with toddlers, establish a pre-bedtime routine. If he screams, check in with him every 10—15 minutes, tuck him in and quickly leave. Be firm!

MEETINGS #12, 13, 14, 38, 39, & 40: STAGES OF CHILD DEVELOPMENT

Meetings #13 & 39: Age 3 Through Middle Childhood

Read the information below. Which problems have you had, and how have you dealt with them?

3-YEAR-OLDS

CHILD CHARACTERISTICS/ NEEDS/TYPICAL PROBLEMS	WHAT PARENTS SHOULD BE DOING
1. *Initiative*—Children build on the independence achieved during the "terrible two's." Excellent memories. Like to make things. Vivid imaginations. Learn from mistakes, more persistent at solving problems, better at delaying gratification. Not yet able to plan ahead—play for the sake of playing.	1. Provide toys and games that challenge him, such as puzzles and markers or paints for drawing. Encourage imaginative play with doll sets, hand puppets, etc., but allow spontaneous play with household objects. Keep television watching to a minimum.
2. *Helplessness*—Fragile sense of identity. Distressed by minor cuts and bruises, because they don't understand that wounds eventually heal. Vivid imagination, along with inability to tell the difference between words and things (if there is a word for something, then it must exist), combine to cause fear of ordinary events, such as ghosts or the dark. Fear of the dark may persist into middle childhood.	2. Continue to be available to the child. Tend to minor injuries, sit with the child, but don't try to correct her exaggerations. Don't try to reason fears away. Acknowledge that the fear is real for her, and reassure her that you are there to protect her from harm. Remain calm. Don't show anxiety or go out of your way to accommodate her—this will only convince the child there really is something to worry about.
3. *Physical awkwardness*—Will often spill things, trip over their feet, stutter, etc.	3. Be patient and supportive. Don't show anger, and don't criticize. If you make a big deal out of it, he'll think he did wrong. If he spills something, help him clean up. If he stutters, don't complete his sentences for him or tell him to slow down. Instead, remain calm, talk slowly, and ask questions that can be answered in a few words.
4. *Imaginary friends*—Indicates an interest in peer relations. Allows them to practice social skills in a way they can control the interaction. Children often project negative aspects of themselves onto these imaginary playmates, as they do with dolls.	4. Never question the existence of imaginary playmates.

5. *Social relations*—At this age, children are very social and can make instant friends. Imitate others, as a way to develop social bonds and acquire more problem-solving skills. Able to take turns and play with others, and not just parallel play. Often, they will rush too quickly into a relationship and be hurt. Will want parents to play with them instead.

5. Provide adequate supervision and guidance. If possible, put her in a good day care program a few days a week. Don't be over-concerned about play interactions that don't go well—making friends is a trial-and-error process for her. Resist her attempts to make *you* her constant playmate.

6. *Morality—Lie and take things.* Until they are six or seven, don't fully understand the meaning of responsibility, or what is the "truth," and understand "good" and "bad" as what their parents approve or disapprove of. Feel empowered when lying works to avoid punishment. Don't understand pronouns, and the difference between "mine" and "yours."

6. *Don't give him a chance to lie. Tell* him what he did wrong—don't ask. Punish the behavior. Disregard the dishonesty. Don't promise to make things easier if he tells the truth or threaten more punishment if he lies. Don't preach or moralize—he cannot understand abstract concepts. If he takes something, focus on his *behavior*, and have him return what he took.

FOURS AND FIVES

CHILD CHARACTERISTICS/NEEDS/ TYPICAL PROBLEMS	WHAT PARENTS SHOULD BE DOING
1. *Purposeful behavior*—Can set goals and work towards them.	1. Provide more complex play materials. Suggest simple projects. Assign tasks, such as cleaning room, and set up reward systems to motivate good behavior.
2. *Verbal skills*—Talk constantly, with vocabulary of 1,500 words by age 4. Ask searching questions, want to know the meaning of words.	2. Be patient! Calmly answer his questions. If you're irritated, tired, etc., change the subject or divert his attention to another activity.
3. *Gender awareness*—Indicate preference for doing "boy" or "girl" things, and seek approval from same-sex parent. Want to know where babies come from. Curious about their genitals, may want to masturbate, or to play "doctor."	3. Don't interfere with the child's natural choices. Pushing a child to be "gender neutral" can be as futile and damaging as prohibiting interest in opposite-sex activities (e.g., boys who want to play with dolls, or girls who like rough-and-tumble play). Reacting to self-exploration of her genitals with anger and disgust, or punishing the child, will give the message that she is bad, and that there is something wrong with bodily pleasures. Teach her that

one's genitals are private. Separate children who are playing "doctor," tell her it's not appropriate, but avoid sermons. Divert her attention to something else. Stay low-key.

4. *Cognitive and ethical limitations*—At this age, children see things in black and white, and don't understand abstractions. Will say "I hate you" if they are angry with something you have done. Understand what is right or wrong based on what the parents specifically approve and disapprove. Can't generalize beyond each particular circumstance.

4. Reacting too strongly or defensively will only reinforce his negative feelings for you. Avoid taking the words seriously, but teach him alternative ways to express feelings (e.g., "I'm angry with you!") Don't expect him to understand ethical terms such as "polite" or "responsibility." Address misbehavior immediately after it happens. Be brief, and focus on his actions.

5. *Clinging behavior*—Although more socially adept, their primary relationships remain with their parents. May demand help, follow mom or dad around the house. May seek reassurance that parents still love them, and will return after going somewhere.

5. Assist with difficult problems, but insist that she figure out for herself those problems she can handle. Don't show discomfort to the question, "Do you love me?" Instead, teach her that saying "I love you" is special, and better used sparingly, like a surprise.

6–11: MIDDLE CHILDHOOD

CHILD CHARACTERISTICS/NEEDS/ TYPICAL PROBLEMS	WHAT PARENTS SHOULD BE DOING

1. *Achievement*—This stage is sometimes known as one of "industry versus inferiority." Children at this age need to build on the independence, initiative, and imaginary play previously acquired to succeed at school and with peers. Starting to understand some abstractions, such as "morning" or "afternoon." Interested in concept of "God." Moral judgment expands from learning peer group rules, competitive play, and the classroom. More cooperative at school than at home.

1. Accept that your child will be preoccupied with school and peers. Problems in these areas will upset him, but don't expect him to always want to talk to you about them. Don't feel rejected. Understand that his loyalties have become divided. Lesser cooperation at home is not your fault, but due to simpler rules at school, and the fact that teachers can be objective, without emotional bonds to the children. Encourage school success by providing a quiet place and time to do homework. Help him learn to study; assist, but *don't* do his homework for him. Also encourage him to engage in activities that give him a feeling of competence. Some kids are good in sports, while others excel in music, etc. Keep him away from organized sports

2. *Peer problems*—Fitting in with peers is a difficult task for all children, and more so for some. As they learn their roles and how they fit in, they may be bossy and aggressive, overly compliant and sensitive, or detached.

3. *Fighting with siblings*—Siblings who are close together in age will often argue and compete, and fighting may escalate to physical brawls.

in which adults are too involved—it's not fun for him, but a burden.

2. Usually, it is best to let her work out her own problems with peers—otherwise, she will depend too much on you and will have a harder time fitting in. Remember that natural consequences are the most effective for learning. Understand that bossiness at home is normal, where the child is being territorial. If she is overly aggressive and rude, send her friends home. If your child is teased or rejected, help her find solutions to the problem. Be supportive without showing pity—pity only reinforces the victim role. If your child isolates, it may be due to shyness or her preference—some children are more introverted, and that is okay. Look for opportunities to pair her up with similar children, but don't force them on her.

3. Separate the siblings. Unless one child is clearly abusing a totally innocent victim, assume that they both participated in the problem. Don't send them to separate time outs—they won't learn a lesson. Ignore their arguments and have them apologize to each other, including shaking hands. Afterwards assign a shared task that will force them to cooperate. If fighting persists, assign more shared tasks but also make them do extra favors for each other.

MEETINGS #12, 13, 14, 38, 39, & 40: STAGES OF CHILD DEVELOPMENT

Meetings #14 & 40: Pre-Adolescence to Young Adulthood

Read the information below. Which problems have you had, and how have you dealt with them?

11–14: PREADOLESCENCE AND EARLY ADOLESCENCE

CHILD CHARACTERISTICS/NEEDS/ TYPICAL PROBLEMS	WHAT PARENTS SHOULD BE DOING
1. *Transition problems*—An extremely awkward stage, between childhood and adolescence. Increasing capability for abstract thinking along with surging hormones and body changes create confusion, intense feelings. Developing sense of morality causes them to have strong opinions about what is right and wrong. Rebel against parents, sulk, impossible to please. Want freedom but unwilling to take on responsibility. Seek out peer group. Constantly evaluating themselves, and wondering what their peers think about them. Seek negative attention to mask their insecurities. Preoccupied with appearance.	1. Be understanding and tolerant. Don't let your buttons get pushed. Listen to her feelings and opinions, even when she is wrong, contradictory, irrational, or just plain angry. Find the proper balance between increased freedom and the restrictions she needs to feel safe. Don't be intimidated by her tantrums or manipulations. Refuse to engage in a power struggle. Don't dismiss her or make fun of her but don't take her too seriously either. Do your best to accept her, while setting appropriate limits, and she'll feel more empowered. And remind yourself that this period in her life won't last forever.
2. *Emotional isolation*—Children at this age often feel lost. Self-esteem dependent on their success at finding a satisfying, stable role in their peer group, so they deliberately push parents away. Unwilling to talk to parents about inner turmoil because this would be admitting dependence on them. However, due to shifts in peer group loyalties, competition, etc., may be reluctant to share feelings with peers and be perceived as weak. Present a front of aloofness, to hide their vulnerability. Especially won't ask parents questions about sex.	2. Don't force him to talk with you about his emotional difficulties. Keep in mind that in the peer group culture, it isn't "cool" to be too friendly with your parents. Let him know that you understand what he's going through, that you once went through similar problems, and that you are there for him if he needs you. Don't subject him to an uncomfortable, embarrassing lecture about sex. Start by focusing on relationship values, such as respecting oneself and one's partner, rather than the mechanics of sex. Tell him that his friend may give him misinformation, and that you are available if he has any further questions. (Girls need to be prepared for their period, and this discussion cannot be avoided.)

3. *Declining grades*—Because of their emotional state and preoccupation with peers, it is not unusual for preadolescent and early adolescent children to "forget" their homework, or turn in reports long past when they are due, and to generally exhibit poor school performance.

3. Make sure that she goes to school. Insist that she put in the time to do homework, without loud music or other distractions. Consult with teachers if you need to. However, accept that there may be some decline in grades, that her preoccupation with other matters may affect her ability to concentrate and follow through.

15–19: LATER ADOLESCENCE

CHILD CHARACTERISTICS/NEEDS/ TYPICAL PROBLEMS

WHAT PARENTS SHOULD BE DOING

1. *Independence and identity*—The developmental task of adolescents is to move towards independence from parents and to establish their own, secure identity. Find their place within the peer group. Want additional freedoms. Idealistic. After 14, usually become more confident and less intensely emotional, but may continue to test limits.

1. Continue to maintain healthy limits. Make increasing freedoms contingent on ability to take more responsibility. Have him earn your trust. For example, extend his curfew only if he regularly comes in on time over a period of several months, and allow him to drive if he gets a job and is willing to pay for the insurance.

2. *Coping*—May be rude and oppositional, taking out on parents the problems they have with school, peers, and opposite sex. May become depressed, overeat, threaten to run away, and/or try alcohol and drugs.

2. Be patient. Accept expressions of anger, but not name-calling or other types of abuse. Keep lines of communication open. Let her know, without rubbing it in, that her acting-out is a sign of internal distress. Offer her the choice of resolving the issue with you or talking with a professional counselor. Don't be overly concerned about threats to run away if you have provided a healthy, secure environment for your child. Insist that she get involved in at least one extra-curricular activity and/or hobby, but give her a wide range of choices. This will keep her constructively engaged, lessen her dependence on the peer group, and help her build confidence and self-esteem.

3. *Privacy*—As they are establishing independence, they will want you to respect their personal boundaries, such as the right to leave their room messy and

3. As much as possible, honor his privacy and personal choices. Be flexible, and willing to compromise. Make privileges contingent on keeping room

play loud music, and for you to not go in without their permission. They will also insist on their right to choose their friends and not have to inform you of their whereabouts.

somewhat clean and keeping music at tolerable levels. Reserve the right to search his room if there is evidence that something may be wrong—for instance, if he has been lying about his whereabouts, skipping school, acting or looking different than usual. Insist on meeting his friends, and ask that he check in regarding his whereabouts, but don't be intrusive if you don't need to.

4.   *Young adulthood*—At 18, a person becomes an adult and no longer the parents' responsibility. Some adolescents will be eager to move out and go to college or get a job. Others will want to stay home for a while, or maybe indefinitely. This may be a mutual choice between parents and adolescent, or because they are not ready or too fearful to get on with their lives.

4.   Allow your child to live at home until she is ready to leave, as long as it is convenient for *you.* Tolerate a few months of goofing off, but then insist that she begin taking on adult responsibilities by either getting a job, going to school, or both. Stay out of her personal life, unless her behavior directly affects you and the family—for example, coming home at 2 a.m. intoxicated, waking everyone. Have her contribute to the maintenance of the household by doing chores and/or paying some rent.

MEETING #26: RESPONDING TO TEMPER TANTRUMS*

A.   Below are some of the ways parents react to their children's tantrums. Put a check mark next to the ones you have used, and then indicate the extent to which they worked:

Response	Check if used	What happens when I use this approach
1. Yelling and shouting		
2. Insults		
3. Thre ats, dirty looks		
4. Physical punishment		
5. Talking about it		
6. Time out		
7. Sending child to their room		
8. Going without dinner		
9. Removal of privileges		
10. Grounding		

B.   Dealing with tantrums is similar to dealing with most negative behavior. Although some of the above responses may be appropriate and work some of the time, the following steps give you the best chance of effectively dealing with tantrums in your children:

STEP 1: Stay calm, and don't take tantrums personally

- Don't overanalyze tantrums. Children throw tantrums for attention and because they aren't getting their way.
- Don't find adult reasons for the tantrums. It's not personal.

STEP 2: Ignore the outburst

- Don't look, point, glare at or talk to the child, or show anger.
- Don't explain, give child what he/she wants, promise anything, or show any signs of affection (e.g, hugs).

STEP 3: Deal with the "burst" (high point of the tantrum)

- Verbal abuse—Ignore it and leave the room
- Physical abuse against you or destruction of property—Remove breakable items and either ignore the child or leave the room
- Tantrum harms other children—Ignore tantruming child, give sympathy and attention to injured or frightened other child

---

*For more information on parenting difficult children, obtain a copy of the manual *Parent Empowerment: Counseling Parents in Positive Child-Rearing Practices*, by Douglas Ruben, 2002. Available on the web: www.abduct.com/acoa/acoa.htm.

- Tantrum attracts attention from other children—Distract other children away. If you must, promise them a treat for ignoring the tantrum and doing something else
- Child with tantrum hurts self—Treat injury if you need to, but don't talk to the child

STEP 4: After the outburst

- Don't talk about the tantrum
- Ask the child to carry out a simple task (e.g., bring you something), and praise him and/or give him physical affection
- If child refuses to comply with this task, or is still huffy and upset, forget about it.
- Return to STEP 1 if child starts the tantrum again.

C.   Coping with Special Problems

Tantrums that won't stop—Children who have gotten a lot of negative attention and/or have experienced a great deal of abuse may continue to act out no matter how long you ignore the behavior, because the tantrum itself has become rewarding (e.g., the tantrum "rush" makes them feel good, tantruming makes them feel stronger).

Violent tantrums by older children and adolescents—As a child gets older and bigger, he/she may present a significant threat to others in the home.

SOLUTIONS:

Physical restraint—For children ages 3 to 9, who are small and physically controllable by the parent, you can wrap your arms and legs around the child from the back or use a mild form of restraint known as "Response Movement Suppression." The latter is preferred, because it involves less physical contact, which can be reinforcing to the child. At the start of an angry outburst, tell the child to "look at the wall." Take the child by the upper arm and move directly to an adjacent wall. Bring that arm up and stretch it against the wall, then do the same with the other arm, so that the child is now in a "frisk" position. At the same time, curl your leg around the child's left ankle, pulling it out and to the left, then do the same for the right ankle. Once all the limbs are extended, stand behind the child facing sideways, with one arm *gently* resting against his/her backbone, pressing *slightly* forward.

> IMPORTANT!—DO NOT ATTEMPT THIS UNLESS YOU HAVE FIRST LEARNED TO MANAGE YOUR OWN ANGER IMPULSES!

Early intervention—You can't wait until the tantrum "burst" with children that may cause significant harm to others. Instead, look for the first signs of aggression (e.g., stomping feet, making gestures or faces, looking agitated) and *immediately divert the child to another activity that is incompatible and/or competes with the tantrum behavior* (e.g., help you put away groceries). Then be sure to reinforce the child for doing what you asked.

Outside intervention—No adolescent wants the embarrassment of outside family members, friends, or law enforcement showing up at the house to help you cope with his/her acting out. After you have tried ignoring, having other family members leave, remove breakable items, etc., give the tantruming child a choice: "You have one minute to quiet yourself down. You can stay here or go outside. That is your choice. But after one minute, I will _____ (friend, outside family, police, etc.) and they will come over to help."

SAY THIS IN A FIRM BUT NON-THREATENING MANNER. DO NOT SAY ANYTHING ELSE. DO NOT TRY TO REASON WITH THE CHILD, OR TO "COACH" HIM. IF YOU OR A COUNSELOR HAD PREVIOUSLY TAUGHT HIM WAYS TO MANAGE HIS ANGER, LET HIM DO THIS ON HIS OWN. ANGRY PEOPLE DON'T WANT TO BE TOLD WHAT TO DO!

IF *YOU* ARE NOT IN CONTROL, HE WON'T BE IN CONTROL.

D.   Tantrums in Public Places

Dealing with a child's tantrums in public poses a special challenge because ignoring the misbehavior may be upsetting to others. Simply leaving is inconvenient to you and risks rewarding the misbehavior. Here are some helpful alternatives:

Make your expectations clear in advance—Inform your child *before* you go out exactly what you expect from her. Be specific. For example, if you are going to a restaurant, don't ask her to "behave," but rather to sit still, not stand in her seat, eat with her utensils, etc. If you are about to go to the supermarket, instruct her to stay in the cart or by your side at all times, refrain from demanding things, etc.

Have rewards for good behavior—Remember that sitting quietly in a restaurant, or patiently following you around in a store without being allowed access to the wonderful items on the shelves, is a lot to ask from a child. An older child may be able to control himself, knowing that he'll retain his TV privileges if he does. However, younger children can't think very far ahead. Be sure to have *immediate* rewards. For instance, let him bring a picture book or toy, which he can play with if he cooperates, allow him a treat, or the opportunity to choose the family's dessert for the night. Use whatever works!

MEETING #34: HOW TO REINFORCE POSITIVE BEHAVIOR

A. Facts about reinforcement
    1. Children are rewarded in various ways all the time, naturally. Parents can use rewards in a conscious, deliberate manner to teach and maintain positive behavior in their children.
    2. Both good and bad behaviors may be rewarded. Examples:
        a. (good) Suzie gets an "A" on her test, and the teacher praises her in class
        b. (bad) Jimmie throws a pen across the classroom, and everyone laughs
        c. Intermittent reinforcement: Bad behavior can be strengthened and become ingrained when the parent refuses to give in, but then eventually lets the child have his/her way—e.g., giving a child candy on the sixth request, after he/she had asked and been refused five previous times. THIS ONLY TEACHES THE CHILD TO BE MORE PERSISTENT AND OBNOXIOUS IN MISBEHAVIOR. EITHER GIVE IN RIGHT AWAY, OR NOT AT ALL!
    3. Preferable to use rewards (given *after* the desirable behavior), as opposed to bribery (reward given *before* the desirable behavior)
    4. Types of reinforcers (rewards)
        a. Social: smile, give pat on the back, praise with words—e.g., "great job!"
        b. Non-social:
            Tangible rewards—e.g., candy, toys
            Privileges—e.g., getting to stay up late, watch TV
    5. Suggestions on using reinforcers

        • Reward immediately after the behavior (especially with younger children), so they get the connection between action and consequence
        • Be specific about what you reward—e.g., praise the behavior, not the child
        • Be consistent
        • Reward frequently and generously when teaching a new behavior, then fade
        • Reward approximations when teaching something new
        • When possible, rewards should be natural and logical, and match the deed

B. Questions for discussion
    1. Do you tend to use bribery or rewards? How often do you reward?
    2. What are some examples of "natural" consequences that might be effective at home?

MEETING #52: CONDUCTING FAMILY MEETINGS

It is a good idea for families to have regularly scheduled meetings (weekly, bi-monthly or monthly) to resolve family problems. In a family meeting, everyone, except for very young children, is allowed to participate.

Parents function as group leaders. They use their leadership skills to help the meetings go as smoothly and efficiently as possible, and they enforce the meeting rules. Each parental team can institute whatever rules they believe will make the meeting better. *Such rules ought to apply to everyone, and include the following:*

1. Listen while others are talking, even if you don't agree with what is said.
2. Wait until they have finished speaking before responding.
3. Speak with respect—do not shout, threaten, swear, or put down any one else.
4. Be clear and brief in presenting issues for discussion.

It is the responsibility of the parents to enforce these rules. Violators can be handled with a stern warning or by being asked to take a time out. Short (5–10 minute) time outs are usually more effective than excessively long ones. When parents violate any of the rules, it is up to them to apologize and take a voluntary time out if necessary. By providing a good example themselves, the parents help the kids better follow the rules.

An excellent way for the parents to get the kids more seriously involved in the meetings is to have them take turns acting as "master of ceremonies." As master of ceremonies, or "mc," the child's task is to write down, in order, the various issues individual family members want to bring up for discussion, and then keep track of them so that everyone has a turn. *Here is a suggested family meeting format:*

1. The mc announces to the group that the meeting is about to begin, reads the rules, and reminds everyone that the parents are the leaders and have the right to enforce the rules.
2. The mc asks if there are any issues, writes them down on paper, then calls on the first person on the list.
3. Each issue is discussed, facilitated by the parents, until all issues have been discussed or the meeting time is expired (meetings can be open-ended, or time-limited).

Keep in mind that many problems can't be resolved in a single meeting, so be patient!

References

Aldarondo, E., & Straus, M. (1994). Screening for physical violence in marital therapy. *Family Process, 33*, 425–439.

Allen, S., & Hawkins, A. (1999). Maternal gatekeeping: Mother's beliefs and behaviors that inhibit greater father involvement in family work. *Journal of Marriage and the Family, 61*, 199–212.

American Psychiatric Association. (1994). *Diagnostic and statistical manual of mental disorders* (4th ed.). Washington, DC: Author.

Apsler, R., et al. (2002). Fear and expectations: Differences among female victims of domestic violence who come to the attention of the police. *Violence and Victims, 17*(4), 445–453.

Archer, J. (1999). Assessment of the reliability of the Conflict Tactics Scale. *Journal of Interpersonal Violence, 14*(12), 1263–1289.

Archer, J. (2000). Sex differences in aggression between heterosexual partners: A meta-analytic review. *Psychological Bulletin, 126*(5), 651–680.

Archer, J. (2002). Sex differences in physically aggressive acts between heterosexual partners: A meta-analytic review. *Aggression and Violent Behavior, 7*, 313–351.

Arndt, J. (1994). Treatment of borderline personality disorder: A challenge for cognitive-behavioral therapy. *Behavior Research and Therapy, 32*(4), 419–430.

Austin, J., & Dankwort, J. (1998). A review of standards for batterer intervention programs. Available online at: http://www.vaw.umn.edu/Vawnet/standard.htm

Averil, J. (1983, November). Studies on anger and aggression: Implications for theories of emotion. *American Psychologist*, 1145–1160.

Babcock, J., Waltz, J., Jacobson, N., & Gottman, J. (1993). Power and violence: The relation between communication patterns, power discrepancies, and domestic violence. *Journal of Consulting and Clinical Psychology, 61*(1), 40–50.

Bagarozzi, D. A., & Wordarski, J. S. (1977). A social exchange typology of conjugal relationships and conflict development. *Journal of Marriage and Family Counseling, 3*, 53–60.

Bartholomew, K., Henderson, A., & Dutton, D. (2001). Insecure attachment and abusive intimate relationships. In C. Culow (Ed.), *Adult attachment and couple psychotherapy* (pp. 43–61). New York: Brunner-Routledge.

Bartholomew, K., & Shaver, P. (1998). Methods of assessing adult attachment: Do they converge? In J. Simpson & W. Rholes (Eds.), *Attachment theory and close relationships* (pp. 25–45). New York: Guilford.

Björkquist, K. (1994). Sex differences in physical, verbal and indirect aggression: A review of recent research. *Sex Roles, 30*(3/4), 177–187.

Bograd, M. (1984). Family systems approaches to wife battering: A feminist critique. *American Journal of Orthopsychiatry, 54*, 558–568.

Bookwala, J. (2002). Adult attachment styles and aggressive behaviors in dating relationships. *Journal of Social and Personal Relationships, 15*, 175–190.

Bowlby, J. (1988). *A secure base: Clinical applications of attachment theory.* London: Routledge.

Brannen, S., & Rubin, A. (1996). Comparing the effectiveness of gender-specific and couples groups in a court-mandated spouse abuse treatment program. *Research on Social Work Practice, 6*(4), 405–424.

Brennan, K., Clark, C. & Shaver, P. (1998). Self-report measurement of adult attachment: An integrative overview. In J. Simpson & W. Rholes (Eds.), *Attachment theory and close relationships* (pp. 46–76). New York: Guilford.

Brownell, P. (1998). *Family crimes against the elderly: Elder abuse and the criminal justice system.* New York & London: Guilford.

Brygger, M., & Edleson, J. (1987). The domestic abuse project: A multisystems intervention in woman battering. *Journal of Interpersonal Violence, 2*(3), 324–326.

Burman, B., John, R., & Margolin, G. (1992). Observed patterns of conflict in violent, nonviolent, and nondistressed couples. *Behavioral Assessment, 14,* 15–37.

Cahn, D. (1996). Family violence from a communication perspective. In D. Cahn & S. Lloyd (Eds.), *Family violence from a communication perspective* (pp. 1–19). Thousand Oaks, CA: Sage.

California Attorney General's Office. (1996). *Child abuse: Educator's responsibilities.*

Campbell, J. (1986). Nursing assessment for risk of homicide with battered women. *Advances in Nursing Science, 8*(4), 36–51.

Campbell, J. (1995). *Assessing dangerousness: Violence by sexual offenders, batterers and child abusers.* Thousand Oaks, CA: Sage.

Campell, J., et al. (2003). Risk factors for femicide in abusive relationships: Results from a multisite case control study. *American Journal of Public Health, 93*(7), 1089–1097.

Carrado, M., George, M., Loxam, F., Jones, L., & Templar, D. (1996). Aggression in British heterosexual relationships: A descriptive analysis. *Aggressive Behavior 22,* 401–415.

Carrillo, R., & Goubaud-Reyna, R. (1998). Clinical treatment of Latino domestic violence offenders. In R. Carrillo & J. Tello (Eds.), *Family violence and men of color* (pp. 53–73). New York: Springer.

Carter, J., Stacey, W., & Shupe, A. (1988). Male violence against women: Assessment of the generational transfer hypothesis. *Deviant Behavior, 9,* 259–273.

Cascardi, M., et al. (1995). Characteristics of women physically abused by their spouses and who seek treatment regarding marital conflict. *Journal of Consulting and Clinical Psychology, 63,* 616–623.

Coker, A., Davis, K., Arias, I., Desai, S., Sanderson, M., Brandt, H., & Smith, P. (2002). Physical and mental health effects of intimate partner violence for men and women. *American Journal of Preventive Medicine, 23*(4), 260–268.

Coleman, D., & Straus, M. (1990). Marital power, conflict and violence in a nationally representative sample of American couples. In M. Straus & R. Gelles (Eds.), *Physical violence in American families* (pp. 287–304). New Brunswick, NJ: Transaction.

Coleman, V. (2002). Treating the lesbian batterer: Theoretical and clinical considerations—a contemporary psychoanalytic perspective. In D. Dutton & D. Sonkin (Eds.), *Intimate violence: Contemporary treatment innovations* (pp. 159–206). New York: Haworth Maltreatment & Trauma Press.

Contra Costa Office of the Sheriff. (2000). *ACAD Conference,* Fall.

Contra Costa Sheriff. (2002, September). Presentation at *ACAD Training Conference.*

Cook, P. (1997). *Abused men: The hidden side of domestic violence.* Westport, CT: Praeger.

Cordova, J., Jacobson, N., Gottman, J., Rushe, R., & Cox, G. (1993). Negative reciprocity and communication in couples with a violent husband. *Journal of Abnormal Psychology, 102*(4), 559–564.

Crozier, J., & Katz, R. (1979). Social learning treatment of child abuse. *Journal of Behavioral Therapy and Psychiatry, 10,* 213–220.

Cusik, M. (2000, October). Seminar presented at 2000 ACAD Conference: Advanced Training on Domestic Violence Issues, Contra Costa County, CA.

Dalpiaz, C. (2004). *Breaking free, starting over: Parenting in the aftermath of family violence.* Westport, CT: Praeger.

Davis, K., & Frieze, I. (2000). Research on stalking: What do we know and where do we go? *Violence and Victims, 15*(4), 473–487.

Davis, M., Eshleman, E., & McKay, M. (1988). *The relaxation & stress reduction workbook,* 3rd ed. Oakland, CA: New Harbinger.

Department of Justice. (2002). Crime in the United States, 2001. Uniform Crime Reports. Washington, DC: Federal Bureau of Investigation.

Deschner, J. (1984). *The hitting habit: Anger control for battering couples.* New York: Simon & Schuster.

Dinkmeyer, D., & McKay, M. (1983). *The parent's guide: STEP teen, systematic training for effective parenting of teens.* Circle Pines, MN: American Guidance Service.

Dobash, R. E., & Dobash, R. P. (1979). *Violence against wives: A case against the patriarchy.* New York: The Free Press.

Dunford, F. (2000). The San Diego Navy Experiment: An assessment of interventions for men who assault their wives. *Journal of Consulting and Clinical Psychology, 68*(3), 468–476.

Dutton, D. (1994). Patriarchy and wife assault: The ecological fallacy. *Violence and Victims, 9*(2), 167–182.

Dutton, D. (1998). *The abusive personality.* New York: Guilford.

Dutton, D., & Painter, S. (1993). Emotional attachments in abusive relationships: A test of traumatic bonding theory. *Violence and Victims, 8*(2), 105–120.

Eagly, A., & Steffen, V. (1986). Gender and aggressive behavior: A meta-analytic review of the social psychological literature. *Psychological Bulletin, 100*(3), 309–330.

Edleson, J. (1999). Children's witnessing of adult domestic violence. *Journal of Interpersonal Violence, 14*(8), 839–870.

English, D., Marshall, D., & Stewart, A. (2003). Effects of family violence on child behavior and health during early childhood. *Journal of Family Violence, 18*(1), 43–57.

Faigman, D. (1986). The battered woman syndrome and self-defense: A legal and empirical dissent. *Virginia Law Review, 72,* 619–647.

Fals-Stewart, W., Kashdan, M., O'Farrell, T., & Birchler, G. (2002). Behavioral couples therapy for drug-abusing patients: Effects on partner violence. *Journal of Substance Abuse Treatment, 22,* 87–96.

Fantuzzo, J., & Lindquist, C. (1989). The effects of observing conjugal violence on children: A review of research methodology. *Journal of Family Violence, 4,* 77–94.

Fantuzzo, J., DePaola, L., Lambert, L., Martino, T., Anderson, G., & Sutton, S. (1991). Effects of interparental violence on the psychological adjustment and competencies of young children. *Journal of Consulting and Clinical Psychology, 59,* 258–265.

Farrell, W. (1988). *Why men are the way they are.* New York: Berkley Books.

Faulkner, K., et al. (1992). Cognitive-behavioral group treatment for male spouse abusers. *Journal of Family Violence, 7*(1), 37–55.

Felson, R., & Messner, S. (1998). Disentangling the effects of gender and intimacy on victim precipitation in homicide. *Criminology, 36*(2), 405–424.

Felson, R., & Messner, S. (2000). The control motive in intimate partner violence. *Social Psychology Quarterly, 63*(1), 86–94.

Fiebert, M., & Gonzalez, D. (1997). College women who initiate assaults on their male partners and the reasons offered for such behavior. *Psychological Reports, 80,* 583–590.

Follingstad, D., Wright, S., Lloyd, S., & Sebastian, J. (1991). Sex differences in motivations and effects in dating relationships. *Family Relations, 40*, 51–57.

Fontes, D. (1998). *Violent touch: Breaking through the stereotype.* (Available online at www.safe4all.org)

Frodi, A., et al. (1977). Are women always less aggressive than men? *Psychological Bulletin, 84*(4), 634–660.

Ganley, A. (1989). Integrating feminist and social learning analyses of aggression. In P. Caesar & L. Hamberger (Eds.), *Treating men who batter: Theory, practice, and programs* (pp. 196–235). New York: Springer.

Geffner, R., Mantooth, C., Franks, D., & Rao, L. (1989). A psychoeducational, conjoint therapy approach to reducing family violence. In P. Caesar & L. Hamberger (Eds), *Treating men who batter: Theory, practice and programs* (pp. 103–133). New York: Springer.

Geller, J., & Wasserstrom, J. (1984). Conjoint therapy for the treatment of domestic violence. In A. Roberts (Ed.), *Battered women and their families: Intervention strategies and treatment programs* (pp. 76–98). New York: Springer.

Gelles, R. (1983). An exchange/social control theory. In D. Finkelhor, R. Gelles, G. Hotaling, & M. Straus (Eds.), *The dark side of families* (pp. 151–165). Thousand Oaks, CA: Sage.

Gelles, R., & Loseke, D. (Eds.). (1996). *Current controversies on family violence.* Newbury Park, CA: Sage.

Goldner, V. (1998). The treatment of violence and victimization in intimate relationships. *Family Process, 37*(3), 263–286.

Gondolf, E. (1996). Characteristics of batterers in a multi-site evaluation of batterer intervention systems. Available online at http://www.mincava.umn.edu/documents/gondolf/batchar.html

Goode, W. (1971). Force and violence in the family. *Journal of Marriage and the Family, 33*, 624–636.

Goodman, D. (1974). *Emotional well-being through rational behavior training.* Springfield, IL: Charles C. Thomas.

Gottman, J. (1999). *The marriage clinic.* New York: W. W. Norton & Company.

Graham-Kevan, N., & Archer, J. (2002). *Does controlling behavior predict aggression and violence to partners?* Unpublished manuscript, available by contacting the author at Ngraham-kevan@uclan.ac.uk

Graham-Kevan, N., & Archer, J. (2004). *Using Johnson's domestic violence typology to classify men and women in a non-selected sample.* Unpublished manuscript, available by contacting the author at Ngraham-kevan@uclan.ac.uk

Greene, K., & Bogo, M. (2002). The different faces of intimate violence: Implications for assessment and treatment. *Journal of Marital and Family Therapy, 28*(4), 455–466.

Grych, J., & Fincham, F. (1990). Marital conflict and children's adjustment: A cognitive-contexual framework. *Psychological Bulletin, 108*, 267–290.

Gutierrez, K. (2000). *Male batterers and their children: Transmission of narcissistic wounding and violent coping.* Unpublished doctoral dissertation available by contacting the author at kkgypsy@yahoo.com

Gutierrez, K. (2003, Fall). Transmission of violent coping. In *FAVTEA Bulletin*, www.FAVTEA.com

Hamberger, K., & Hastings, J. (1986). Personality correlates of men who abuse their partners. *Journal of Family Violence, 1*(4), 323–341.

Hansen, M., Harway, M., & Cervantes, N. (1991). Therapists' perceptions of severity in cases of family violence. *Violence and Victims, 6*(3), 225–235.

Hare, R. (1993). *Without conscience: The disturbing world of the psychopaths among us.* New York: Guilford.

Healey, K., et al. (1998). *Batterer intervention: Program approaches and criminal justice strategies.* (U.S. Department of Justice, Office of Justice Program.)

Hendrix, H. (1988). *Getting the love you want.* New York: Harper & Row.

Hershorn, M., & Rosenbaum, A. (1985). Children of marital violence: A closer look at the unintended victims. *American Journal of Orthopsychiatry, 55,* 260–265.

Hesse, E. (1999). The Adult Attachment Interview: Historical and current perspectives. In J. Cassidy & P. Shaver (Eds.), *Handbook of attachment theory, research, and clinical applications* (pp. 395–433). New York: Guilford.

Heyman, R., & Schlee, K. (2003). Stopping wife abuse via physical aggression couples treatment. In D. Dutton & D. Sonkin (Eds.), *Intimate violence: Contemporary treatment innovations* (pp. 135–157). New York: Haworth Maltreatment & Trauma Press.

Hines, D., & Malley-Morrison, K. (2001). Psychological effects of partner abuse against men: A neglected research area. *Psychology of Men & Masculinity, 2*(2), 75–85.

Holden, G. (1998). The development of research into another consequence of family violence. In G. Holden, R. Geffner, & E. Jouriles (Eds.), *Children exposed to marital violence* (pp. 1–18). Washington, DC: American Psychological Association.

Holden, G., & Ritchie, K. (1991). Linking extreme marital discord, child rearing and child behavior problems: Evidence from battered women. *Child Development, 62,* 311–327.

Holmes, T. H., & Rahe, R. H. (1967). The Social Readjustment Rating Scale. *Journal of Personal and Social Psychology, 21,* 296–301.

Holtzworth-Munroe, A., & Stuart, G. (1994). Typologies of male batterers. *Psychological Bulletin, 116*(3), 476–497.

Holtzworth-Munroe, A., Stuart, G. L., & Hutchinson, G. (1997). Violent vs. nonviolent husbands: Differences in attachment patterns, dependency, and jealousy. *Journal of Family Psychology, 11*(3), 314–331.

Hotaling, G., & Sugarman, D. (1986). An analysis of risk markers in husband to wife violence. *Violence and Victims, 1,* 101–124.

Housecamp, B., & Foy, D. (1991). The assessment of post-traumatic stress disorder in battered women. *Journal of Interpersonal Violence, 6,* 367–375.

Jackson, D. (1965). The study of the family. *Family Process, 4,* 1–20.

Jacobsen, N., & Gottman, J. (1998). *When men batter women.* New York: Simon & Schuster.

Jacobsen, N., Gottman, J., Waltz, J., Rushe, R., Babcock, J., & Holtzworth-Munroe, A. (1994). Affect, verbal content, and psychophysiology in the arguments of couples with a violent husband. *Journal of Consulting and Clinical Psychology, 62*(5), 982–988.

Jacobsen, N., Gottman, J., Gortner, E., & Berns, S. (1996). Psychological factors in the longitudinal course of battering: When do couples split up? *Violence and Victims, 11*(4), 371–392.

Jaffe, P., Wolfe, D., & Wilson, S. (1990). *Children of battered women.* Newbury Park: CA: Sage.

Jennings, J. P., & Jennings, J. L. (1991). Multiple approaches to the treatment of violent couples. *The American Journal of Family Therapy, 19*(4), 351–362.

Johnson, M. (2000, November). *Conflict and control: Symmetry and asymmetry in domestic violence.* Paper presented at the National Institute of Justice Gender Symmetry Workshop. Available online at mpj@psu.edu

Johnston, J., & Campbell, L. (1993). A clinical typology of interparental violence in disputed-custody divorces. *American Journal of Orthopsychiatry, 63*(2), 190–199.

Johnston, J., & Roseby, V. (1997). *In the name of the child.* New York: The Free Press.

Kadushin, A., & Martin, J. (1981). *Child abuse: An interactional event.* New York: Columbia University Press.

Kasian, M., & Painter, S. (1992). Frequency and severity of psychological abuse in a dating population. *Journal of Interpersonal Violence, 7*(3), 350–364.

Kitzmann, K., Gaylord, N., Holt, A., & Kenny, E. (2003). Child witnesses to domestic violence: A meta-analytic review. *Journal of Consulting and Clinical Psychology, 71*(2), 339–352.

Kolbo, J., Blakely, E., & Englemen, D. (1996). Children who witness domestic violence: A review of the empirical literature. *Journal of Interpersonal Violence, 11*(2), 281–293.

Koonin, M., Cabarcas, A., & Geffner, R. (2002). *Treatment of women arrested for domestic violence: Women ending abusive/violent episodes respectfully.* San Diego, CA: Family Violence & Sexual Assault Institute.

Lane, G., & Russell, T. (1989). Second-order systemic work with violent couples. In P. Caesar & L. Hamberger (Eds.), *Treating men who batter* (pp. 134–162). New York: Springer.

Langhinrichsen-Rohling, J., Neidig, P., & Thorn, G. (1995). Violent marriages: Gender differences in levels of current violence and past abuse. *Journal of Family Violence, 10*(2), 159–175.

Laumakis, M., et al. (1998). The emotional, cognitive, and coping responses of preadolescent children to different dimensions of marital conflict. In G. Holden, R. Geffner, & E. Jouriles (Eds.), *Children exposed to marital violence* (pp. 257–288). Washington, DC: American Psychological Association.

Lee, M. (2000). Understanding Chinese battered women in North America: A review of the literature and practice implications. *Journal of Multicultural Social Work, 8*, 215–241.

Lehmann, P., & Rabenstein, S. (2002). Children exposed to domestic violence: Assessment and treatment protocols. In A. Roberts & G. Greene (Eds.), *Social worker's desk reference* (pp. 673–678). Oxford, UK: Oxford University Press.

Leisring, P., Dowd, L., & Rosenbaum, A. (2003). Treatment of partner aggressive women. In D. Dutton & D. Sonkin (Eds.), *Intimate violence: Contemporary treatment innovations* (pp. 257–277). New York: Haworth Maltreatment & Trauma Press.

Letellier, P. (1994). Gay and bisexual male domestic violence victimization: Challenges to feminist theory and responses to violence. *Violence and Victims, 9*(2), 95–106.

Litrownik, A., et al. (2003). Exposure to family violence in young at-risk children. *Journal of Family Violence, 18*(1), 59–73.

Lloyd, S. (1996). Physical aggression, distress, and everyday marital interaction. In D. Cahn & S. Lloyd (Eds.), *Family violence from a communication perspective* (pp. 177–198).

Lynch, M., & Ciccheti, D. (1998). An ecological-transactional analysis of children and contexts. *Developmental Psychopathology, 10*, 235–257.

Maccoby, E. (1980). *Social development: Psychological growth and the parent–child relationship.* New York: Hartcourt Brace Jovanovich.

Makepeace, J. (1986). Gender differences in courtship violence victimization. *Family Relations, 35*, 383–388.

Malley-Morrison, K., & Hines, D. (2004). *Family violence in a cultural perspective: Defining, understanding, and combating abuse.* Thousand Oaks, CA: Sage.

Mann, C. (1988). Getting even? *Justice Quarterly, 5*, 33–51.

Margolin, G., & Burman, B. (1993). Wife abuse versus marital violence: Different terminologies, explanations, and solutions. *Clinical Psychology Review, 13*, 59–73.

Margolin, G., John, R., & Gleberman, L. (1993). Affective responses to conflictual discussions in violent and nonviolent couples. *Journal of Consulting and Clinical Psychology, 56*(1), 24–33.

Marshall, L. (1992a). The Severity of Violence Against Men Scales. *Journal of Family Violence, 7*(3), 189–203.

Marshall, L. (1992b). Development of the Severity of Violence Against Women Scales. *Journal of Family Violence, 7*(2), 103–121.

Marziali, E. (2002). Borderline personality disorders. In A. Roberts & G. Greene (Eds.), *Social worker's desk reference* (pp. 360–363). Oxford, UK: Oxford University Press.

Marziali, E., & Munroe-Blum, H. (1994). *Interpersonal group psychotherapy for borderline personality disorder.* Boulder, CO: Perseus.

Maupin, D. (2002). Family violence prevention services. Available at www.serve.com/fvps/

Mills, L. (2003). *Insult to injury: Rethinking our responses to intimate abuse.* Princeton, NJ: Princeton University Press.

Milner, J. (1986). *The child abuse potential inventory,* 2nd ed. Webster, NC: Psyctec.

Milner, J., & Chilamkurti, C. (1991). Physical child abuse perpetrator characteristics: A review of the literature. *Journal of Interpersonal Violence, 6,* 345–366.

Moffitt, T., & Caspi, A. (1999, July). *Findings about partner violence from the Dunedin Multidisciplinary Health and Development Study.* (National Institute of Justice, No. NCJ 170018.)

Moore, T., & Pepler, D. (1998). Correlates of adjustment in children at risk. In G. Holden, R. Geffner, & E. Jouriles (Eds.), *Children exposed to domestic violence* (pp. 157–184). Washington, DC: American Psychological Association.

Morse, B. (1995). Beyond the conflict tactics scale: Assessing gender differences in partner violence. *Violence and Victims, 10*(4), 251–269.

Mun Wah, L. (1998). Asian men and violence. In R. Carrillo, et al. (Eds.), *Family violence and men of color* (pp. 128–146).

Murphy, C., & O'Leary, D. (1989). Psychological aggression predicts physical aggression in early marriage. *Journal of Consulting and Clinical Psychology, 57,* 579–582.

National Research Council/Institute of Medicine. (1998). *Violence in families.* Washington, DC: National Academy Press.

Neidig, P., Friedman, D., & Collins, B. (1986). Attitudinal characteristics of men who have engaged in spouse abuse. *Journal of Family Violence, 1*(3), 223–233.

Neidig, P., & Friedman, D. (1984). *Spouse abuse: A treatment program for couples.* Champaign, IL: Research Press.

Nowicki, S., & Marshall, D. (1974). A locus of control scale for college as well non-college adults. *Journal of Personality Assessment, 38,* 136–137.

O'Leary, K. (1988). Physical aggression between spouses: A social learning theory perspective. In R. Van Hasselt, R. Morrison, A. Bellack, & M. Hersen (Eds.), *Handbook of family violence* (pp. 31–55). New York: Plenum Press.

O'Leary, K., Barling, J., Arias, I., & Rosenbaum, A. (1989). Prevalence and stability of physical aggression between spouses: A longitudinal analysis. *Journal of Consulting and Clinical Psychology, 57*(2), 263–268.

O'Leary, K., Heyman, R., & Neidig, P. (1999). Treatment of wife abuse: A comparison of gender-specific and conjoint approaches. *Behavior Therapy, 30,* 475–505.

O'Leary, K., & Murphy, C. (1999). Clinical issues in the assessment of partner violence. In R. Ammerman & M. Hersen (Eds.), *Assessment of family violence: A clinical and legal source book* (2nd ed., pp. 46–94). New York: John Wiley & Sons.

Paul, J., & Paul, M. (1983). *Do I have to give up me to be loved by you?* Minneapolis, MN: Comp Care.

Pearson, P. (1997). *When she was bad: Women and the myth of innocence.* New York: Penguin Books.

Peled, E., Eisikovits, Z., Enosh, G., & Winstok, Z. (2000). Choice and empowerment for battered women who stay. *Social Work, 45*(1), 9–25.

Pence, E., & Paymar, M. (1993). *Education groups for men who batter: The Duluth model.* New York: Springer.

Perilla, J. (2000). Cultural specificity in domestic violence interventions: A Latino model. *The Family Psychologist, 16,* 6–7.

Petracek, L. (2004). *The anger workbook for women.* Oakland: New Harbinger.

Pimlott-Kubiak, S., & Cortina, M. (2003). Gender, victimization, and outcomes: Reconceptualizing risk. *Journal of Consulting and Clinical Psychology, 71*(3), 528–539.

Potter-Efron, R., & Potter-Efron, P. (1991). *Anger, alcoholism and addiction.* New York: W. W. Norton & Company.

Potter-Effron, R., & Potter-Effron, P. (1995). *Letting go of anger.* Oakland: New Harbinger.

Renzetti, C. (1992). *Violent betrayal: Partner abuse in lesbian relationships.* Newbury Park, CA: Sage.

Roberts, N., & Noller, P. (1998). The association between adult attachment and couple violence: The role of communication patterns and relationship satisfaction. In J. Simpson & W. Rholes (Eds.), *Attachment theory and close relationships* (pp. 317–350). New York: Guilford.

Roberts, M., & Powers, S. (1990). Adjusting chair timeout enforcement procedures for oppositional children. *Behavior Therapy, 21,* 257–271.

Rosemond, J. (1990). *Parent power!* Kansas City, MO: Andrews & McMeel.

Rosenbaum, A., & O'Leary, K. (1986). The treatment of marital violence. In N. Jacobsen (Ed.), *Clinical handbook of marital therapy* (pp. 387–405). New York: Guilford.

Rosenbaum, A., & Maiuro, R. (1989). Eclectic approaches in working with men who batter. In P. Caesar & L. Hamberger (Eds.), *Treating men who batter* (pp. 165–195). New York: Springer.

Ruben, D. (2002). *Parent empowerment: Counseling parents in positive child-rearing practices.* Available at www.abduct.com/acoa/acoa.htm

Salzinger, S., Feldman, R., Ing-mak, D., Mojica, E., Stockhammer, T., & Rosario, M. (2002). Effects of partner violence and physical child abuse on child behavior: A study of abused and comparison children. *Journal of Family Violence, 17*(1), 23–52.

Saunders, D. (1986). When battered women use violence: Husband-abuse or self-defense? *Violence and Victims, 1*(1), 47–60.

Saunders, D., & Hamill, R. (2003). Violence against women: Synthesis of research on offender interventions. National institute of justice, NCJ 201222.

Schore, A. (1994). *Affect regulation and the origin of the self: The neurobiology of emotional development.* Hillsdale, NJ: Erlbaum.

Sheridan, D. (2001). Treating survivors of partner abuse: Forensic identification and documentation. In J. S. Olshaker, M. Jackson, & W. Smock (Eds.), *Forensic emergency medicine* (pp. 203–228). Philadelphia: Lippincott Williams & Wilkins.

Shupe, A., Stacey, W., & Hazlewood, L. (1987). *Violent men, violent couples: The dynamics of domestic violence.* New York: John Wiley & Sons.

Siegel, D. (1999). *The developing mind: How relationships and the brain interact to shape who we are.* New York: Guilford.

Simmons, C., Lehmann, P., & Cobb, N. (2004, September). Personality profiles & attitudes toward violence of women arrested for domestic violence: How they differ from and are similar to men arrested for domestic violence. Paper presented at the Family Violence & Sexual Assualt Institute 9th International Conference on Family Violence, San Diego, CA.

Simonelli, C., & Ingram, K. (1998). Psychological distress among men experiencing physical and emotional abuse in heterosexual dating relationships. *Journal of Interpersonal Violence, 13*(6), 667–681.

Sommer, R. (1994). Male and female perpetrated partner abuse. (Doctoral dissertation, University of Manitoba. University Microfilms International, ISBN-0-315-99064-3.)

Sommer, R. (1995). *Controversy within family violence research.* Paper presented at Women's Freedom Network Conference. Available at www.reenasommerassociates.mb.ca/a_wfn.html

Sonkin, D., & Dutton, D. (2003). Treating assaultive men from an attachment perspective. In D. Dutton & D. Sonkin (Eds.), *Intimate violence: Contemporary treatment innovations* (pp. 105–133). New York: Haworth Maltreatment & Trauma Press.

Stacey, W., Hazelwood, L., & Shupe, A. (1994). *The violent couple.* Westport, CT: Praeger.

Sternberg, K., et al. (1993). Effects of domestic violence on children's behavior problems and depression. *Developmental Psychology, 29,* 44–52.

Stets, J., & Straus, M. (1989). The marriage license as a hitting license: A comparison of assaults in dating, cohabitating and married couples. *Journal of Family Violence, 41*(2), 161–180.

Stimmel, B. (1993). *The facts about drug use.* New York: Haworth Medical Press.

Stith, S., Rosen, K., & McCollum, E. (2002). Developing a manualized couples treatment for domestic violence: Overcoming challenges. *Journal of Marital and Family Therapy, 28*(1), 21–25.

Stith, S., Rosen, K., & McCollum, E. (2004, July). Treating intimate partner violence within intact couple relationships: Outcomes of multi-couple versus individual couple therapy. *Journal of Marital and Family Therapy, 30*(6), 305–315.

Stosny, S. (2004). *Manual of the Core Value Workshop.* North Charleston, NC: Book Surge Publishing.

Straus, M. (1992). Children as witnesses to marital violence: A risk factor for lifelong problems among a nationally representative sample of American men and women. Paper No. VB48, available online at Murraystraus@unh.edu

Straus, M. (1993). Physical assaults by wives: A major social problem. In R. Gelles & D. Loseky (Eds.), *Current controversies on family violence* (pp. 67–87). Newbury Park, CA: Sage.

Straus, M. (1999). The controversy over domestic violence by women. In X. Arriaga & S. Oskamp (Eds.), *Violence in intimate relationships* (pp. 17–44).

Straus, M., Gelles, R., & Steinmetz, S. (1980). *Behind closed doors: Violence in the American family.* Newbury Park, CA: Sage.

Straus, M., & Gelles, R. (Eds.). (1990). *Physical violence in American families.* New Brunswick, NJ: Transaction.

Straus, M., & Donnelly, D. (2001). *Beating the devil out of them.* New Brunswick, NJ: Transaction.

Straus, M., & Stewart, J. (1999). Corporal punishment by American parents: National data on prevalence, chronicity, severity, and duration, in relation to child and family characteristics. *Clinical Child and Family Psychology Review, 2*(2), 55–70.

Sugarman, D., & Frankel, S. (1996). Patriarchal ideology and wife-assault: A meta-analytic review. *Journal of Family Violence, 11*(1), 13–39.

Swann, S., & Snow, D. (2002). A typology of women's use of violence in intimate relationships. *Violence Against Women, 8*(3), 286–319.

Tannen, D. (1990). *You just don't understand.* New York: Ballantine.

Tavris, C. (1989). *Anger: The misunderstood emotion.* New York: Touchstone.

Teichman, M., & Teichman, Y. (1989). Violence in the family: An analysis in terms of interpersonal resource-exchange. *Journal of Family Violence, 4*(2), 127–142.

Telch, C., & Lindquist, C. (1984). Violent versus nonviolent couples: A comparison of patterns. *Psychotherapy, 21*(2), 242–248.

Tjaden, P., & Thoennes, N. (1998). Prevalence, incidence and consequences of violence against women. *National Institute of Justice,* NCJ 172837.

Tolman, R. (1989). The development of a measure of psychological maltreatment of women by their male partners. *Violence and Victims, 4*(3), 173–189.

Van Horn, P., Best, S., & Lieberman, A. (1998, November). Breaking the chain: Preventing the transmission of trauma in children of battered women through parent–child psychotherapy. Paper presented at the 14th annual meeting of the International Society for Traumatic Stress Studies, Washington, DC.

Vivian, D., & Langhinrichsen-Rohling, J. (1994). Are bi-directionally violent couples mutually victimized? A gender-sensitive comparison. *Violence and Victims, 9*(2), 107–124.

Walker, L. (1979). *The battered woman.* New York: Harper & Row.

Walker, L. (1983). The battered woman syndrome study. In D. Finklehor (Ed.), *The dark side of families* (pp. 31–48).

Wallace, R., & Nosko, A. (2003). Shame in male spouse abusers and its treatment in group therapy. In D. Dutton & D. Sonkin (Eds.), *Intimate violence: Contemporary treatment innovations* (pp. 47–74). New York: Haworth Maltreatment & Trauma Press.

Watzlawick, P., Beavin, J., & Jackson, D. (1967). *Pragmatics of human communication: A study of interactional patterns, pathologies and paradoxes.* New York: Norton.

Webster-Stratton, C. (1990). Enhancing the effectiveness of self-administered videotape parent training for families with conduct-problem children: Comparison with two cost-effective treatments and a control group. *Journal of Abnormal Child Psychology, 18,* 479–492.

Weisinger, H. (1985). *Dr. Weisinger's anger workout book.* New York: Quill.

West, C. (1998a). Leaving a second closet: Outing partner violence in same-sex couples. In J. Jasinski & L. Williams (Eds.), *Partner violence: A comprehensive review of 20 years of research* (pp. 163–183). Thousand Oaks, CA: Sage.

West, C. (1998b). Lifting the political gag order: Partner violence in ethnic minority families. In J. Jasinski & L. Williams (Eds.), *Partner violence: A comprehensive review of 20 years of research* (pp. 184–209). Thousand Oaks, CA: Sage.

Williams, O. (1994). Group work with African American men who batter: Toward more ethnically sensitive practice. *Journal of Comparative Family Studies, 25*(1), 91–101.

Wolak, J., & Finkelhor, D. (1998). Children exposed to partner violence. In J. Jasinski & L. Williams (Eds.), *Partner violence: A comprehensive review of 20 years of research* (pp. 73–112). Thousand Oaks, CA: Sage.

Ziegler, P., & Hiller, T. (2002, March/April). Good story/bad story: Collaborating with violent couples. *Psychotherapy Networker,* pp. 63–68.

Index